# Bridal Intercession

*Authority in Prayer
through Intimacy with Jesus*

**Gary Wiens**

**OASIS HOUSE**

**Oasis House**
P.O. Box 127
Greenwood, Missouri 64034-0127
www.oasishouse.net

Printed in the United States of America on acid-free paper.

ISBN 0-9704791-1-5
Library of Congress Control Number: 2001118179

**Ordering Information**
Burning Heart Ministries, Inc.
13309 Corrington Ave.
Grandview, MO 64030

www.burningheartministries.com
816-965-9336

# DEDICATION

To Mary, my bride, who for 30 years
has stood in the gap for me.

# ACKNOWLEDGEMENTS

I am grateful to the Lord Jesus for the contributions of many that have made this book possible. At the head of the line is Mike Bickle, whose teaching on the passionate heart of Jesus has been so profoundly used by the Holy Spirit to heal my heart, and to fill me with desire to know and love the Son of God.

Behind him stand the voluntary lovers who make up the International House of Prayer in Kansas City, who have strengthened me again and again through their prayers. They fervently and faithfully stand in agreement with the opinions of God concerning His purposes in the world, and in agreement with His purposes in my life. My heart has been particularly stirred by the ardor of those who stand in the Night Watch, ministering to Jesus in the hours during which no one else hears except Him. He has been their sure reward. Thank you all!

Particular thanks go to a group of folks who have committed to pray for Mary and me daily. These intercessors have carried us in their hearts before the throne of God with unfailing love and have sustained us more than they know.

Finally, I am grateful to Deb Hvass, whose wisdom and persistence in the process of editing the manuscript have made this effort deeper and stronger than it ever could have been without her.

Blessings on you all.

# FOREWORD
## BY MIKE BICKLE

It has been my pleasure to know Gary Wiens since 1985 in a friendship that has gone from mere acquaintance to partnership in ministry. Since he and Mary came with their family to Kansas City in 1996, I have watched him grow in his relationship with the Man Christ Jesus to the place where his heart burns with the desire to go deeper and deeper in the knowledge of the beauty of the Lord. I have watched his children become established as godly young people, and have appreciated deeply the contributions this family has brought to this city, first to Metro Christian Fellowship, and now to the House of Prayer.

In recent years, I have sensed from the Lord a specific calling and anointing on Gary's life, that he would preach the Forerunner message to the Bride of Christ with passion and skill, but also that he would grow in scholarship and artistry in the expression of this message. As he began to embrace God's purpose for this phase of his life, I observed Gary in the prayer room. I sensed the fire of the Spirit of God ignited in his heart. He is a skilled and articulate spokesman for the International House of Prayer, a preacher whose messages are profound and appealing. While many today are brokers of the most recent hot topic, Gary has invested deeply to become a voice and not merely an echo of someone else's message. He is an excellent communicator, and I find his messages instructive and challenging to me personally.

Gary has also discovered a wonderful part of God's gifting to him in the area of writing poetry. With passion and artistry, Gary expresses the beauty and emotion of the human heart in the place of longing after the Person of God. He has recently released his first compilation of poems entitled "Songs of a Burning Heart," in both written and recorded form. (His poems have stirred the hearts of many and have been the inspiration for the release of other artistic expressions in the arenas of music and painting. I am convinced that part of the Forerunner nature of Gary's ministry is as one of the voices calling forth the arts to be restored to the house of the Lord, where they belong.

Bridal Intercession is an inspiring and challenging book that calls the Bride of Christ to come forward into her favored place of authority in prayer, which is found through intimacy with Jesus. In these early days of the release of the Forerunner ministry in the earth, there is needed a compassionate and fervent call to those who long to choose the most excellent part: sitting in the presence of the Lord to hear His heart and gain the place of authority in prayer available only to His Bride. This book provides such a call.

In a unique way, Gary has grasped the reality of God's purposes in drawing His people to the place of prayer as never before in history. In this treatment, prayer is seen as an invitation to intimacy rather than a dutiful religious activity to convince God to do something on behalf of the human race. Jesus Christ is presented as the Chief Intercessor, whose longing is to bring His people into partnership with Him in His eternal work of redemption. Gary establishes this reality as the seedbed of intercession, prayer that grows not out of our place of need, but out of God's passionate desire to commune with us as His Beloved.

I want to call attention to three important sections of Bridal Intercession. The first is the discussion of the difference between the widow's petition and Bridal Intercession. Gary contrasts the desperate prayers of the persistent widow in Luke 18 with the effective intercession rooted in intimacy, as illustrated by the Old Testament character of Esther. If the body of Christ could get a grasp of this concept alone, the reality of it would revolutionize the way Christians pray.

Another emphasis I believe is so relevant for this time in history is the concept of strategic delay. Gary's treatment of the parable of the 10 virgins in *Matthew 25* and the stories of Mary and Martha in *Luke 10* and *John 11* gives me additional motivation to invest all my energy in the pursuit of knowing Jesus through the presence of the Holy Spirit. As we approach the last days, nothing is more important than growing in our understanding of the ways of God, so that even when we find His strategies unexpected or confusing, our hearts can be firmly established in the knowledge of His goodness and trustworthiness.

Finally, I am grateful for Gary's treatment of spiritual warfare. As natural history moves toward its culmination, God's people will find it more and more important to have our warfare grounded in worship and in the knowledge of God's purposes and His passionate heart for us as His Bride. Hearing the Word of God and coming to a place of agreement with God's agenda from the perspective of intimacy in worship is absolutely essential.

I am delighted to endorse *Bridal Intercession* as a challenging and inspiring invitation to go deeper in intimacy and authority in prayer. I look forward to more coming from Gary's heart to strengthen the body of Christ. Go for it, man of God!

Mike Bickle, Director
International House of Prayer in Kansas City
Spring 2001

(*Songs of a Burning Heart* is available in book form and on compact disc from Gary's ministry website, www.burningheartministries.com.)

# CONTENTS

# INTRODUCTION
## THE PERSUASIVE VOICE

The lifelong journey toward intimacy with Jesus, once we begin to taste His beauty and understand His passion for us, is a journey that is compelling and irresistible. Learning how to pray from a posture of intimacy may be the most important part of that journey. For until we as the Bride of Christ begin to understand His language of love, and begin to respond to Him in the language He prefers, we will be left with a stunted prayer life and unsatisfied hearts.

Early in the year 2000, I was on a ministry trip with Chris DuPre, my golfing buddy, confidant and prayer partner. Chris is a worship leader and songwriter par excellence and a wonderful husband and father.

We were sharing together at a conference in Dallas, Texas, and Chris was speaking about the place of intimacy in intercession. He used a word picture that touched my heart and greatly assisted me in rooting my own prayer life in the exalted reality of bridal intimacy with Jesus.

As we discussed the things that influence our actions and attitudes, our conversation turned to advertising. In our culture, the world of the media gives itself extravagantly to the task of swaying our opinions about issues and products, and it does so with no sense of remorse or contrition over the use of manipulative techniques, sensuality, distorted perspectives and downright lies.

I find some of the strategies obnoxious, and sometimes I respond to them simply to eliminate the sound of their pleas. Some of the messages, however, because they are artistic and appealing or funny, succeed in grabbing my interest for just a second. Advertisers know that if they can catch my attention briefly, sooner or later, when I need that specific product, I may buy theirs. These tactics have some measure of success in your life and mine. If they didn't, the advertisers would find another way.

Another type of influence—empathy perhaps—works on my actions and attitudes when neighborhood children come to my door wanting me to buy overpriced candy or magazines I don't read so their band or team can purchase equipment or go somewhere fun. If my son or daughter is in the band, I buy more. My personal commitment is that if a young person is selling something useful to raise money for something legitimate, I'll buy one. Kids who are motivated enough to knock on my door ought to be rewarded with my cooperation.

I also can be moved to action by a sense of responsibility or guilt. The promise of reward is often sufficient to move me to do something someone else wants done. Sometimes that reward is positive—the satisfaction of having fulfilled my duty, the pleasure of having done the right thing. Sometimes the reward is earthy and viscerally motivated—I want that raise or I envision the comfort a certain product will bring me. Other times, I'm simply so tired of being pestered that I'll cave in and do what is demanded just to get the person who is trying to motivate me off my back.

But there's one influence that has more power to move me to activity than all the other factors combined. I'm a husband, and I'm in love with Mary, my wife. There is no human influence more powerful than her voice whispering to me in the context of the intimacy of our marriage. We've been married nearly 30 years, and she and I have come to understand one another. Our perspective of how we want our lives to be worked out has come to a place of unity. Even if the activity she desires is distasteful to me, my heart tells me it will be good for me to hear her and, if at all possible, to answer her request.

In addition to that, she has endured me lovingly for all these years and I love her for it. I want to give her what she wants if I can. If for some reason we disagree about what needs to happen, we don't refuse one another but we talk, and in the dialogue comes resolution. We come to agreement about the next steps of activity.

Now, Mary could approach her position of influence in different ways. She could whine, nag, scream or manipulate, and she would have a measure of power. I might not like it much—in fact I might hate it—but I would be influenced, if for no other reason than the fear of reprisal or the specter of withheld affections.

But Mary is not like that. She's strong but she's gentle. She's clear in her opinions but patient in her style. She tends to me; she is a vehicle of nurture to me and to our children, and she does it day in and day out. She loves me, and I know that if she really needs or wants something, it's important enough for me to do my best to satisfy her. My wife's voice, expressing her desires in the context of intimacy, is the most powerful human influence in my life.

I believe the same is true in our relationship with our heavenly Bridegroom, the Lord Jesus Christ. He is my Beloved and I am His, and there is nothing sweeter in all the earth than the sense of His presence and affection. And when we are in that place of intimacy—when I am attuned to His purposes and His grace and understand the kind intentions of His heart, when I am willing to trust His sense of timing—there is only one more powerful influence in the universe than my voice whispering in His ear.

That force is none other than His whole Church, dressed in the garments of holiness, prepared as a Bride for her Bridegroom, coming into the place of intimacy and agreement with His heart that will release the infinite power of God Most High upon the earth. He is moving us toward that reality, and the purpose of this book is to encourage you, its readers, along the way to seek His presence with hope and joy, and to invest all that you are and have in the magnificent obsession: the knowledge of His love for you and me, the Bride of Christ.

## CHAPTER 1

# MOTIVATIONS OF THE HEART

## WHY WE PRAY

This morning at just after 6 o'clock, I walked into the International House of Prayer in Kansas City, Missouri, and entered into a reality that has been going on 24 hours a day, seven days a week, since September 19, 1999. A team of five young adults, all in their early 20s, was ministering to the Lord in the prayer room, singing well-known worship songs, creating spontaneous songs directly from the Scriptures, and weaving short, spoken prayers with the phrases of the songs. Ministering from a perspective of intimacy, they gave expression to the longing in their souls to know God and be known by Him.

These young people are part of an emerging community of intercessory missionaries who are giving their lives to the work of prayer. They are declaring the purposes of God over the cities and nations of the earth and seeking to understand and agree with His intentions for the remaining years of human history. During the course of this day, in the same way it happens every day, several hundred people will come through the prayer room and participate in this adventure in intercession. Many will be on the staff of the House of Prayer, individuals and families who have raised their own financial support to give themselves to a life of intercessory worship. Others will come from the Kansas City area and from other cities and nations to join in night-and-day prayer.

This form of prayer is called the Harp and Bowl model of intercessory worship, and it is but one expression of the emerging prayer movement that is exploding all over the earth. In a way unprecedented in human history, the Spirit of God is stirring the hearts of Christians everywhere to seek Him in prayer. As a staff member of the House of Prayer, and one who is privileged to travel around this country and around the world to call believers to a life of intimate prayer, I am becoming increasingly aware of the scope of God's search for true worshippers who will seek His face and His will for the earth.

Many are aware of the wondrous work of prayer that has been going on in places like Seoul, Korea, where tens of thousands of people pray every day at the Prayer Mountain associated with the ministry of Pastor Paul Yonggi-Cho. But fewer know that this yearning to seek the Lord's face is exploding among believers all over the world, and that God is stirring the hearts of believers everywhere to call upon His name until He intervenes directly in the affairs of men and women.

Jon Petersen, a friend who joined the pastoral staff of Metro Christian Fellowship in Kansas City in the spring of 2000, for years has given his attention to building relationships among pastors in the cities of North America. Jon shared some rather startling information with me about prayer in the United States: There are about 6,000 cities with a population of more than 15,000 people. In 1993, only a few of those cities had groups of pastors organized specifically to pray for the cities in which they serve. But by the year 2000, more than 90 percent of those cities had interdenominational groups of pastors meeting regularly to pray over their cities.[1]

In fact, groups of intercessors are meeting all over the world, some in very organized fashion, such as Intercessors for America, The International Fellowship of Intercessors, America's National Prayer Committee and others.[2] Less-organized intercessory groups are popping up all over as God moves on the hearts of His people to pray with fervency. In the spring of 2000, a team was sent from Metro Christian Fellowship in Kansas City to meet with believers in Nepal and strengthen the Church there. The leaders of the Kansas City team asked the Nepalese believers what the Holy Spirit was saying to them as the current emphasis of His activity. The response was that the focus of God's heart seemed to be intercessory prayer and that the Lord would move in the land to bring revival.

In the past year and a half I have personally traveled to India, Cyprus, Israel, Ecuador, Kenya, England, Canada and many cities in the United States, and in all those places I have witnessed this stirring to pray.

As I sit in the International House of Prayer this morning, there is a young man praying over this very issue: that the Lord would raise up intercessors all over the earth to worship and seek Him concerning His intervention in the affairs of human beings. It is out of these emerging realities that the need for this book has arisen. Its purpose is not only that we might pray, but that our prayers would be brought forth in the context of intimacy with Jesus, Whose heart burns with passion for the human race. We want to touch His heart. As we grow in our understanding of His desire and will, we will find increasing strength to pray with the kind of fervency and hope required by the day in which we live.

**WHY DO WE PRAY?**

The first question that comes to me as I make these observations is, "Why?" Why are people calling on the name of the Lord as never before? What is causing the hearts of human beings to turn toward the Lord in unprecedented numbers and take the time and energy to seek Him?

In *Ezekiel 22:30* is recorded a time in which the Lord God articulates through the prophet the sins and failings of the nation of Israel. He is poised to bring judgment on the land,

and the anguish of His heart is that there is no one to "stand in the gap," to stand before the Lord on behalf of the land. Though He finds no one at the time and judgment is released upon the land, this is a prophetic picture that later would be completed in the work of Jesus Christ upon the cross, the one Man Who would stand effectively before God on behalf of the people of the earth.

This posture of standing before the Lord God on behalf of other people is the essence of intercession. It is the ongoing work of Jesus, even as He is in the presence of God today.[3] We as His people, His Bride, are being summoned by the Spirit of God to join with Jesus Christ in this labor of intercession. We are invited to stand as His partners in the priestly ministry of holding the nations before the throne of God, that He might pour out His mercy instead of His wrath upon human beings.

Because this is so, it is imperative that we have a clear understanding of the heart of God concerning intercessory prayer, so that we might fulfill our destiny as His people with maximum effectiveness and joy. Before we do this though, we must begin to move away from false perceptions about prayer and consider some prevalent—but inaccurate—ideas about intercession.

Like most Christians, I have been aware for a long time that prayer is an important part of my life as a follower of Jesus. The problem was that I didn't like to pray. I didn't enjoy prayer, whether in the context of corporate prayer meetings or in my virtually non-existent personal prayer life. Although my heart was stirred by the testimonies of others about prayer, my motivations were almost always in the realm of guilt, shame and religious pressure.

When I first began to hear about people who would give themselves to prayer in an extravagant way, I vacillated between holding those people up as heroes in my mind and succumbing to a self-condemning attitude of hopelessness. Since I really don't enjoy being depressed, I would simply put the matter out of my mind and get on about the business of ministry. When I did pray, I focused almost exclusively on what I needed God to do, either for me personally or for the ministry in which I was involved.

My suspicion is that many believers find themselves in this same boat. We know we should pray but we don't like to pray, and the fact for 21st century Americans is that unless something is enjoyable at some level, or unless it has a relatively quick payoff, we simply won't engage in the activity long term. In order to address this dilemma, I want to present some suggestions of what intercessory prayer is *not,* so that we might then be able to look with clearer eyes at what it is.

**Prayer as Christian Duty**

Perhaps the most common misconception about prayer with which believers struggle is the idea that prayer is our duty. Somehow, we have gotten it in our minds and hearts that God is a religious entity Who, unfortunately, just happens to be the all-powerful Lord of the universe. Therefore, though we don't really like to talk to Him, we sort of need to anyway. We don't really understand why God wants us to beg Him for our provisions. Our emotional perception is that since He is somewhat disinterested and distant, He must be persuaded to give us what we need.

I'm reminded of a little poem written by a friend years ago. Entitled *"Protocol,"* it is a poignant assessment of duty-bound prayer. It goes like this:

**I hold my hands like this to pray,**
**Was told to do four times a day.**
**With friends I talk and reminisce;**
**Only God wants my hands like this.**[4]

In reality, this kind of dutiful exercise is completely opposite of God's heart for His people in the place of prayer. We are told through the prophet Isaiah that at the end of the age even those who are foreigners to God's covenants will be brought to a place of *joyful* prayer. Consider these words:

"Also the sons of the foreigner who join
themselves to the LORD, to serve Him,
And to love the name of the LORD,
to be His servants—
Everyone who keeps from defiling the Sabbath,
and holds fast My covenant—
Even them I will bring to My holy mountain,
and make them joyful in My house of prayer.
Their burnt offerings and their sacrifices
will be accepted on My altar;
For My house shall be called a house of prayer
for all nations."
Isaiah 56:6-7

Notice the themes. Prayer will be initiated by God. It will be about loving the name of the Lord and experiencing joy in the house of prayer, a ministry in which all the nations of the earth shall participate. Religious duty is not the motivation for intercessory prayer.

**Prayer as a Tool for Changing Things**

The perception of prayer that seems the most common today is that it is God's way of changing things. While there is truth in this statement, in itself it is an inadequate perspective of prayer. Since I will explore this theme more fully in Chapter 4, I will treat the issue only briefly at this point. It is my perception that most intercessory prayer today is stimulated by the awareness that so much is wrong with the world, and that God must be persuaded through fervent and even anguished prayer to extend His hand and bring about change. The measuring stick for effectiveness in prayer is the degree to which the circumstances around us change, either in personal situations or in relationship to any other specific external state of affairs.

As an underpinning of this desire for personal and social intervention, much attention has been given recently to discovering the root sin problems of geographical areas. The "spiritual mapping" process yields much understanding as to the generational "sins of the fathers" that have polluted a city or a region. Once that information has been obtained, intercessors attempt to discern the identity of the spiritual principalities and powers that have exerted their influence in the region. The intercessors then repent from the sinful choices of which the forebears were guilty in order to bring about a measure of restoration.

Certain kinds of "prophetic acts" are often part of the practice of spiritual mapping, such as administering salt to river waters that flow through a city or marching around certain geographical areas with musical instruments such as rams' horns and tambourines.[5] In some cases, efforts are put forth to address the demonic principalities and powers that have authority over a particular city or region, although this has become a less frequent practice in recent years. John Paul Jackson, in his helpful book entitled *"Needless Casualties of War,"*[6] demonstrated that this activity can be very damaging to those who involve themselves in it.

This kind of prayer has had significant and measurable effect in cities all over the world. George Otis, Jr., a well-known student of church growth and revival, has produced two videos, both entitled *Transformations,*[7] that give objective and observable evidence of the impact of city-wide prayer based on this methodology.

In this method of prayer, however, there is a danger that the continual focus on an area's sinfulness and the spiritual forces of darkness behind the problems may have a negative impact on intercessors. There has emerged in many places a sense of overwhelming fatigue and even despair that are gripping numerous prayer warriors, and I am convinced that much of it may come from focusing on the wrong things. When the focus of prayer is consistently placed on what is wrong in an area, we tend to develop eyes that see only the corruption, and we may lose our sense of the beautiful.

We were created to become what we behold, and God's intention is that we gaze on the beauty of His Son, Jesus

Christ, and become like Him in the process. Then, in the context of intimacy with Jesus, filled with His Spirit of compassionate power, we will begin to accompany Him as He visits the cities of earth and brings the restoration of all things to the will of the Father, one person at a time.

## Prayer to Increase Our Boundaries

As I write this in May 2001, the runaway best-selling book on every chart is a little 96-page volume entitled *The Prayer of Jabez*. Written by Bruce Wilkinson,[8] it is a meditation on the two-verse historical record of a man named Jabez, whose life story is encapsulated in *1 Chronicles 4:9-10*. To be sure, Jabez was born into a difficult situation. His "story" is tucked in the middle of the genealogies of Chronicles, and the first thing that sets him apart is that his mother named him. This indicates that she was probably a single mom, either widowed before his birth, or perhaps even an unwed mother. In the Middle Eastern culture of that day, this would have been among the worst possible scenarios.

Jabez' name means "to cause pain." Now there's a heritage for you! Beset by pain, Jabez is spoken of in the biblical text as being "more noble than his brothers," since he calls out to God to increase the boundaries of his life so that he will be blessed and not cause pain in the lives of others.

The beauty of this prayer is that it begins to touch the desire of God's heart to bless His children, particularly those who realize the brokenness of their lives. This passion in the heart of God for the well-being of His people is the right motivation for prayer, and I have personally been blessed and encouraged by the use of this prayer. There are individuals who pray the prayer of Jabez over my life daily, and I am tremendously grateful. I want to explore this deep desire in God's heart to bless His own more fully in the paragraphs to come.

The prayer of Jabez, however, quickly can become just a newer version of the "bless me" theology that has degenerated into selfishness over the years, with God becoming no more than the cosmic Santa Claus. The good news about this little prayer is that millions more are praying because of it. The danger is in staying focused on our own blessing instead of having our eyes filled with the wonder and majesty of the Person of Jesus as we entrust ourselves to His generous care and provision. Once again the focus of prayer becomes the changing of our circumstances, rather than having our hearts ravished with the beauty and majesty of God.

The desire of God's heart is to have a relationship of loving intimacy with human beings. Our role in that relationship is the one we must grapple with as we continue to explore the question of why we pray.

## CONSIDER THE END TO FIND THE BEGINNING

The place to begin is at the end. We need to see where this whole thing called human history is headed in order to get an accurate picture of God's intentions in leading us through the experiences of life. Consider these amazing words:

> Then I, John, saw the holy city, New Jerusalem,
> coming down out of heaven from God,
> prepared as a *bride* adorned for her husband.
>
> And I heard a loud voice from heaven saying,
> "Behold, the tabernacle of God is with men,
> and He will dwell with them,
> and they shall be His people.
> God Himself will be with them and be their God.
>
> And God will wipe away every tear from their eyes;
> there shall be no more death, nor sorrow, nor crying.
> There shall be no more pain,
> for the former things have passed away."
> **Revelation 21:2-4, italics mine**

*The culmination of human history is a wedding ceremony!* The final state of the people of God when all the evil has been removed, when all the pain is dealt with, when every tear has been wiped away by the personal touch of the Lord Himself, is that of a Bride adorned for her husband! It is this reality that God has held in His heart from the beginning of time. Because this has always been the goal, *we can therefore interpret all of His dealings with human beings in the light of this exhilarating fact.* My goal in the next two chapters is to provide evidence from the Scriptures that the bridal analogy is indeed a central theme (if not *the* central theme) of God's revelation to us, which provides an interpretive key for understanding His dealings with us.

Once we begin to see that this is so, and begin to interpret the realities of Scripture—the history of Israel, the coming of Christ, His life, death and resurrection, His dealings with us as we attempt to walk out the life of faith—from the perspective of His heart as the eternal Bridegroom, we begin to understand the unfolding realities of our lives in a completely different way. He has always dealt with us from this perspective.

## The Preparation of the Bride

There is a passage in Paul's letter to the Ephesians that has long been one of my favorites. Consider the power of these words as they speak to us of God's decision to love us and draw us to Himself from before time began:

**Blessed be the God and Father of our Lord Jesus Christ, who has blessed us with every spiritual blessing in the heavenly places in Christ, just as He chose us in Him before the foundation of the world, that we should be holy and without blame before Him in love, having predestined us to adoption as sons by Jesus Christ to Himself, according to the good pleasure of His will.**

**Ephesians 1:3-5**

These are strong words and they serve to settle our hearts in the knowledge of the Father's love for us. They are words of healing and encouragement, for they declare to us the truth that we are valued and precious to our heavenly Father. It is in His identity as our Father that God has adopted us to be His "sons."[9] But our understanding of the passage is made complete when we begin to realize that the "good pleasure of His will" extends beyond His desire to merely have a large family of children, all of whom have been conformed to the image of Jesus.

If we go on in the Ephesian letter, we come to realize that the "good pleasure" of God's will for us is fulfilled when Jesus, Who is God in the identity of the Son, receives us from the Father's hand, and forms us to be His Bride! Consider this:

**Husbands, love your wives, just as Christ also loved the church and gave Himself for her, that He might sanctify and cleanse her with the washing of water by the word, that He might present her to Himself a glorious church, not having spot or wrinkle or any such thing, but that she should be holy and without blemish. . . . "For this reason a man shall leave his father and mother and be joined to his wife, and the two shall become one flesh." This is a great mystery, but I speak concerning Christ and the church.**

**Ephesians 5:25-27, 31-32**

The whole reason we were chosen from the beginning of time was so that the passionate heart of Jesus would be satisfied! We were redeemed and adopted for a purpose, and that purpose was that Jesus might present us to Himself as His perfect counterpart, washed in His blood, filled with glorious beauty and made fully like Him. We were created and redeemed for romance, and because of that fact, we now have the hope that our deepest longings for intimacy and significance will be satisfied through relationship with Jesus.

The fire that has burned in the heart of God since the beginning of the beginning is the passion to have a partner for His Son! We were chosen to be holy and blameless in Christ before the worlds were made, so that we might become a Bride suitable for Him, a partner who is like Him. The good pleasure of the will of God the Father was to have this kind of relationship with human beings, that He might nurture us with perfect love and prepare us to be joined to His Son Jesus in the romance of the ages.

The idea of God being both our Father and our Bridegroom is somewhat difficult for us who approach the Scripture with a Western mindset, and may even sound inappropriate. But in the biblical record, we have two significant prophetic pictures of this reality in the story of Ruth and Boaz, and in the record of God's relationship with Israel found in *Ezekiel 16.*[10] Both of those passages give evidence of an initial fatherly covering and nurturing similar to an adoptive relationship. In both instances, in a way that is not inappropriate at all, the relationship takes on a romantic dimension, and the father figure becomes the bridegroom. From that point on, any break in the bond between the two can only be categorized as infidelity.

There is another passage of Scripture that has repeatedly thrilled my heart over the last couple of years. Found in *Proverbs 8:30-31*, it speaks of the emotional dynamics of relationship that characterized the Triune God during the time of creation. The passage reads like this:

> **Then I was beside Him as a master craftsman;**
> **and I was daily His delight,**
> **Rejoicing always before Him,**
> **rejoicing in His inhabited world,**
> **And my delight was with the sons of men.**
> **Proverbs 8:30-31**

This statement is made by the "master craftsman" during the time of the creation of the worlds. We know from *John 1:3* that Jesus Himself is the master craftsman, having fashioned all that is made simply by speaking it into existence. The thing I want to point out here is that the process of creation was carried out in the context of a delightful rela-tionship between Father and Son. Jesus was and is the Father's constant delight,[11] and the expression of the Son's delight before the Father is constant "rejoicing." This is a rich word, carrying all the emotional content of laughing, sing-ing, dancing, leaping, whirling—and even joking![12]

What makes this passage stunning is that in verse 31, we are told that the focus of the Son's joy and delight is the human race—the sons of men! There was such an ardent, eager love in the heart of the second person of the Trinity that He danced and whirled and sang and told jokes with the Father as He made the worlds and formed us to be His own special treasure (I believe with all my heart that some of God's creation—the platypus is a wonderful example—is simply God's version of a joke!). God was delighted with you from the beginning because He knew what the end was go-ing to be—a Bride made perfect for His Son.

The attitude God has taken toward us has never been one of pity, irritation or impatience. He has succumbed nei-ther to despair nor to a performance orientation. His attitude has always been that of the delighted Father, preparing the perfect partner for His perfect Son. The Son's posture has eternally been that of the enthralled Bridegroom, captured by the beauty of one created specifically to be His counter-part. The assurance of the power of God guarantees that at the end of it all we will be what He has intended.

My family is currently focused on a very exciting event that is about to occur. Our older daughter, Alyson, will be getting married this summer to Benjamin Alberts, and we are thrilled about the prospect. I want to tell you, there is nothing more thrilling to the heart of a father than to see his children become godly young adults and, in the beauty of holy living, meet the ones who will become their life part-ners. This has been our experience over the past few years as Ben and Alyson met and became friends, and then best friends. They finally realized that the friendship had blos-somed into a true romance.

I remember the morning in October 2000 that Alyson called me to inform me of her engagement to Ben. I was out of town that weekend, teaching a conference (actually, Ben had taken me to the airport in order to inform me of his intentions), and as I heard her voice on the phone that morning, I knew what was coming: "Daddy! I got engaged last night!" And in that moment, a stunning revelation of God exploded in my heart. I suddenly realized that my entire relationship with Alyson through the 22 years of her life had been for the purpose of preparing her to meet her beloved. My job was to establish her in the freedom necessary to become a faithful and loving wife to him, so that through the beauty of this relationship they might come to know the joy of intimate relationship with Jesus as the heavenly Bridegroom.

As I have reflected on that experience, I have come to understand the heart of God in a deeper way. He wants us to be ready for the ultimate wedding ceremony, and all of His dealings with us can be interpreted through that desire that burns in His heart. During Alyson's childhood, as I interacted with her about her choices, disciplined her, took her on dates, she was being prepared for this culminating event—her marriage to her beloved. And as she looks back on our relationship from the perspective of a bride, she sees that it all was good, for the thing that has been produced is lovely.

## Prayer: The Great Romance

Since the focus of God's heart from the beginning of time has been preparing a Bride for His Son, He has always desired an intimate relationship with His people. And so He has spoken to us in various ways, *with the consistent goal of engaging us in a dialogue about life in relationship with Him.* This dialogue is called prayer, and its primary purpose is that we might come to know the heart of the One Who loves us and understands who we are and what we will become.

He alone knows my true identity, and His words empower me to live in that identity. What could be more helpful, more healing than listening to Him? What could be more beneficial than speaking with Him in loving dialogue? Out of His heart of love, He draws us to the place of prayer, that He might communicate His intentions.

When He spoke to Abram in *Genesis 15*, informing this Middle Eastern nomad that He, God Almighty, was Abram's very great reward, He addressed Abram as a representative of the human race, one who would become known as the father of faith. This means that in His conversation with Abram, God was speaking to you and me, and it is just as normal for Him to communicate with you and me as it was for Him to communicate with Abram. His purpose is that we, through dialogical prayer, might come to understand His purposes and will for our lives and that we, like Abram, would come to know Him as *our* great reward.

As we listen, the Spirit of God works within our hearts and convinces us that God loves us and that we are indeed His children, called according to His purposes.[13] He speaks to us about His plans for us, just as He spoke to Jeremiah in the Old Testament:

**For I know the thoughts that I think toward you, says the LORD, thoughts of peace and not of evil, to give you a future and a hope.**
**Jeremiah 29:11**

He knows the plans He has for us and He's in the mood to talk about them! God is a communicator. He has romance on His mind, He is preparing us for an eternal relationship of joy and gladness with His Son Jesus Christ and He longs to speak with us about it. Consider this statement:

**From the beginning . . . when, in temporal terms, we did not exist at all, God's gaze fell upon us and knew us. . . . His gaze is creative, generative, originative, by His utterly free decree. "This is what, in my eyes, you**

**are; this is what you mean; no other truth can have
any validity but this, for me, for you, or for anyone
else."[14]**

As He speaks and we listen, we come to agree with His
agenda for us and for the rest of the human race. Because
God is a lover, His strategy is not simply to invade the earth
with overwhelming power and authority, but to woo and
win a Bride through gentle persuasion. He wants voluntary
lovers who become convinced of His honorable intentions.
From that place of confidence, we become partners in accomplishing His purposes, first in personal matters, then in the
redemption of all mankind and the restoration of the created
order, and finally in a place of shared rulership for eternity
over His ever-increasing Kingdom.[15]

This partnership is realized through intercessory prayer.
We begin to say back to God that we agree with His agenda
and His strategies, not only for ourselves and the things that
concern us, but for every situation outside ourselves for which
He gives us the strength to pray. In doing so, we stand alongside the Man Christ Jesus before God as heirs of His Kingdom.
As we begin to agree with Him, He begins to release more
and more of His influence, until at the end of the age all things
are conformed to His pleasure and will. Those who have come
into agreement with His assessment of reality will stand together with His Son Jesus Christ, the Lord of all that is, as His
royal Bride and ruling partner.

## OUR INTERCESSION ORIGINATES IN THE
## INTERCESSION OF JESUS

In the first section of this chapter, under the heading of
"Why Do We Pray?" I mentioned the passage in *Ezekiel 22* in
which God is seeking for someone to "stand in the gap" for
the nation of Israel. This gap-standing posture, standing in
the place of another to make an appeal, is the fundamental
role of intercession, and it points to the amazing fact that

God has given human beings the right to come before Him as representatives of the human race and agree with His agenda, thereby releasing that agenda to the reality of earthly experience. Having stood before God on behalf of mankind, we also then have the right to stand before people on behalf of God and declare His blessings to them.[16]

Why have we been given this favored place? How is it that we can presume to come before God and simply by listening and agreeing, set in motion powerful forces of righteousness? It is simply because of the work of one Man, the Lord Jesus Christ. Jesus Christ is the Great High Priest and Intercessor, the One Who has stood in the gap for us and called us to be His partners in standing in the gap for the rest of mankind.

## The Original Intercessor

The most significant intercession in history is the work Jesus accomplished on the cross of Calvary. Early in the history of the human race, the first people were internally aware that a glorious place of rulership was their birthright. They made a conscious choice to disagree with God's agenda and timetable for their exaltation to the place of full authority as His bridal partner (though they could not have understood the implications of their decision at the time).

Grasping after that position but not trusting the Father to release it to them in His own way and time, Adam and Eve listened to the jealous manipulations of the serpent and decided to promote themselves in their own way. In doing so, they introduced sinful self-will into the spiritual "DNA" of all humanity, and estrangement from God was the inevitable result.[17] The only adequate ransom to purchase the Bride back from sin's captivation was a perfectly obedient Man—since in God's economy only a flawless Intercessor could "stand in the gap" on behalf of the guilty.[18]

Thus, in an unthinkable expression of His goodness and passion, God's own Son took on the very form of a man, be-

coming a human being and thereby forever joining humanity with the true divine nature. As the full expression of the
Godhead in bodily form,[19] Jesus walked out a life of perfect
human obedience to the will of God and took His place on
the cross, that the judgments of God might be poured out
where they belonged—on the ultimate Intercessor. God provided Himself as the required sacrifice, the Lamb. In doing
so, through Jesus He restored to the human race the position
of righteousness that a relationship with God requires, and
with it, all the promises and intentions that were in His heart
from the beginning.[20] The intercession was complete.

The stunning thing about this historical occurrence is that
God had made provision for it before He ever began the process of creating. Before creation was established, God the
Father and God the Son instituted an eternal agreement that
God Himself, in the Person of Jesus Christ, would become
the one true Man Who would stand as Intercessor between
the Father and the human race.

*Revelation 13:8* informs us that the Lamb was "slain from
the foundation of the world," establishing our redemption
before the first sin was ever committed![21] From eternity past
He stood in our place, the true Adam, perfectly agreeing with
the Father's will where the earthly Adam did not, and taking
upon Himself the just and right judgment of death for the
sin of all humans. From eternity, long before the incarnation,
He was pouring Himself out that we might live through His
life—the ultimate picture of intercession.

### Jesus' Continuing Intercession

When Jesus was resurrected, the body that came forth
from the grave had a different kind of humanity from the
one that was buried. In His bodily resurrection, Jesus, the
eternal Bridegroom, released to us the power to become the
children of God,[22] and now lives in the presence of the Father
to sustain us in that relationship by His constant intercession.[23] Through the power of Christ's resurrection, we stand

even now in that place of intimate authority,[24] anticipating the full realization of our identity as the Bride, which is the corporate identity of all who accept His invitation to the ultimate wedding feast at the end of the ages.[25]

Even as the wrath of God was poured out upon the perfect Intercessor, so the pleasure of God is now poured out on the Bridegroom, and righteousness is imputed to His yet imperfect Bride. He is gathering to Himself all who will respond, so that when the time comes, a holy and blameless Bride might be called forward to reign with Him.[26]

And so the Man Christ Jesus still stands in the place of intercession, ever before the Father, ever living to intercede.[27] Assisted by the Holy Spirit, the constant posture of Jesus now is to agree with the Father concerning the position of the Bride before God. He is our Advocate, pleading our case before the Father, our just Judge.[28] By the power of the Spirit, we are constantly being transformed into His image,[29] becoming one with Him as a man and woman become partners in the context of intimacy in a marriage relationship.

## Partners in Intercession

Now and throughout eternity, we have the privilege as His bridal partners to intercede in the same way Jesus does, standing in the gap on behalf of the rest of mankind and agreeing with God's desires. We come boldly and confidently before His presence, the throne of grace, because the way has been opened for us by the true Man, Jesus Christ, our Bridegroom.[30] We receive His mercies afresh every day[31] and we are empowered by His presence to walk out the new life He has given us by the blood of Christ.[32] In that place of safety and intimacy, we take our place as His Bride and bring before Him the needs of the people around us, declaring over them the will of God by agreeing with His agenda as revealed in the Word of God.[33]

In this process, we come to an ever-increasing awareness of His goodness and the truth of His ways. We begin to understand that the heart of God is for us and not against us, and that His purposes for the human race are more wonderful than we ever imagined.[34] We come into glad-hearted agreement with the Son of God concerning Who He is, Who the Father is and who we are.

We are the objects of His delight, the focus of His affections, and because He speaks this to our hearts in such a personal and convincing way, we begin to comprehend that He can feel the same way about every person without leaving any individual unattended. We start to share His perspective of our cities and nations and of the situations in which our families and friends find themselves. When we experience His love poured out upon us, we become convinced of His power to set right every situation for every person. When His powerful affections touch our hearts, we realize that the true reward of prayer is not changed circumstances, but the reality of intimate experiential friendship with Jesus Christ, the Lover of our souls. In that place of intimacy, we are free to affect the world around us with the knowledge of His love.

As we come to know His heart, there is a point at which He invites us to walk the streets of the cities with Him, personally touching those who need Him—the "dimly burning candles" and "bruised reeds"[35] of this world—until their lights burn brightly and their countenances are lifted up. The power is His. The new identity is ours. The methodology is intercession.

And so, we pray.

CHAPTER 2

# SEEING WITH NEW EYES

## THE BRIDAL PARADIGM, PART 1

T hrough my years in full-time ministry, a number now approaching 30, there are some things I have come to observe with a measure of clarity. For example, I've come to understand that how we see reality and truth is a major factor in our ability to experience the Christian life in the way we desire. Back in the early 1980s my wife, Mary, and I were privileged to be associated with John Wimber and the emerging Vineyard movement, with their emphasis on the release of a new style of intimate worship. One distinctive was that the gifts of the Holy Spirit, particularly healing, were not merely to be believed in, but experienced as a normal part of the Christian life. It was an exhilarating and lively time in the body of Christ, and much excitement and exuberance accompanied our times of worship and ministry.[1]

In order for us to move freely into those kinds of experiences, we needed to make some adjustments in the way we perceived reality. We needed to have a way of seeing that made room for the incursion of the miraculous into what we called "normal" life. Not only that, but we desired to see these supernatural realities lived out in a way that was not culturally weird or offensive in unnecessary ways.[2] In short, we needed a paradigm shift, a way of re-defining normalcy that included opportunities for the power of God to invade our usual experience.

The wonderful thing was that as we developed this new perspective according to the biblical examples of God's insurgent power, we began to experience that power somewhat more regularly and some of our experiences began to resemble more closely the dynamic of the New Testament accounts. As that perspective was received through the body of Christ during subsequent years, more and more believers began to experience new dimensions of God's miraculous presence in their everyday lives.

I believe we need a paradigm shift once again among God's people with regard to prayer. In the activity-addicted, performance-oriented entity that is the Church, we have largely lost sight of the experiential intimacy with Jesus to which we have been called, and we need a restoration of that understanding. The new perspective makes room for believers to define their lives before God not on the basis of what they do for Him, *but on the basis of the declarations of His ravished heart as the Heavenly Bridegroom.*

We need a shift in the way we read the Scriptures, with a resultant shift in our theological thinking and ultimately a shift in the way we relate to Jesus, to ourselves, and to what we do in His Name. Our experience of the Christian life needs to be deepened and changed. The path the Holy Spirit is opening into this deeper experience is the way of intimacy with Jesus as our Bridegroom. My goal in this chapter is to begin building a foundation of biblical understanding that will enable believers to see with new eyes, to begin to experience the presence of the Lord in new and sweeter ways.

I readily acknowledge at the outset that this "bridal paradigm" is not a new thing. It has been a central part of biblical theology all through history, and has been preserved through the life of the Church in marvelous ways in the experiences of mystics and contemplatives, most of whom have lived within the Catholic and Orthodox expressions of Christianity. There have been, however, a precious few saints within the Protestant ethos who have gone deep into the understanding of Jesus' love for His Bride, and whose personal experiences of these depths have enabled them to write in helpful ways.

Like Martha of Bethany, Protestant Evangelicals have been concerned with many necessary things, to the point that we have excluded the needful thing Mary chose—sitting at the feet of the Bridegroom to hear His heart and voice. But God is changing that, and my prayer is that this little contribution to the process will be of assistance to those who read it.

Let's look at this theme of bridal relationship as it is presented through the Scriptures, beginning with the Old Testament record, that we might know and believe what is in His heart.

## OLD TESTAMENT PICTURES

This section is by no means exhaustive. My hope is merely to begin to open your eyes to the reality that the bridal paradigm is found everywhere in the Scriptures. My desire is that you might see it for the dominant theme that it is, and thus interpret the rest of the story through that grid. Having said that, I have chosen to include several of the most significant snapshots, though I will be developing others in subsequent chapters.

### The Joining of Adam and Eve

When the Lord God first set man in the Garden, He did an interesting thing. He allowed the newly formed human to experience what it was like not to have a counterpart right from the beginning as all the other creatures did. It was the only thing in the whole of creation that God said was "not good." The question comes to me: Why did the Lord follow this plan? Why did He not establish man and woman at the same time, and give them to one another in the fullness of intimacy that He intended humans to experience together?

Was there something churning in God's heart that could only be understood by Adam through the sense of being incomplete, knowing first-hand the experience of loneliness and deprivation? Why the man's sense of exhilaration and wonder at the completeness he realized only when the woman came on the scene? Surely from his observation of the animal realm, he sensed there was something "wrong," something "missing," and yet how could that be, since Adam had known no other existence? How can one long for something that does not exist?

C.S. Lewis wrote that the fact that a man is hungry does not ensure that he will be fed, but it certainly indicates that somewhere there is food designed to meet his need. *In the same way, the fact that Adam knew he was incomplete demanded the existence of a fulfilling reality.* Adam's longing had to have its root somewhere other than in his own experience.

And what of the strange idea that a man must therefore leave father and mother, and cling to his wife? Adam left no one to cling to Eve. Was this merely the starting point for future reference, or was there already a reference point in place, one that stretched backward beyond the boundaries of time? The answer to these musings would be mere speculation except for the understanding that comes much later through the writings of Paul the apostle. In *Ephesians 5*, he quotes some of the same phrases as the basis for commitment in human marriage, then shows us that the reference point for these ideas is none other than Christ and the Church.[3] The statement about leaving and cleaving was an early reflection of God's plan for Jesus to come in the flesh, leaving the heavenly home of the Father to cling to a human Bride.

Adam's longing, his sense of being unfulfilled, his exhilaration at the discovery of his counterpart, had its genesis in the heart of Christ and His desire for the Bride that was the standard before mankind was ever created! Adam's experience of longing was, from the first moment, a reflection of the chosen longing in the heart of the Triune God to have a counterpart suitable for His beloved Son, the living Word in Whom was formed everything that exists.

The taking of the woman from the side of the man, out of his very flesh and bone, must have seemed to Adam a bizarre methodology compared with the one God employed for the rest of creation. We see it now as a picture of the Bride taken from the riven side of the crucified Christ, the Lamb slain from the foundation of the world.[4] He identified permanently with her humanity without negating His divinity, thereby leaving Himself with no alternative but to exalt her to the incredible place of fellowship and partnership in the triune life of God. Truly a magnificent picture! And it's only the beginning.

### The Story of Isaac and Rebekah

One of the clearest representations of the Gospel in the Old Testament is in the twenty-fourth chapter of *Genesis*, in the story of Abraham's search for a suitable wife for his son, Isaac. What appears on the surface to be merely a nice, romantic story in the lives of two children of Middle-Eastern nomadic tribes becomes, when seen through the perspective of the bridal metaphor, an astonishing prophetic picture of what God had in mind for His people as He pursued them for the sake of His beloved Son.

The fact that Abraham's relationship with Isaac is a prophetic picture of God's relationship with Jesus is no surprise. We see that reality in the supernatural birth of Isaac and in the fact that he is named "Son of Laughter." Since Christ is portrayed in *Psalm 45:7* as the most joyous human being because of His love for righteousness, it is easy to see Isaac's name as a preview of the heart of the true Bridegroom. We see the "type" of Christ in the beautiful and gripping portrayal of Isaac being sacrificed as a burnt offering, only to be rescued at the last moment when God declared that He would provide Himself as the sacrificial Lamb.[5] But the prophetic portrayal goes even further as we consider the elements of chapter 24.

At the beginning of that section of Scripture, Abraham declares that his longing to have a suitable bride for Isaac will not be fulfilled in the land of Canaan, but among his kindred people, his family. The old and trusted servant, Eliezer, is commanded by the father not to settle for one of the local girls, but to go to the country that is the focus of the father's heart, among his own people, there to find a wife suitable for his son.

It is my belief that Eliezer fills a dual role in this picture of the Gospel. At first he stands in the role of the Man Christ Jesus, coming to earth as God incarnate, yet not presented in the regal disclosure of His power and majesty, but in the hiddenness of the Servant's identity.[6] He takes with him gifts from the father's house to woo the prospective bride, gifts meant to indicate the wealth of the father's house without overwhelming her freedom to accept or reject the offer of a husband.

The servant sets out on the long journey to the bride's country (a picture of the incarnation) and meets her in a place designed to reveal her spirit of servanthood. He arrives at the well near Rebekah's hometown at about the time the women come to draw water. His test for the prospective bride is that she be not only beautiful, but that she also have the willingness to serve with gladness of heart. This part of the picture is very important, for the Lord also is looking for a Bride with a servant's spirit. This is not because He is a task-master looking for help, but because He Himself is the Servant and is seeking a like-minded partner. Only a Servant-Bride completes the picture adequately.

It is in this arena of servanthood that there are some dangers for those seeking to move out of a "Martha" mentality into more of a "Mary" posture before the Lord. If we are not careful, in our attempts to grasp the place of intimacy we can turn our backs on the servant dimensions of that relationship. Our key role model is Mary, the mother of Jesus, who presented herself first as the "handmaid of the Lord," then moved into a place of greater intimacy.

In many of the biblical examples of the bridal analogy, the posture of the *handmaiden* is clearly in focus at the beginning of the story. In the story of Isaac and Rebekah, it is part of the initial encounter between Eliezer and the girl as he asks her for a drink of water from the well. It is this part of the story that convinces me of the servant's place as a picture of the first coming of Jesus, for this prophetic shadow is fulfilled in the encounter between Jesus and the woman at the well in *John 4*. As Eliezer encountered Rebekah, so Jesus encountered the woman—and so He encounters us in the places of our thirst and need.

Of course, Rebekah serves him gladly, going the extra mile of watering his 10 camels until they are satisfied, no small task. Eliezer inquires about her family and eventually meets them and joins them for a meal, another picture of Jesus' willingness to have fellowship with human beings and share the elements of covenant with them. Upon disclosing to them his identity and mission, Eliezer inquires about the possibility of Rebekah going with him to become Isaac's wife.

Although the girl has never seen Isaac, she realizes that something has happened in her heart through this encounter with the servant: She loves Isaac.[7] She is eager to go with Eliezer to realize her destiny. In the same way, Jesus came to the Bride's country in the guise of a Servant, sharing the gifts of the Father's house: healing, deliverance, the truth about the Kingdom of God. The Servant-Bride, having seen the Father's heart through the life of the Servant, falls in love with the Son. And she loves Him even though she has not yet seen Him in His eternal power and glory. She's only seen the disguise of his humanity, which by comparison has no form or comeliness that He should be desired at all.[8]

Rebekah decides to take the long journey with Eliezer back to the father's home, to meet the son face to face. She is released from her father's house with the blessing of her family members, who speak a powerful prophecy over her life that finds its final fulfillment in the victorious Church occupying the territory of her enemies. This journey is a picture of the Christian life, a journey through the wilderness, the bride making herself ready in the difficult context of riding through the desert on the back of a camel. Could there be a better picture of the preparatory journey of the believer's walk of faith on the way to heaven? At this point, in my imagination, Eliezer takes on the role of the Holy Spirit, functioning as Rebekah's guide and friend, keeping her focus fixed on the beauty of the son so she will have the grace to endure the journey.

Finally, the ordeal is complete, and Rebekah sees Isaac walking in the field near Abraham's home. She alights from the camel and finishes her preparation just in time to be introduced to the son. He is delighted with her, and his heart is captured by this beautiful woman ("Rebekah" means "snared by beauty"!) who has been provided for him by the desire of the father's heart. Their union is a full-blown picture of the culminating day of human history, when we will meet our Bridegroom. The veil will be taken away. We shall see Jesus as He is and we shall be like Him, forever joined with Him as His Bride.

This story is historically true. It really happened. The reason it is recounted here is that we might understand, through the picture presented, God's heart as He pursues His people. He is after a Bride for His Son, the One in Whom is all His delight. He finds the beautiful Bride and His heart is fully satisfied with her.

It is my conviction that as we begin to experience this kind of affection from God with greater depth and in greater frequency, we will be established in a place of increasing strength and so equipped to face the coming days.

## The Story of Boaz and Ruth

This story, again historically accurate, stands as a pro-phetic illustration of the heart of God toward His people. The story is powerful in that it centers on God's embrace of Gen-tile peoples in His plan to find His Bride. It is one of the first pictures in the Scriptures demonstrating that relationship with God is established in the heart arena of faith, not within the confines of ethnic heritage. Many elements of this story are worthy of deeper study but they are beyond the scope of this work.[9] I will focus on a few aspects of the truth that are illustrative of the bridal paradigm.

The dimension of the handmaiden is perhaps even more in focus here than in the previous example. Ruth is the Moabite daughter-in-law of Naomi, who years earlier had left her Jewish homeland due to a famine to sojourn in Moab with her husband and sons. The sons had married Moabite women and, in a tragic twist, had become sick and died, as had their father. Only the three women were left and they were in crushing circumstances. We join the story as the fam-ine in Judah has broken. Naomi decides to go back to her homeland and, in the desperate state of her widowhood, try to find a relative who will have mercy on her. One of the daughters-in-law decides to remain in Moab, but the other, Ruth, follows her heart and goes with Naomi to discover her fate.

As they arrive in the area around Bethlehem, Ruth must give herself to working in the fields of the region, gleaning the grain left over by the harvesters. In those days, this was the Lord's way of making provision for the needy.[10] It is in this place of humility and servanthood, the place of the widow/handmaiden with no expectation of privilege or inti-macy, that Ruth is brought into an encounter with Boaz. He is the owner of the land and the one who in this story takes the place of the God-figure, opposite Ruth's characterization as the Bride.

As Ruth labors in the field, Boaz comes to check on the workers. Having heard the reports around town of this new girl who has been faithful to Naomi and who works with such diligence, he extends his protection and blessing to her. He ends up giving her more grain than she is able to collect on her own, and begins to model the grace of the Lord shown to those who come to Him for help.

When Ruth returns to Naomi at the end of the day, a wonderful truth is uncovered: Boaz is in fact a relative, one who would be in line to be a "kinsman-redeemer," with the right and dutiful privilege of claiming these women as members of his household since their husbands are no longer present to provide for them. As the story progresses, Boaz becomes aware of this situation and wants to fulfill this role. He eventually takes Ruth as his wife, and it is out of their union that Obed, the grandfather of King David, is born and the lineage of the Messiah is established.

Two little realities in this story grab my heart in a significant way, and speak to me of God's grace as He embraces me as His own and touches me with the tenderness of His romantic heart. First, there is the reality that Boaz' first posture toward Ruth is that of a father. In a poignant encounter in which she submits herself to his care, this relationship is established.[11] It is here that Ruth presents herself to Boaz as a maidservant, making no claim to bridal intimacy, but simply coming in the humility and purity of one who needs covering and protection.

Ruth, however, does not realize the extent to which Boaz' heart has been ignited by her beauty and her humble willingness to serve him. In a previous segment,[12] Boaz has instructed her to stay by the young women and keep her eyes focused on what she has been given to do in the field. Later, in an endearing mis-reporting of the encounter, she informs Naomi that she was instructed to stay by the young men, at which point Naomi corrects her, and settles her into the appropriate role for the situation.

As Ruth presents herself to Boaz for his fatherly covering, he gives the first indication that there is more in his heart
than being her protector. Boaz has also experienced the
emerging love of a bridegroom for this girl, and he takes initiative toward that end. This is an example of the earthly
portrayal of the dual role of Father and Bridegroom that characterizes God's love for His people. He loves us first of all as
Father, to establish us in our fundamental identity as His
people, the children of His family. And then in His great love
for the Son, He prepares us to be joined to Him as the Bride:
One God deals with us in the dual roles of Father and Son,
and all of it is directed by the third Person, the Holy Spirit.[13]

As the fatherly Boaz takes initiative with Ruth, he becomes
smitten with her beauty and character, and he is glad she has
kept her attentions from the young men. In a surprising revelation of the Lord's heart for His Bride, Boaz speaks to her
of the kindness she has shown to him by *"not going after the
young men, whether poor or rich."*[14] She has shown him a great
kindness! Here is the initial emergence of the heart of a passionate Bridegroom being revealed in a startling vulnerability—God's heart filled with delight that the girl would choose
Him over the more immediately appealing but far inferior
loves of her daily experience. His heart is made glad by the
choice of a servant-girl! What a romantic reality!

My heart is staggered by the thought that this Old Testament saint is merely a model of the eternal heart of my
Redeemer, Whose heart is made glad by *me*, Who considers
it a *kindness shown by me to Him* that I would keep my affections for Him alone, not turning my eyes away to lesser loves,
but keeping a single focus, gazing upon Him, longing for no
one but Him. And the wonder of it is, He will touch me with
this truth. He will speak it to my heart by the power of the
Holy Spirit as I sit quietly in His presence, giving Him a chance
to impress this upon me at the level of my heart-understand-
ing. This is communicated to me more deeply than that of a
theology that merely touches my mind. This is the kind of
truth that must be burned into my heart experientially, that

my innermost being may become convinced and transformed by the knowledge of His extravagant love.

### The Story of Hosea and Gomer

Perhaps the most jarring and unexpected story of the Bridegroom's love for His Bride is found in the prophetic parable of Hosea and Gomer. The story line is not difficult to follow, except that the reality of it is so astounding. The book of *Hosea* stands as an unfathomable declaration of the ravished heart of God that will not be dissuaded from loving the Bride of His choice, regardless of her rebellious and foolish ways.

As we are introduced to the drama in the first few verses of chapter one, we are stunned by the command given to the prophet Hosea: *"Go, take yourself a wife of harlotry, and the children of harlotry. . . . "* As if it is not enough to take a wife of harlotry, in chapter three Hosea is again commanded concerning this woman, only this time in a more intensive fashion: *"Go again, love a woman who is loved by a lover and is committing adultery, just like the love of the Lord for the children of Israel, who look to other gods and love the raisin cakes of the pagans."* Hosea is commanded not only to take an adulterous wife, but he is commanded to love her, *"like the love of the Lord for . . . Israel."*

It is clear that the Lord knows exactly what kind of woman He is embracing—one who "loves the raisin cakes" of the pagan peoples. Raisin cakes were a symbol of sexual desire, often used in the rites of pagan religions as an aphrodisiac to stimulate lewd desire and ritual promiscuity. God is fully aware whom He is loving here, and in order to demonstrate His love to the people of the earth, He arrests, commands and empowers a human male to love such a woman with His kind of love.

At first glance we might think, "How nice that the Lord would give such a love to Hosea!" But this love is anything but "nice." The Holy Spirit gives Hosea a supernatural, burning passion for this woman Gomer, a love that will not be dissuaded by the vilest practices. This is an agonizing love, a love rooted in the covenant of a burning heart, one that cannot change. It is a love poured forth through a man held in the grip of God so that the people of the nation may have an undeniable example of God's heart for them. This is raw and unrelenting passion, terrible and inextinguishable love, the kind of strong love that will face the shame of the cross so the Bride may be purchased once and for all.

In one of the most powerful encounters of the entire Scriptures, the Lord speaks to Israel in chapter two of *Hosea*, and charges her with the vileness of her sin against God. In the first 13 verses, God charges Israel with repeated unfaithfulness and vows to expose the vile nature of her sin and shame. Her sin is spoken of in the most explicit sexual terminology,[15] and in a stroke of unimaginable judgment God strips her naked, exposing her before the leering eyes of her false lovers. It is made clear in these records that Israel's sin was not the result of being misled or unwittingly enticed. She has been purposeful in her sin,[16] pursuing false lovers with zeal, even stooping to the place of paying them for her pleasure.

This is such a thorough judgment that the false lovers themselves turn away in disgust. Yet, in the aftermath of this radical exposure, when every expectation is that God will reject this people who bring Him nothing but pain, He speaks these startling things:

> **"Therefore, behold, I will allure her,**
> **will bring her into the wilderness,**
> **and speak comfort to her.**
> **I will give her her vineyards from there,**
> **and the Valley of Achor as a door of hope;**
> **She shall sing there, as in the days of her youth,**
> **As in the day when she came up**
> **from the land of Egypt.**

**"And it shall be, in that day," says the LORD,
"That you will call Me 'My Husband,'
and no longer call Me 'My Master,'
For I will take from her mouth
the names of the Baals,
And they shall be remembered
by their name no more."
Hosea 2:14-17**

It is in the context of her extreme, purposeful failure that God comes to His Bride, re-focuses her attention on Him, and informs her that now He is going to restore her to the place of bridal relationship. He is going to do this for His own pleasure and by His own profligate goodness and passion, that she might once again know Him as "Husband" and not "Master."[17] He will not stand for His Bride to be unfaithful. The way He deals with the situation is not to reject her, but to woo her and win her back to Himself out of her foolishness, rebellion and devastation.

In New Testament terms, it is this reality that causes the Man Jesus to relate the way He does to the woman caught in adultery,[18] for she is the personification of the devastated Bride. His mercy is not motivated by the pity-filled heart of someone who merely understands the wretchedness of the human condition and wants to be kind to one who is broken and weak. Rather, it is the inflamed heart of the Bridegroom Whose radical, terrible kindness is driven by jealous and passionate romance in a pure sense. His rescue of this woman is the daring intervention of a Kinsman-Redeemer in Whose heart this woman has been defined from before the foundation of the world as a faithful Bride.

She has been held in the clutches of an enemy and her life can only be healed by the most extreme kind of love. He does not condemn her, though she was caught in the very act of adultery, and in a profound act of empowering grace He tells her she will not return to this place of sin but she will love Him in return, as passionately and perfectly as He loves her. This is the love of a Bridegroom God, Who comes to the broken and shamed of the earth, and exchanges their ash-heap brokenness for the headpiece of beauty that He Himself wears in the wedding ceremony.[19]

You see, the so-called fairy tales of history really are true. The Prince really has kissed the girl, the humble handmaid really is the Princess, and the Beauty who has been under the spell of the poison apple really will be brought to life. The King will have His glorious Bride and the desires of His heart will be satisfied. The stories are clear and you'll find them throughout Scripture. Our God is a God in love, and His burning heart is the heart of a Bridegroom Who will not be dissuaded from His task. His zeal burns for the restoration of His people, and He will not relent until the broken woman, whose name is also called Jerusalem, shines forth in the way He intended, as a praise in all the earth.[20]

It is out of this reality that Isaiah writes passages such as that found in chapter 62 of his prophecy:

> **For Zion's sake I will not hold My peace,**
> **and for Jerusalem's sake I will not rest,**
> **Until her righteousness goes forth as**
> **brightness, and her salvation as**
> **a lamp that burns.**
>
> **The Gentiles shall see your righteousness,**
> **and all kings your glory.**
> **You shall be called by a new name,**
> **which the mouth of the LORD will name.**
>
> **You shall also be a crown of glory in**
> **the hand of the LORD,**
> **And a royal diadem in the hand of your God.**
>
> **You shall no longer be termed Forsaken, nor shall**
> **your land any more be termed Desolate;**
> **But you shall be called Hephzibah,**
> **and your land Beulah;**
> **For the LORD delights in you,**
> **and your land shall be married.**

**For as a young man marries a virgin,
so shall your sons marry you;
And as the bridegroom rejoices over the bride,
so shall your God rejoice over you.
Isaiah 62:1-5**

Notice the progression of the passage: God Himself insists that He will not hold His peace, He will not rest until the lamp of the passionate life of His people burns brightly. His intention is that she become a crown of glory in the hand of God, an enhancement of God Himself! This is an amazing reality in itself, but He goes on to clarify. His people will no longer be forsaken or desolate, and He declares over them the realities of marital provision and delight. God's testimony over this people is that they are the focus of His delight, and that the joy He has is nothing less than the joy of a Bridegroom over His Bride.

Surely in that kind of heart there lies hope for me, if only I have eyes to see as He sees. If we as His people at the end of the age are going to have what it takes to stand firm in the face of surging evil, before the evil one's increasingly overt strategies to distract and dissuade us from His purposes, it will be because we have heard the sweeter song of the Bridegroom's voice, quickening our hearts to what is true and pure. We are loved, and passionately, by the King of the Universe. It is His desire to let me know by the power of the Holy Spirit the reality of this love in my deepest experience.

CHAPTER 3

# THE SONG OF
# THE BRIDEGROOM

## THE BRIDAL PARADIGM, PART 2

A s a male Christian raised in the rugged indi-
vidualism of American culture, I have found it
relatively easy to view God as super-powerful, all-
wise and all-knowing. I can visualize Jesus as the Son of God,
the living Word, the manly Man Who strides over the earth
with purpose and dedication, strong yet compassionate, determined to fulfill the Father's purposes. I've even been able
to fathom the theological concept of Jesus the heavenly Bridegroom, Whose passion is for the redemption of a people called
the Bride of Christ.

Like most men, though, experientially I found myself
struggling to see Jesus as a Bridegroom gazing over me with
the kind of passion I was hearing others speak about. To echo
the words of so many men in response to this message of the
ravished heart of God, I just couldn't picture myself in that
white dress!

Then I began to give myself to the study of this theme in
the Scriptures and began to see how, in Jesus' personal encounters with human beings like me, male and female, He
*was* the experiential fulfillment of those prophetic pictures
given in the Old Testament. Once I began to worship the Lord
in the context of that understanding, I began to experience

the touch of intimacy on my own heart. I began to know what it is to be loved personally, deeply and romantically by the Lover of my soul. I began to comprehend C.S. Lewis' comment: *"God is the Masculine before which all of us are feminine."* I began to know the inexpressible joy of being romanced, of being cherished, of having the Lord touch me in a personal way purely out of affection.

I had known His touch of healing, conviction and forgiveness, of empowering for ministry, of compassion for others, but I had never known the tender touch of His Spirit upon my heart—a touch released simply because of love for me, personally and intimately. I tell you, it is a life-changing experience to know that touch!

Out of the growth in my own life, I want to continue to unfold this biblical perspective so that we all, as contemporary Western believers, can more readily embrace the idea that Jesus would love us like that, personally and existentially. It is my conviction that there is no better place in which to consider this theme than the *Song of Solomon,* the book in Scripture that begins with the bold statement that it is "The Song of all Songs." This is an astonishing claim, for it demands that we consider it in comparison with every song ever composed in heaven or on earth, and come to the agreeable conclusion that this Song is the culminating expression of the art of music-making in the entire history of the universe. The Song of all Songs! This declaration alone confronts us with the truth that what is burning in the heart of God is a romantic reality, that the basis of all music in the universe is romantic love, and that out of that reality, God communicates to us His passion.

## EIGHT PICTURES OF THE BRIDEGROOM

In this chapter I will focus on a number of snapshots of the bridegroom king in the *Song of Solomon* that are fulfilled in the Person of Jesus, as documented in the Gospel accounts of the New Testament. There are eight such pictures upon which I want to focus your attention,[1] and my prayer is that as you meditate on them, your own heart will be stirred to come to know Him more deeply in this place of intimacy.

## The Inviting Shepherd

The dimension of Jesus' character that I call "The Inviting Shepherd" is found in the prophetic picture of the invitation of the king (the picture of Jesus) to the Shulamite shepherd girl (the picture of the Bride of Christ) in the first chapter of the allegory. The young maiden opens the text of this *Song* with a startling expression of desire: *"Let Him kiss me with the kisses of His mouth—for Your love is better than wine."*

It is essential right from the beginning to understand that the imagery here is symbolic. Our interpretation is allegorical; the story is a picture of Jesus' relationship with the Church. Therefore, "the kisses of His mouth" does not refer to a dynamic of sexuality between Christ and His people, but rather to the touch of the Word of God upon the human heart, empowered by the Holy Spirit.[2] When His Word pierces through the emotional and theological barriers of our hearts, and touches us with the existential truth of His love, it is a kiss that is better than any other, it is the exhilaration we were meant to enjoy, the reality of which a human kiss is merely a dim reflection.

As the Shulamite speaks about the king, she inquires concerning his presence (v. 7): Where is that predictable place in which she might feast upon his beauty? She has decided there is no reason she should remain veiled in his presence. Why should she hold herself back from intimacy when he is present specifically to release such a dynamic? It is in the king's reply that we see the face of the Inviting Shepherd:

> **If you do not know, O fairest among women,**
> **follow in the footsteps of the flock,**
> **and feed your little goats**
> **beside the shepherds' tents.**
> **Song 1:8**

In this little phrase, the Shulamite is being invited to join the ranks of the saints throughout history who have pursued the place of intimacy with Jesus extravagantly. One of the things we contemporary evangelical Protestants must face is the fact that throughout history countless human beings have experienced the reality for which our hearts are longing. They have found in that reality the satisfaction of all human desire. In the king's invitation to the Shulamite, I too am being solicited to join the procession of those who have pursued Him with extravagance and passion, and my answer is a resounding "Yes!"

The prophetic Word becomes flesh in the Person of Jesus as He, the incarnate Bridegroom, extends the same invitation to real men to come and join Him in living out this relationship. *John 1:35-39* gives the account of John the Baptist and two of his disciples as they are standing together the day after the baptism of Jesus. John declares that this is the One for Whom he has been waiting. The men see Jesus walking along and they begin to follow Him. He notices and, turning to them, asks what they want. In their response we find the poignant echo of the heart of the Shulamite, voiced in the real words of manly men of the first century: *"Teacher, where are You staying?"*

Can you hear the reverberating sounds of her heart-cry? *"Tell me, O you whom I love, where do you feed your flock?"* And the incredible reality is that on an actual day in history, at about four o'clock in the afternoon, the eternal Word made flesh—the Bridegroom-God Who from ages past has desired intimate relationship with human beings—gazed upon these two flesh-and-blood men, men like me, and gave the Bridegroom's answer: *"Come and see."* And so they followed, and their lives were never the same.

As I write this in the House of Prayer in Kansas City, the worship team is singing from *Psalm 27:4* that like King David, there is nothing I desire more than to spend my life gazing upon the beauty of the Lord.

*I will draw near to You, Jesus! You are my life and my joy! Thank You for inviting me to come and see. My heart burns to know You more, and my longing is that I might find You and hear Your voice more clearly. Kiss me again, Lord, with the kisses of Your mouth, and let me know the truth of Your love for me.*

## The Passionate Suitor

As I consider my own life before the Lord, I am aware that one of my deepest longings is to be desired, to be cherished and seen as the delight of the heart of another. While this can happen to a wonderful degree at the level of human relationships, the reality is that down deep inside, we have a sense that we were made to love Someone and to be loved by Someone in an infinite way. We know there is something inside us that will not be satisfied until we are able to release our love in a fervent single-mindedness that brings focus and passion to everything we do. The awareness of this longing causes an ache in the human soul that simply cannot be assuaged except by the touch of the infinite Lover, and by our response—a fervent commitment to Him. Only He can go that deep, only He can love that way. Only He can elicit that kind of response.

This is the reality that is at play in the staggeringly beautiful encounter between the Shulamite and the king at the end of chapter 1 and the beginning of chapter 2 of the *Song*. In verse 12 of chapter 1, having been invited to the place of intimacy in which she could come to know the heart of the king, she begins to express the romantic inclinations of her heart by declaring that her perfume is drawing his attention, even as he sits at the dinner table. She muses on the passions of her heart, giving poetic expression to that which burns inside:

**A bundle of myrrh is my beloved to me,
that lies all night between my breasts.
My beloved is to me a cluster of
henna blooms in the vineyards of En Gedi.
Song 1:13-14**

The king responds, articulating the very thing she longs to hear, his fiery words instilling in her heart a passion deeper than she has ever known:

**Behold, you are fair, my love! Behold,
you are fair! You have dove's eyes.**
**Song 1:15**

To be considered fair by the king! In his words are the power of life and death. And he calls her fair! The power of it grips her soul, entering deep within the secret chambers of her heart, the places of insecurity and fear that have not been completely healed. She is not yet the mature bride who will emerge later in the *Song*. She is still the immature maiden who knows there is weakness in her, who is painfully aware of her propensity to unfaithfulness and sin.

His words begin to change that. He speaks of her as having *"dove's eyes."* To us, that sounds poetic but sort of meaningless until we understand that a dove has the capacity to focus its eyes on only one thing at a time. It sees only one thing. And when the king is speaking this reality over the Shulamite, he is declaring to her that in his view she has already reached the single-minded fervency of love that her heart desires. He sees her as fair and faithful, and this at the very beginning of their relationship. How can this be?

In his wisdom and foresight, the king sees the Shulamite as she will be when his love for her has completed its work, and he relates to her on that basis from the beginning. He knows that the power of her true identity and the dynamic of his love will transform her as certainly as the dawn comes in the morning. In the place of intimate fellowship, he can speak these things in such a way that her heart will hear them and believe. And so he invites her to the place of nearness and intrigue, the banqueting house,[3] and there sustains her with expressions of his deepest love.

This delightful and beautiful picture of the love language exchanged by these two is given expression in the life of Jesus, this time recorded for us in the Gospel of Matthew. But in the New Testament portrayal, the heart of Jesus is filled with pathos and grief. *Matthew 23:37-39* is the record of Jesus' lamentation over Jerusalem because the city, as the representation of the Bride of Christ,[4] has refused His invitation to intimacy and instead has continued the historic practice of killing those who come in His Name to draw her to His side. The emotion of the heart of Jesus is palpable:

> **O Jerusalem, Jerusalem, the one who kills the prophets and stones those who are sent to her! How often I wanted to gather your children together, as a hen gathers her chicks under her wings, but you were not willing!**
>
> **Matthew 23:37**

Jesus is here giving testimony to the passion burning in the heart of God, the same passion that caused Him to speak in such loving terms over the life of His dark but lovely bride in the *Song*. He longs to gather His people to the House of Wine (more on this in Chapter 5), to stir our emotions of being cherished and seen as fervent and single-minded. He deeply desires to speak to our hearts of how He sees us, of the delight that is within Him, of the confidence He has in the power of His love to do the things He has promised.

Those during the course of history who have experienced this "gathering," this stirring of the Lord's intimate love, bear witness: Nothing else matters when the touch of Christ's love fills our hearts. This is why Paul the apostle could cheerfully consider every other important thing to be so much refuse compared with the pleasure of knowing Jesus.[5] It is why Stephen exulted as he stared death in the face, for he saw the Lord's glory in the face of his Bridegroom standing at the right hand of the Father to welcome him into eternity.[6] Because of this reality the martyrs of history have gladly given their lives for the sake of a better resurrection—one fully conformed to the life of the Beloved.[7] Jesus fulfills the promise, and He calls you and me to that place.

*Jesus, I will receive Your invitation to the place of intimacy in prayer. I long to hear Your voice telling me the truth of who I am, and how You love me. I long to live out of the place of affirmation that comes from Your heart, and that liberates me to love You in return and live in the beauty of Your holiness. Draw me, Lord, and I will follow after You.*

## The Challenging Leader

In the life of every believer comes a time that is often very disconcerting. It is the time when the Holy Spirit chooses to reveal to us that the Lover of our souls and the King of the universe are one and the same Person. We are gripped by a sense of awe and wonder that is pleasant and exhilarating on one hand yet terrifying on the other, because we begin to see the implications of intimacy with this Man, Christ Jesus.

In C.S. Lewis' *The Lion, the Witch, and the Wardrobe* there is a delightful section in which one of the citizens of Narnia, Mr. Beaver, is leading the newcomers (children from England who will one day rule in the Kingdom of Narnia) to meet Aslan the Lion, the Christ-figure in the story. As they approach the place where they will meet him, the children begin to experience feelings of holy dread and numinous, which cause them to tremble with appropriate fear. One of the children asks Mr. Beaver a question that capsulates the fears that well up in any human soul when confronted by that which tran-scends us: *"This Aslan—is he safe?"*

That's the question, isn't it? Part of us wants to experi-ence an exhilarating love, but at the same time we want to know that it's safe to go there, especially in an era when adventuresome romance is so frequently unsafe.

Mr. Beaver's answer shines with the wisdom of the ages, the understanding of one who has walked with the Lord for long years: *"Safe? No one said anything about safe. But he's good! He's the king, I tell you!"* It is because of the reality of God's goodness that we can have confidence as we approach Him, knowing that wherever He may lead us, we are ultimately safe. We begin to be confident about ultimate things, that no matter what we may encounter, our eternal well-being is a settled issue.

To the surprise of the Shulamite, her beloved appears one day in a thoroughly unexpected persona. She describes his coming in this way:

**The voice of my beloved!**
**Behold, he comes leaping upon the mountains,**
**skipping upon the hills.**
**Song 2:8**

In these delightful phrases we are informed of the sovereign power of the king over all the obstacles of life, the hills and mountains that seem to us unconquerable hindrances to a life of faithful and single-minded fervency for the Lord. Her response to the king's activity is filled with wonder and delight, and there is an initial sense of enjoyment at what he is doing:

**My beloved is like a gazelle or a young stag.**
**Behold, he stands behind our wall;**
**He is looking through the windows,**
**Gazing through the lattice.**
**Song 2:9**

Suddenly, though, her mood changes, because as the king draws near to the Shulamite in disclosing his sovereign authority over difficult things, he invites her to join him in the exhilarating dance of victory over the seemingly undefeatable realities of her life:

**My beloved spoke, and said to me:**
**"Rise up, my love, my fair one, and come away.**
**For lo, the winter is past,**
**the rain is over and gone.**
**The flowers appear on the earth;**
**the time of singing has come,**

**and the voice of the turtledove
is heard in our land.
The fig tree puts forth her green figs, and the vines
with the tender grapes give a good smell.**

**Rise up, my love, my fair one, and come away!
"O my dove, in the clefts of the rock, in the secret
places of the cliff, let me see your face,
let me hear your voice; for your voice is sweet,
and your face is lovely."
Song 2:10-14**

In our parallel relationship with Jesus, we must confront a crucial question: Will He be allowed to draw us past the things that have regularly defeated us in our attempts to be faithful in following Him? But the wondrous emphasis here is clearly on the majesty of the king, his beauty and power, and his ability to take the Shulamite with him as he leaps and dances over the mountains of her life. He draws her after him, reminding her that she is hidden in the cleft of the rock—a euphemism for the riven side of Christ on the cross.[8] It is in the context of his sacrifice and redeeming power that she is safe, and his voice draws her to come and follow.

But she can't do it. Her fears are too strong, and in the first real crisis of the Song, the Shulamite declines his invitation:

**Until the day breaks and the shadows flee away,
turn, my beloved,
and be like a gazelle or a young stag
upon the mountains of Bether.
Song 2:17**

*"Turn, my Beloved, and be like a gazelle or a young stag. . . ."* In effect, the Shulamite is saying "Go, my friend, and do what you do. I am unable to come, but I will delight in your power and majesty." This is the first crisis of faith, and the first point at which the Shulamite must face her own

failure to experience the life she longs to live. Restoration will come later, but for now she experiences a time of defeat.

I believe a powerful story in the *Gospel of Matthew* corresponds directly to this prophetic scene. In chapter 14, the disciples are trying to cross the Sea of Galilee in a raging storm in the middle of the night, and Jesus comes walking to them on the water. Consider the power of the text:

> **And when the disciples saw Him walking on the sea, they were troubled, saying, "It is a ghost!" And they cried out for fear. But immediately Jesus spoke to them, saying, "Be of good cheer! It is I; do not be afraid."**
>
> **And Peter answered Him and said, "Lord, if it is You, command me to come to You on the water." So He said, "Come." And when Peter had come down out of the boat, he walked on the water to go to Jesus.**
>
> **But when he saw that the wind was boisterous, he was afraid; and beginning to sink he cried out, saying, "Lord, save me!"**
>
> **And immediately Jesus stretched out His hand and caught him, and said to him, "O you of little faith, why did you doubt?"**
>
> **And when they got into the boat, the wind ceased. Then those who were in the boat came and worshiped Him, saying, "Truly You are the Son of God."**
>
> **Matthew 14:26-33**

In a stunning fulfillment of the allegory, Jesus, a real flesh-and-blood Man, comes walking on top of the stormy seas. What's more, He invites Peter to come and join Him. I wish I could communicate the sense of majesty I am feeling as I write this. We have read this story so often and interpreted it (appropriately) in a spiritual sense, but it really happened! Jesus was really out there, dancing on the waves. It was impossible, but it happened! And then Peter really said, in time and space, during the fourth watch of the night (between 3:00 and 6:00 a.m.), "Call me out there with You, if it's really You!"

I've wondered why the time of day is included in some of these stories. It seems incidental, but I believe it's because God is communicating that these incredible encounters happened in real time, during a real storm in a real night, with real water and the real possibility of disaster. This is no fairy tale—there are no rocks under the water for Him to stand on, and no computer-generated special effects. It really happened!

Jesus loves Peter's request, and answers him without hesitation: *"Come!"* Imagine the scream in Peter's heart. *"OH NO! He's calling my bluff!"* We can hardly imagine the moment. But he went for it. He dared, if only for a moment, to dance upon his fears, and the Bridegroom's heart was thrilled. Even though Peter lost his focus, even though he began to sink, the Lord was there, and *that's the whole point!* When the King invites us to come, we can presume upon His power to save. The subsequent statement about "little faith" is not so much a rebuke as it is the affectionate and playful response of a fatherly Bridegroom Whose heart is absolutely exhilarated at the willingness of His child-friend to dare to trust Him. Far from being critical of Peter, I believe Jesus is saying *"O Peter! If you only knew what is possible! Trust me, and I will take you through places and events you never even dreamed of, for with me all things are possible!"*

*O, Sovereign King! O, Majestic Lord of all things! I long to dare to run with You! I long for the courage of the leap of faith, the joy of the victorious dance upon the stormy waves, upon the mountains and hills of my fears. Call me again, Lord! Don't give up on me! Sooner or later, I will trust You.*

## The Glorious Bridegroom

As we face our own fears, there is often a sense of unrest rooted in the fear that God will measure us by our standards rather than by His, and that we will be judged unworthy of His affections. While these feelings may rightfully accompany true conviction and repentance, all too often they are simply the recurrent accusations of the enemy and of our own minds, passing judgment on ourselves based on the faulty assumption that God has done so, too.

What is almost impossible for us to understand (indeed, it requires the ministry of the Holy Spirit![9]) is that His assessment is based on totally different information from what we see. He is gazing upon a Bride who is fully formed, whose life is hidden in the life of His Son at the Father's right hand,[10] and who therefore can embrace with total confidence the character we already have been given. We, like any child growing up into the identity made certain by his or her heritage, are becoming who we are.

In the aftermath of the Shulamite's hesitancy to follow the king, she experiences this kind of restlessness, the fear that she has lost the one her heart desires:

> **By night on my bed I sought the one I love;**
> **I sought him, but I did not find him.**
> **"I will rise now," I said, "And go about the city;**
> **in the streets and in the squares**
> **I will seek the one I love." I sought him,**
> **but I did not find him.**
> **Song 3:1-2**

When my own passion for intimacy with Jesus was being birthed, there came such a crisis moment. My soul was awakening to His wooing, and I had begun to ask the Holy Spirit to increase my sense of longing for the presence of the Lord. I continued in this mode for some days, until early one morning I had a profound and powerful encounter with the Spirit of God. It was as though He decided, in a quite literal way, to take me up on my request for a greater sense of longing.

In that hour-long confrontation (my wife awoke to the sounds of my anguish and knew it was the Lord, but feared

I was having a heart attack!), I began to feel an overwhelming sense of desire, an experience that was not wholly positive. I had been asking for a longing to know the Lord, but wrapped in that awakening desire were the memories of all the disappointments and anguish associated with unfulfilled dreams and deferred hope. My heart was sick in a more desperate way than I had been able to express, and in this moment the Spirit of God was inviting me to dance upon the waves of those fears and disappointments. And I said *"No."*

It was too frightening to go there. I couldn't bear the thought of facing all that "stuff," so I did what the Shulamite did, what Peter did. I looked at the mountains of difficulties instead of at the strength of the King, and said, *"You go ahead. I'll be along some other time."* In the days immediately following that decision, His presence withdrew (or was it I who cowered away?), and I could not find that sweet voice anywhere.

At first I didn't even care to look for His presence, because the memory of the terror I had felt was too fresh. Over time I began to miss Him, but it wasn't until several months later, after a long "night" of feeling no sense of His nearness, that I heard His quiet, internal voice inviting me onward once again. This time there was no hesitation—I simply missed Him too much to say "no" again. That's the reality that drives us onward, isn't it? We *miss Him,* and our hearts know that, at the end of the day, only His presence is going to be enough. And so like the Shulamite, we swallow our fear and go out to find Him once again.

She wanders through the city streets, past the watchmen, inquiring about the king, seeking him until she suddenly finds the one she loves! She clings to him, not wanting to let go, and cleaves to him until he promises to come to her home and see her.[11] The Shulamite begins to realize that the love she is experiencing is powerful and nothing to trifle with. I imagine her going to her home to await his arrival.

And does he ever show up! The next thing the Shulamite knows, there is a royal cavalcade approaching her house. She realizes the king is coming and his intent is to take her away! Look at the text:

> **Who is this coming out of the wilderness**
> **like pillars of smoke,**
> **perfumed with myrrh and frankincense,**
> **with all the merchant's fragrant powders?**
> **Go forth, O daughters of Zion,**
> **and see King Solomon with the crown**
> **with which his mother crowned him**
> **on the day of his wedding,**
> **the day of the gladness of his heart.**
> **Song 3:6,11**

The king is coming and he has bridal intentions! His crown is on his head, and he has been made ready. Suddenly all the fears are gone, her unfaithfulness is a distant memory, and she is swept up in the overwhelming realization that she is at the center of his heart. She is his focus on *"the day of the gladness of His heart."*

It would seem that the logical fulfillment of this picture in the New Testament would be the time of Jesus' triumphant return to claim His Bride at the end of the age, and it certainly will be that in the fullness of time. But I believe a dramatically different understanding must come first. The picture of the final triumph is the second side of the equation; first comes a darker reality, a stunning turn of events.

Often the prophetic pictures of Christ in the Old Testament were based on an incomplete understanding of His suffering as it relates to the redemption of His people. The old saints had no difficulty imagining the victorious Messiah, but the suffering Christ was another matter. Inherent in the picture of the crowned king coming in gladness and victory are the crucifixion and death of Jesus. The elements are powerfully present in the text of the *Song*, chapter 3, verses 6-11. First, the bridegroom is escorted by soldiers on the way, as Jesus was on the way to the cross. He is accompanied by his royal throne, even as Jesus carried the cross that would lift Him up in triumph for all to see. The women go out to see him and in the most gripping picture of all, he is crowned by his mother on the day of the gladness of his heart.

Likewise, the crown of thorns is placed upon the head of Christ by the nation that gave Him birth, and we are told in *Hebrews 12:1-2* that the emotion that drives Him there is joy. His gladness is rooted in the anticipation that at the end of the journey, even as the Shulamite awaited the king, you and I will be awaiting His arrival.

We think that by our little failures and inconsistencies we abort the process of our redemption and discourage the Lord from His pursuit of us. Our shortcomings are real and not without consequence. But there is a much sterner thing going on here. Jesus withdraws from us for a moment not to abandon us, but to perform the act that will result in the release of the power necessary for us to follow Him forever. By His suffering He will make atonement, and by His resurrection and ascension the Holy Spirit will be released to us. We will become in fact what He has promised, and therefore the death and the gladness are one. The crown of thorns and the regal crown are one and the same. It is with the crown of suffering that Jesus purchases the Bride who will become the glorious diadem of *Isaiah 62:3*, and His suffering is also, finally and fully, His joy.

*O Jesus! How do I begin to think about this? The stunning realization that the day of Your crushing is the day of Your delight is beyond my ability to comprehend. Teach my heart, O God. I want to know You and the fellowship of Your sufferings and the power of Your resurrection, that I may finally know what You have in Your heart concerning me.*

## The Heavenly Husband

In chapter 4 of the *Song*, the king begins to strengthen the Shulamite in the most powerful and practical way. He speaks directly into her heart about his heart concerning her.

When we begin to understand the poetic language of this passage, the section from verses one through 15 is one of the most penetrating passages in the Scripture. The following contains a few of the more piercing thoughts:

**Behold, you are fair, my love!**

**Behold, you are fair!**
**You have dove's eyes behind your veil.**
**You are all fair, my love,**
**and there is no spot in you.**
**How fair is your love, my sister, my spouse!**
**How much better than wine is your love,**
**and the scent of your perfumes than all spices!**

**A garden enclosed is my sister, my spouse,**
**a spring shut up, a fountain sealed.**
**A fountain of gardens, a well of living waters,**
**and streams from Lebanon.**
**Song 4:1,7,10,12,15**

It is one thing for us to consider this passage as a poetic piece of history—we've all read romantic stories about the love of an exhilarating man for a ravishing woman—but it becomes quite another matter when we begin to realize this passage is only a reflection (and a dim one at that) of the kind of love that rages in the heart of Jesus for His Bride. When we begin to comprehend this, the truth causes our heads to spin. I am loved in a staggering way. This is not just a story—it's my story! This is the heart of Jesus concerning me.

Consider the second line above, verse seven in the biblical text. The king's testimony concerning the Shulamite is that she is *"all fair,"* and that *"there is no spot in you."* All fair?! No spot?! Wait a second! How can this be? How can I think those thoughts concerning myself? And yet in *Ephesians 5:27* we are told that Jesus has in mind to present us to Himself as a *"glorious Church, not having spot or wrinkle, or any such thing."* That is where this is going, and since in the heart and mind of God we already are in this completed state, He can speak these things over me without exaggerating *because they are true.* This is how things are. And this only a few minutes removed from my refusal to go on with Him because I didn't trust His love and power!

The life-changing power of this Scripture is centered in the fact that Jesus sees us and relates to us now in the light of what He knows is coming. He sees the end from the beginning. In other words, since before He began the process of creating us, redeeming us and drawing us to be with Him, He has known *with certainty* that the desired result would be brought about by the power of His own strength. His right hand and strong arm have won the victory.[12] The zeal of the Lord of hosts is accomplishing this work.[13] And the goal of the whole thing is the perfection of His people as His Bride!

Therefore, when the king speaks to the Shulamite in the language of romantic love and declares her perfection, it is not merely flattery or the pretension that love is blind. His love is not blind! His eyes are wide open, for in the middle of this passage in chapter 4 he again refers to his sufferings:

> **Until the day breaks and the shadows flee away,**
> **I will go my way to the mountain of myrrh**
> **and to the hill of frankincense.**
> **Song 4:6**

The *"mountain of myrrh"* and the *"hill of frankincense"* are references to the sufferings of Jesus, and they are presented again in the midst of his declarations of love. These are not the fatuous ramblings of a hormone-driven teenager trying to sell something to an unsuspecting paramour. These are the sober, truthful assessments of a ravished-hearted God Who is fully prepared to do whatever is necessary to bring about the desired result. In fact, because He embraced the sacrificial dimension of this plan before the foundation of the world,[14] He understands that in actuality the work stands completed. He sees her as she is! He does not see in the natural realm but after the Spirit, and what He sees is the truth.

This is why Jesus could relate to the disciples the way He did. This is why He could see that ragtag group of fishermen, tax collectors and thieves and call them apostles.[15] It is for this reason that He could forgive sins and heal lameness— He saw those folks as they are in the beauty of holiness, not in the grip of the fallen world's evil. That son of thunder, John the beloved apostle, understood it somehow. The truth pierced his heart, and he was able to speak of himself all through his own Gospel as "the disciple Jesus loves." The epitome of arrogance? Not if it's true! And you see, it *is* true. This is how He sees us and relates to us. When I begin to comprehend the fact that in first-century conversations He was including me as a recipient of that grace, something inside me begins to change.

It is essential for us to grasp that these words are spoken to us in the place of personal intimacy with the Bridegroom in such a way as to change our heart's perception of reality. In the secret place of prayer, as I minister to Him and see the beauty of His Person, that compels me to believe Him, and as I receive His tender ministrations to me, I begin actually to accept and agree with this report. I begin to acquiesce to His assessment. I begin to stand in the truth of His opinions because they are the truth about me that I always longed to believe. I've always wanted to be loved like that! I've always known—somehow, deep inside—that this ought to be the way it is. And the stunning truth is: *This is how it is!* I *am* loved this way! And so are you. It changes everything.

*O Lord, thank You that in Your Mercy, You suffered for me in order to give me a new identity: forgiven and beloved, whole and healed. Help me to grasp that truth. Help me to agree with Your assessment of me. You have declared my loveliness as Your Bride now and for eternity. Let me begin now to experience the life-changing power of that identity.*

## The Suffering Servant

I remember some years ago watching an instructional video on paradigms—the belief lenses through which we experience reality. The video used an interesting tool to demonstrate the amazing ability of human beings to edit what we experience by the subconscious use of paradigms. A deck of playing cards was shown, one card at a time, in very rapid sequence—each card was shown for only one-twentieth of a second. Most of the cards were fairly easily identifiable, but there were several I simply couldn't see well enough to recognize.

And that was the point of the video, because when the instructor slowed down the speed of the exposure of each card, I realized that the cards I couldn't see were cards like a red 10 of spades, or a black six of diamonds. See, the issue was that spades are normally black, and diamonds are normally red, and so when they were shown in a way different from what I expected, my brain could not register the new reality it was seeing. This is how paradigms work. We see what we expect, and we are disoriented to the point of non-comprehension when we see or hear or experience something outside our paradigm.

In the midst of the most intimate encounter the king and his Shulamite have had, he introduces a concept, a paradigm that is so foreign to the bride's thinking that it almost passes unnoticed. The Shulamite, like us, possesses the amazing editorial ability to subconsciously eliminate ideas or perceptions that fall outside the boundaries of experience or expectation. We often just simply don't hear or see things that we don't expect to hear or see, and especially things that violate the boundaries of our theology.

The concept introduced by the king is the matter of his imminent suffering on behalf of the bride. The idea is brought to her first in chapter 4, verse 6, which I mentioned in the section above. However, it seems that the Shulamite is so taken with the graces of the king that this revolutionary idea—that a king would suffer to win the love of a peasant girl—completely eludes her. She is hearing his affirming voice, and there is simply no room for suffering in her paradigm of intimacy.

But in the midst of his tender wooing of her heart, as she begins to believe his report, something happens. The Shulamite becomes so enraptured with the king's declarations of love that she does what lovers do. She makes a sweeping avowal of unwavering commitment:

**Awake, O north wind, and come, O south!**
**Blow upon my garden,**
**that its spices may flow out.**
**Let my beloved come to his garden**
**and eat its pleasant fruits.**
**Song 4:16**

In this unrestrained profession of love and commitment, the bride says, *"Let come what may—whatever needs to happen in my life so that the king can fully enjoy who I am—let it be so!"* The "north wind" here symbolizes the difficulties that purge her and prepare her heart for mature love. She welcomes these along with the "south winds" of pleasant circumstances, realizing that both elements are in fact present in the process of maturing. She is awakening to a new paradigm of intimacy that includes the sharing of difficulty for the purpose of maturing in love.

This topic is reinforced in the next chapter:

**I sleep, but my heart is awake;**
**it is the voice of my beloved!**
**He knocks, saying, "Open for me, my sister,**
**my love, my dove, my perfect one;**
**for my head is covered with dew,**
**my locks with the drops of the night."**
**Song 5:2**

As the king comes to the Shulamite's door, knocking and longing for admittance to the place of deeper intimacy, he states that he wants her to open to him because he is suffering. The picture of his head "covered with dew" and his "locks with the drops of the night" is a reference to the anguish of Christ in the Garden of Gethsemane the night He was betrayed.[16]

The king longs to have an intimate partner with him in the place of suffering, and her heart is ready. She is properly clothed, her feet no longer defiled with the pollution of walking in the world's ways, and she opens the door, the anticipation of sharing his suffering dripping from her hands like liquid myrrh. But he is gone! Despite her willingness and desire to join him, this is one path he must walk alone, and the best she can do is follow at a distance, confused and wounded by those who do not understand her passion.

This prophetic picture is lived out by Jesus and the disciples is a most dramatic fashion. When, in the aftermath of Peter's Spirit-inspired declaration of Jesus' true identity, He first begins to reveal the concept of suffering to them, their response is predictable and strong:

> **From that time Jesus began to show to His disciples that He must go to Jerusalem, and suffer many things from the elders and chief priests and scribes, and be killed, and be raised the third day.**
>
> **Then Peter took Him aside and began to rebuke Him, saying, "Far be it from You, Lord; this shall not happen to You!"**
>
> **Matthew 16:21-22**

The thought of a suffering Messiah is just too weird for the disciples. Messiahs are for conquering, not suffering! In their hearts, being with Jesus means winning, not dying. It is a complete paradigm shift, and they don't like it. In characteristic fashion, Peter voices what everyone else is thinking and feeling. He speaks these totally contradictory words: *"No, Lord!"* This shall not happen!

As Jesus silences him and continues to explain what He is saying, the disciples' hearts change. They embrace the new paradigm to a fault, with Peter (again) the spokesman:

> **But he spoke more vehemently, "If I have to die with You, I will not deny You!"**
> **And they all said likewise.**
>
> **Mark 14:31**

I have long believed that when Peter spoke thus he was just making empty, arrogant protestations on which he would not be able to follow through. I now believe he is standing in the place of the Shulamite, his hands dripping with liquid myrrh, as he cries out of the passionate love of his heart for Jesus: *"I will go with You! I don't care what it costs!"* The others agree, not able to imagine that this is a road Jesus must walk alone, and that therefore their best efforts to follow are doomed to failure. Consider His statements to them:

> **Then Jesus said to them, "All of you will be made to stumble because of Me this night, for it is written: 'I will strike the Shepherd, and the sheep of the flock will be scattered.' "**
>
> **Matthew 26:31**

It is not possible in the economy of God for the disciples to follow Jesus at this point. They will be *made to stumble!* His road has to be walked alone, in fulfillment of the prophecies of the Old Testament.[17] But Jesus sees the passionate desire in their hearts and loves them all the more for it. He knows they will be tested beyond their ability to survive but that in His sacrifice will be their strength. Though they fall short, their failure will not be fatal. Through these experiences the disciples will come to know the unconditional nature of the Bridegroom's love as never before. Once again, we are called to consider that in Jesus' interactions with the disciples He encounters us, for His Word is eternal, cutting across all the boundaries of time and space. He speaks these words to me, and I am prepared by them for my own walk of faith.[18]

*Lord, it is with trepidation that I invite the north winds to blow again on my garden. More than I desire personal safety and comfort, I desire that You would enjoy the fruits of my life, that You would revel in Your own character being formed in me, and that even in times of testing, the absolute nature of Your love will become more real in my heart.*

## The Majestic God

In the Western mindset, it is difficult for us to hold in tension ideas and concepts that seem, on the surface at least, to be contradictory. I once read a sermon in a book by Nels Ferre that was entitled "The Extreme Center." Frankly, I don't remember all that much about the content of the sermon, but the title has gripped me for years. One of the major keys to Christian living is to understand that the most radical place to stand is in the center of the truth, being fully committed to all its dimensions, not emphasizing one facet of the truth over another. It's a difficult place to walk, since our tendency is to embrace certain doctrinal or practical truths that support our personal biases.

In our walk with Jesus, we must deal with difficulties such as suffering, but we must hold those in tension with our understanding of Jesus as the glorious, great and beautiful King of the ages. It is precisely this insistence on standing firmly in both places, however, that gives us the solid hope we need in order to face the realities of our life in God. We can know moments of glory and yet not be knocked out of commission when a season of difficulty comes upon us. All things being equal, I much prefer the glory realm! It is His glory, the beauty of His majesty, that is the focus of His role as the majestic God.

In the *Song of Solomon*, we are given a wonderful and exalted picture of the beloved Bridegroom through the eyes of his smitten Bride. While it is not our purpose to do a line-by-line exposition of this text,[19] it is nonetheless good for us to consider for a moment the beauty of the Lord as He is revealed here:

My beloved is white and ruddy,
chief among ten thousand.
His head is like the finest gold;
his locks are wavy, and black as a raven.
His eyes are like doves by the rivers of waters,
washed with milk, and fitly set.

His cheeks are like a bed of spices,
banks of scented herbs.
His lips are lilies, dripping liquid myrrh.

His hands are rods of gold set with beryl.
His body is carved ivory
Inlaid with sapphires.
His legs are pillars of marble
set on bases of fine gold.
His countenance is like Lebanon,
excellent as the cedars.
His mouth is most sweet, yes,
he is altogether lovely.

This is my beloved, and this is my friend,
O daughters of Jerusalem!
Song 5:10-16

It is my conviction that the body of Christ needs a restored understanding of the majestic beauty of the Man Christ Jesus. A renewed emphasis on the specific exaltation of Jesus Christ as the glorious and limitless Lord of the universe is absolutely central to our lives as His Bride, especially as we are called to the place of prayer.

Someone has said that the most neglected topic of preaching and study in the body of Christ today is the Person of God. We have become so focused on our own personal happiness and on the business of solving issues, meeting needs and pursuing our visions that we have neglected to focus on the beauty and majesty of the One Who makes it all worthwhile in the first place.

In the International House of Prayer in Kansas City, the main focus of our time and energy 24 hours a day, seven days a week, is the declaration of the glory of the Lord Jesus Christ by speaking and singing of that glory from the texts of the Scripture. The reality is that as our hearts become more and more exhilarated in His beauty and passion, we become more and more convinced that He is able to do what we need, and to hold until that day the victory He won for us on the cross.

This is precisely why the Lord God calls us in the fourth chapter of John's Gospel to worship Him in Spirit and in truth. It is not that He is some sort of egocentric God Who must be placated by little people telling Him how important He is. That describes the plight of the Wizard of Oz, but it is not the condition of our Lord Jesus Christ. He desires us to be focused on His loveliness and to declare it to Him night and day *for our own benefit*, that we might see His power and glory and become convinced that He is able to keep us. Worship and adoration increase our sense of His majesty and put our hearts at rest in faith and confidence.

When worship is focused on the beauty of the Lord not for the sake of my comfort but simply for the sake of adoring Him, the unexpected happens. I, in fact, come to a greater sense of peace and rest than when attaining peace and rest was my goal. It is the reality of His beauty that enabled Paul the apostle to say, *"I know Whom I have believed, and I am persuaded that He is able to keep the things I've committed to Him until the day of His glorious return!"*[20] The knowledge of Christ sets us at rest. The Shulamite knew that the best way she could come to a place of rest and ease was to focus on the beauty and the excellence of her king.

The disciples experienced this same reality as Jesus disclosed Himself to them in His glory just before His suffering and death:

**Now after six days Jesus took Peter, James, and John, and led them up on a high mountain apart by themselves; and He was transfigured before them. His**

**clothes became shining, exceedingly white, like snow, such as no launderer on earth can whiten them.**

**And Elijah appeared to them with Moses, and they were talking with Jesus. Then Peter answered and said to Jesus, "Rabbi, it is good for us to be here; and let us make three tabernacles: one for You, one for Moses, and one for Elijah"—because he did not know what to say, for they were greatly afraid.**

**And a cloud came and overshadowed them; and a voice came out of the cloud, saying, "This is My beloved Son. Hear Him!"**

**Mark 9:2-7**

What is essential for us to see here is that Jesus opens the eyes of His trusted friends, Peter, James and John, and allows them to see the truth of His identity, undisguised in the Servant garments of the incarnation. They see Him for Who He is and are so stunned that they don't know what to say. They see with real eyes and hear with real ears as Moses and Elijah, two of the major heroes of the Old Testament, come down in bodily form and worship the Lord Jesus Christ, Who just happens to be their friend!

What was the point for the disciples? I believe one reason the disciples were invited to the transfiguration event was that they might be strengthened in the reality of a beauty they had yet to experience here on earth. The revelation of the Lord's beauty, which is His glory made visible to human eyes, is for our exhilaration. It serves as an anchor for our faith and helps us understand the joy of what awaits us when our faith is made complete.

O Beloved, let the knowledge of the glory of the Lord fill your hearts! It's what He has promised for the last days.[21] We as believers get to drink from that stream ahead of time, that we might be filled with joy and firmly set on the rock-solid foundation of His glorious reality, and that we might share the reality of His beauty and majesty with all who will listen.

*Lord God Almighty, show me Your glory. Let me see You even though my eyes are still far too dim for my satisfaction. Touch them, Lord Jesus, and cause me to behold Your beauty, that I might exult in You and be settled in the truth. You are worthy of all praise, Jesus. Let all nations see Your glory, that the Lamb may receive the reward that is due His Name.*

## The Consuming Fire

The final pictorial revelation of Jesus in the *Song of Solomon* is the reality that He is the all-consuming Fire of God, the passionate Lover Who consumes my very soul with His burning love. This final portrait is painted in chapter 8 of the *Song:*

> **Set me as a seal upon your heart,**
> **as a seal upon your arm;**
> **for love is as strong as death,**
> **jealousy as cruel as the grave;**
> **its flames are flames of fire,**
> **a most vehement flame.**
> **Many waters cannot quench love,**
> **nor can the floods drown it.**
> **If a man would give for love**
> **all the wealth of his house,**
> **it would be utterly despised.**
> **Song 8:6-7**

The longing of the heart of the Shulamite is expressed here in this achingly beautiful passage. *"Seal me, O God! Sear my very countenance into Your burning heart, and engrave my name onto Your arm that was stretched out for me. Your love is a vehement flame that cannot be quenched, and I long to know the power of it surging within my heart."*

This is our heart-cry, to love and be loved with this kind of fervency. In order to give ourselves with passion unrestrained, we must come to know that there is Someone Who is worthy to be trusted with that level of commitment. That Person is Jesus Christ.

Once again my heart is thrilled to understand that on a real day, one like today, the Man Christ Jesus came alongside two disciples who were trying to make sense of a very confusing time in their lives as they walked down the road to a village called Emmaus.

In the story recorded in *Luke 24*, these men are devastated and lost in the wake of Jesus' death. Even though they have heard the rumors of the resurrection, they still have not been able to make sense of the events that have occurred, and everything in their world seems turned upside-down.

And then, in the mercy and goodness of a loving God, *the Lord Himself comes to them* in their anguish. He patiently and lovingly takes them through the Old Testament Scriptures and unfolds to them the reality of His identity and all that will happen. He gives them eyes to see, ears to hear and hearts to understand. And once again, in that encounter between Jesus and real humans, I find the truth that He encounters me in the same way.

I often stand in the place of those men, confused and at a loss to understand the ways and workings of God, and then He comes to me just as He did to them and speaks to my heart of the truth of His life, love and purposes. In those moments my heart is ignited and I see the way things are, and I say with my brothers:

**"Did not our heart burn within us while He talked with us on the road, and while He opened the Scriptures to us?"**

**Luke 24:32**

Jesus came to those men and He comes to you and me because He has set us like a seal upon His own heart, and because the fire of His love burns with a violent flame, stronger than death, more powerful than the grave. The touch of that reality invigorates and heals, gives vision and faith, satisfies longings and calls me to realize the destiny of my life, to know why I was created in the first place. His flaming touch is everything to me. Like the Shulamite, I long for His touch.

Human beings are made for the exhilaration of passion, and we will search for the reality of that exalted place until we find it. May we come to understand that only in His presence is the longing for passion fulfilled, and that in a holy and wondrous way.

*Thank You, Jesus, for revealing Yourself in Your Word. Thank You for making my heart burn with passion to know You, to see Your glory and to declare Your worth to all who will hear. I love You, my Lord, and by Your grace I will follow You all of my days.*

## CHAPTER 4

# THE PLIGHT OF WIDOWHOOD

## THE DESOLATION OF ESTRANGED PRAYER

During the past several decades the Holy Spirit has taken the realities of intercessory prayer and branded them on the hearts of His people in every culture, tongue, tribe and nation. Part of what is exhilarating about living at this time in history is that it seems God is choosing to draw believers to prayer in a scope and depth of intensity never before experienced on the earth.

Although I am one who has come only lately to this expanding movement of prayer, I stand among a group of people who are being raised up as forerunners to proclaim a shift in the atmosphere as together we seek the face of God. I believe with all my heart that a new day has dawned in the ministry of intercessory prayer, and the Holy Spirit is intent upon spreading the news. Our God is a God of deep love and desire. His passion is for His people to know His goodness and come to seek Him based on the confidence that He has heard and will act on the prayers He Himself has birthed in our hearts.

In earlier years, when I was involved in pastoral ministry, I had two emotional responses concerning the amazing group of people called "intercessors." The first was, *"Thank God that there are intercessors in the body of Christ."* The second thought that came almost in the next breath was, *"And thank God that I'm not one!"* The reason for this ambivalence was that most of the intercessors I observed were heavily burdened much of the time, seized with concern over the agonizing issues of the day, and continually in the powerful grip of a "spirit of intercession" that, quite frankly, was hard to live with. I saw my role as somehow trying to figure out how to walk the tightrope between blessing the intercessors and trying my best not to get drawn too closely into their circle.

The term "travail" was frequently used to describe the intense times of anguished crying out to the Lord, and when I observed it (or on the infrequent occasions when I, too, was captured by the invisible hand of God and seized with the sense of birthing), it was easy to comprehend why that term was employed. While I sympathized with the intercessors because of what they endured in the Name of the Lord, my participation in their ministry was a reluctant one at best, with a deep hope that my involvement would not become chronic.

Please note: I am not defending this posture. It was born out of a lack of understanding, which led to fear. Today, I am fully identified with intercessors and gladly so. My goal in Chapters 4 through 6 is to focus on an arena of intercession that I believe the Lord is changing for the better through a call to bridal intimacy.

In sharp contrast to my perceptions is the life of prayer modeled by the Lord Jesus. There was something about His life in prayer that riveted the attention of the disciples as they observed Him from day to day. They saw Him pray over individuals with profound effect. They watched Him in the intimate moments of His personal times with the Father. There was such vibrancy, such joy in His times alone with God that He would come forth from them refreshed as from a couch of rest. So intrigued were the disciples that they would occasionally inquire about that dynamic and Jesus would instruct them.

Now, what must be seen about the prayers of Jesus is that *they are first and foremost the prayers of a human being uttered in the context of a human relationship with God through the ministry of the Holy Spirit.* When Jesus related to other humans, He was exercising that dimension of the priesthood that consists of God representing Himself to mankind, the Word of God addressing His Beloved. But when Jesus was ministering to the Father in prayer, He was doing so from the opposite dimension of the priestly office, namely that of redeemed mankind coming before the God of grace in order to receive from His hand the necessary provision for the day. In this way, Jesus stands in the place of prayer as the prototypical Bride, the representative of humanity before the Father. His prayer life is the model for bridal intercessory prayer and worship.

Therefore, not only by observing what Jesus says, but also by considering His attitude before the Father, we may discern how we are to pray. His prayers are succinct, often just one or two words, and one never gets a sense of anxiety or embattlement. Even in the Garden of Gethsemane, during the most intense prayer imaginable, one has the sense of deep intimacy and trust as the context of the pleading. Along with His personal examples, Jesus also gives us the Lord's Prayer, that wonderful rabbinic instruction that serves as a topical prayer list, in addition to several passages that specifically instruct us in the matter of prayer.

One of the key points Jesus used to draw the disciples further into prayer was the compelling parable of the persistent widow:

**Then He spoke a parable to them, that men always ought to pray and not lose heart, saying: "There was in a certain city a judge who did not fear God nor regard man. Now there was a widow in that city; and she came to him, saying, 'Get justice for me from my adversary.'**

**And he would not for a while; but afterward he said within himself, 'Though I do not fear God nor regard man, yet because this widow troubles me I will avenge her, lest by her continual coming she weary me.'"**

**Then the Lord said, "Hear what the unjust judge said. And shall God not avenge His own elect who cry out day and night to Him, though He bears long with them? I tell you that He will avenge them speedily. Nevertheless, when the Son of Man comes, will He really find faith on the earth?"**

**Luke 18:1-8**

Because this parable is so profoundly pointed at persistent prayer and is straight from the mouth of the Lord Himself, it must be seen as a paramount teaching on effective intercession. And so it has been, but with what I believe to be a misplaced emphasis, rooted in a misunderstanding of Jesus' intent and of the nature of God. Let's examine it for a moment.

Jesus begins with a clear statement of the parable's purpose, that believers *"should always pray and never give up."* That's clearly the point of the story, and I know of no confusion concerning that issue. However, I believe that what comes next is, in the common interpretation of the parable, a misperception of Jesus' objective. It concerns a widow who had a problem (more likely a number of problems) for which she needed justice[1] to be invoked by someone with the authority to do so. In other words, certain matters of horizontal relationships were desperate for her, and because of the hopelessness of her situation and her inability to bring about justice in any other way, her only recourse was to go to the judge.

What we must understand is that in the Middle Eastern culture of that day, it was difficult at best to be a widow. A widow, especially if she had no living son,[2] was a nonentity in the culture, and could only survive by begging or prostitution, or by being redeemed by a kinsman[3] or becoming a ward of the temple.[4] So the woman in our story was probably alone, with no defender. To make matters worse, she was stuck with a judge who, in the chilling words of the Lord, *"did not fear God nor regard man."*

Jesus, as the Master Teacher and Storyteller, is building tension upon tension to focus our awareness on the critical nature of this woman's circumstances. Her only hope was for intervention from the one who was supposed to be a representative of righteousness, but who apparently was anything but that. In the Rome-dominated, corrupt society of the day, many government officials obtained their positions by fraud, deception or treachery, with the aim of gaining wealth and power. Opportunities to use their authority to establish righteousness or help the poor—these were foreign concepts to the power brokers of the day. This judge, whom Jesus labeled "unjust," was no different. In office for prestige and power, he held his position with arrogance and ruthlessness. This pathetic widow meant nothing to him, and he meant to do nothing for her.

The widow chose *the only weapon she had left at her disposal:* sheer, unrelenting, strenuous and vocal appeal. The text merely states that *"she came to him,"* but the verb tense in the original language indicates a repeated action, that "she kept coming and kept coming." She came to the judge unceasingly and relentlessly asking for her needs to be met. She became a perpetual presence in his court, so much that the judge used the phrase *"she troubles me with her continual coming."* This word *"troubles"* is intriguing here, for it means that she "joined herself to him." She came right alongside him, became his shadow. She tailed him. She was his thorn in the flesh, his right-hand agitator. She grabbed hold of the feet of this judge and would not be denied, until he finally relented and avenged her. Why? Simply because she was wearing him out!

One can almost see the tension mounting in the judge's heart. Hoping to silence her with a curt refusal, he shrugged off her initial appeal and thought that would be the end of it.

But this woman was desperate; she had a need and would not be denied.

In my home lives a 12-year old girl named Rachel, my younger daughter. She is a lovely young lady, and from the time she was conceived, my wife, Mary, and I had a sense that God was preparing her to be effective in intercessory prayer. There is much that has yet to be developed in Rachel's character and in her understanding of her relationship with Jesus, but one thing that is already fully in place is a tenacity of spirit that, once focused on a particular goal, is a wondrous thing to behold. Over the course of her short life, we have had many encounters in which her sheer determination and persistence have won the day. We have acquiesced to her desires simply because she would not relent. I can only imagine what she will be like when the Holy Spirit grips her with the things that are on God's heart and causes her to be persistent before the Lord in the full expression of her gifting and calling. I would not want to be an unrighteous judge standing in her way!

This judge was no match for the widow. She beat him to death with her appeals until he finally could not endure it another moment, and he gave her what she wanted. Justice was served, the widow got what she needed and the parable is complete.

Or is it?

## THE CONTRASTING EXPERIENCE
## OF GOD'S CHOSEN ONES

Almost every time I have heard this story told with regard to intercessory prayer, it has been presented as a model of how we should approach God in intercession. The widow's effectiveness is held up as the standard for dynamic, efficacious prayer, and intercessors are urged to approach the Lord with the same tenacity she exhibited.

Numerous times I have heard intercessors testify to this effect: *"We're going to storm the gates of heaven, get around the throne and get hold of the feet of God, and not let go until He gives us what we're after."* Hearts are stirred, emotions are engaged and fervor is borne on the wings of determined decisions that we, too, can pray like that! The result is that all over the earth there are intercessors who call out to God with great zeal, weeping with anguish over the horizontal issues of the day, pleading with God to hear their appeal, rend the heavens and come down to establish justice on earth.

Further, in order to emphasize and strengthen the call to pray in this fashion, there are frequent references to Old Testament prophetic passages such as *Joel 2:17*, where the priests are enjoined to weep between the porch and the altar. Stirring prophetic prayers such as *Isaiah 64* are emulated, beckoning God to shake heaven and earth until all righteousness is restored.

Please do not misunderstand me. I do not *for a moment* mean to devalue those who pray with tremendous focus and zeal. Would to God that such earnestness could be stirred among all His people! What troubles me, however, is that I believe we have missed the point of the parable. The reality of the story in *Luke 18* is that Jesus *was building tension for the purpose of contrast.* His intent was not to say, "Here is what prayer is about and this is how you should pray." He was in fact saying, "If that kind of appeal by one with no rights or standing is eventually effective even with an unjust judge, *how much more will the prayers of God's beloved Bride be effective with Him Whose heart is ravished with love for her? Will He not hear the cry of His elect ones, and answer them speedily when they call out to Him night and day?"*

You see, Jesus was speaking about a widow because the people of God in that day were living as widows. Yet the Bridegroom was standing in their midst unrecognized and ignored. The ultimate Kinsman-Redeemer had come to earth to embrace and welcome His Bride back into His arms, and they would not come because they had the mentality and emotional make-up of a widow—abandoned, lonely, without hope. The staggering news God Himself was proclaiming through the presence of the Man Christ Jesus was that the day of restoration had arrived! The Bridegroom had come and the abandonment and isolation of the people could end. If only they would turn and see and hear!

Now, historically, the Scriptures speak very tenderly of widows. They are to be taken care of and nourished by the community, not deprived of their rights just because they've met with tragedy and sorrow. In the absence of a welfare system, provision was made through family intervention and, as a last resort, through the oversight of the temple priests. *But it was still tragic to be a widow,* and whenever God spoke to Israel as a widow in the Old Testament, it was to address a spiritual condition, one of being under judgment.

The intimate presence of God caring for Israel as a loving Husband had been strategically withdrawn for a season in the hope that she would repent of her unfaithfulness and sin. God's intent had always been to treat her as a wife, not a widow. But Israel had foolishly turned away from her first love and abandoned the God Who would be as a husband to her.[5] She turned away from His covenant love until He had no choice, in effect, but to annul their marriage for a season and treat her as an enemy would.[6] *But it was never His desire to do that!* His longing was that she would love Him and return to Him so He could have mercy on her and restore her to the place of favor and intimacy.

We see in Isaiah's prophecy the promise that one day the shame of Israel's youth would be set aside and she would no longer be seen as abandoned, but as desirable and married.[7] There would come a time when her fortunes would be restored in spite of her unfaithfulness, and God would return to her and be her Husband again instead of merely her Master.[8] She would no longer relate to God primarily on the basis of what He could do for her, but on the basis of Who He is in the majesty of His eternal love.

But Israel's desperation had not yet reached its peak, and it was not until the nation had been invaded, Jerusalem destroyed and the temple razed that the circumstances of the wife of God sank to the lowest level.

## THE DEVASTATED WIDOW

The section of Scripture describing this situation is as bleak and hopeless as imaginable. Found in the Book of the *Lamentations* of Jeremiah, we have a revelation that is riveting in its horror. Consider the text:

> **How lonely sits the city that was full of people! How like a widow is she, who was great among the nations! The princess among the provinces has become a slave! She weeps bitterly in the night, her tears are on her cheeks; among all her lovers she has none to comfort her.**
>
> **All her friends have dealt treacherously with her; they have become her enemies. Judah has gone into captivity, under affliction and hard servitude; she dwells among the nations, she finds no rest; all her persecutors overtake her in dire straits.**
>
> **The roads to Zion mourn because no one comes to the set feasts. All her gates are desolate; her priests sigh, her virgins are afflicted, and she is in bitterness. Her adversaries have become the master, her enemies prosper; for the LORD has afflicted her because of the multitude of her transgressions.**
>
> **Her children have gone into captivity before the enemy. And from the daughter of Zion all her splendor has departed. Her princes have become like deer that find no pasture, that flee without strength before the pursuer.**
>
> **In the days of her affliction and roaming, Jerusalem remembers all her pleasant things that she had in the days of old. When her people fell into the hand of the enemy, with no one to help her, the adversaries saw her and mocked at her downfall.**

> **Jerusalem has sinned gravely, therefore she has become vile. All who honored her despise her because they have seen her nakedness; yes, she sighs and turns away. Her uncleanness is in her skirts; she did not consider her destiny; therefore her collapse was awesome; she had no comforter. "O LORD, behold my affliction, for the enemy is exalted!"**
>
> **Lamentations 1:1-9**

Notice the second phrase of the very first verse: *"How like a widow she is ...."* The prophet gives us an emotional portrait of the condition in which Israel found herself because of her unfaithfulness to God. Without going into a detailed exegesis of the passage, I want to briefly point out nine realities in which the people of God found themselves, realities encapsulated in the term "widow."

**1. The bondage of slavery.** In verse one, Israel is spoken of as *"lonely."* Notice that, *"the princess has become a slave."* She who was the darling of royalty, the very jewel in God's crown, exhibited before the neighboring nations as the favored Daughter of Zion, is now on the ash heap, forsaken and in bondage.

**2. The bitterness of betrayal.** Verse two informs us that she is filled with bitter weeping, with no one to comfort her, and even her friends have become treacherous. Imagine the emotional condition of being deserted like that—and not merely deserted, but *treacherously so. Treachery* is a horrible word that speaks of betrayal by trusted companions. A previous loyalty had to have been in place in order for treachery to operate, and so the nation experiences not merely loneliness but betrayal.

**3. The displacement of captivity.** In verse three, the people are in captivity, complete with hard servitude and affliction, with no homeland and no place of rest. This is a particularly difficult thing for the Hebrew people to endure, because for nearly a thousand years their entire identity had been settled in the land of promise. The land represents to them God's provision and care. No longer can they enjoy the identity and destiny that will be preserved for them through the graces of the Almighty God Who is their Husband! They are homeless! This is unthinkable in its tragedy. The head has become the tail. The blessed ones have become the accursed.

**4. The boredom of imprisonment.** Verse four tells us that there are no feasts celebrated in the place of captivity. They cannot celebrate the feasts, which are representative of intimacy, deliverance, joyfulness and celebration. The feasts are rooted in the heavenly reality of the one great Feast, the Wedding Supper of the Lamb, and they cannot celebrate the earthly representation of the Lord's Supper in the place of captivity. Whose heart is so stony as to be unmoved by the pathos of *Psalm 137,* when the people, captive in Babylon, are asked to *"sing some of those great songs you used to sing in Zion"?* A feast in captivity would be only empty form with neither life nor power, replete with memories too agonizing to endure.

**5. The agony of children's suffering.** Their enemies prosper and their adversaries rule (does this remind you of *Luke 18?*). Their children are captives afflicted of the Lord. Woe upon woe! It's one thing to experience some difficulty, but to watch one's children captivated by the enemy and afflicted of God is a horror we are loathe to endure.

**6. The demise of princes.** In verse six we are told that the splendor of the nation has departed and their princes are as weak as starving deer. Do you catch the irony and tragedy of this imagery? The Shulamite saw her beloved king as the breathtaking hind that leapt and flew over the mountain peaks, oblivious to danger and difficulty, inviting her to come and dance on the mountaintops of her fears. Now the princes of the nation are not conquering champions but weak and starving specters, their glory having departed.

**7. The anguish of pleasant memories.** As though the present situation is not difficult enough, verse seven informs us that they are afflicted with pleasant memories of how things were when all was right and in order. In other words, they remember the days when faithfulness and justice were the realities of everyday life. Now they have to endure the mocking of their enemies, the ridicule of those who do not fear God. They are laughed at for their impotence, taunted because nothing happens when they pray. The very wonder of their miraculous history in God is used as a weapon of torment by those who hate them.

**8. The mockery of enemies.** In verse eight we see an even deeper horror: The people are despised by their enemies because of the vile nature of their sin. This is perhaps the greatest of ironies. The nations around them remember their glory and can't believe the people of God would turn their backs on this Sovereign Who fought for them while they stood still, Who went before them into battle with power and majesty shining forth from His very presence upon the Ark of the Covenant. The nations had feared the Jews because their Husband had been the Lord of the armies of heaven, and they can't believe that these people have forsaken this God in order to serve their foul and powerless idols. They see the nakedness of Israel and turn away in disgust.

**9. The loss of protection.** Finally, in verse nine, we are given what I believe is the culminating reason for the estrangement and desperation of the wife of God. The text says that because of the uncleanness in her skirts (a euphemism for her unfaithfulness with other gods), Israel does not *"consider her destiny; therefore, her collapse was awesome."*

She does not consider her destiny. I believe this means that as a people, primarily at the leadership level, and then secondarily at the level of the populace, the nation refuses to come into the presence of the Lord of glory and gaze upon the beauty of the One Who called her His Beloved, and in that refusal she loses sight of who she is to God and Who He is and ever shall be. Her identity is lost to her, and her sense of security and protection with it.

Because Israel refuses to consider and meditate upon the ways and means of God, the leaders begin to assume that they have to look to the political and economic strategies of the day in order to compete in the world market, and they leave their Husband. They have lost their sense of destiny as the wife of God, and their collapse is terrible in its scope and implication.

The imagery is profound and pervasive. Israel was in the position of widowhood through her own sin and unfaithfulness, but God, by contrast, was taking every necessary step to change that situation. Again and again He sent prophetic messengers who attempted to draw the nation back to the place of intimacy. He eventually restored a remnant to the land, and continued to give them prophetic pictures of His care and love.[9] And now the Bridegroom Himself had come into their midst, and stood inviting them to pray to a God Whose heart burned with that fiery love the Shulamite knew.

But they didn't recognize Him. They don't to this day. The Orthodox Jews still go to the Wailing Wall, between the porch and the altar, and weep as they appeal to an apparently distant God Whose ears seem closed to their anguished cries. I have stood there and it is a sobering and profound thing to see the little pieces of paper crammed between the rock and mortar of the Wall, the written prayers of those appealing as the persistent widow, a perpetual calling on the Lord in the hope that one day He will change His mind and come to their rescue.

We in the body of Christ feel sorry for them, but the fact is that we continue to pray in much the same fashion—in the anguished, fear-based, issue-oriented style of the widow of *Luke 18, as though God were the unjust judge,* distant and unconcerned. And I believe the reason we do so is that we as the body of Christ still have the experience and the mentality of the widow, when God is poised to reveal to us the ravished heart of the Bridegroom. He is calling us to wake up to that fact so we might begin to appeal to Him in an entirely different mode.

## THE ANGUISH OF INTERCESSORS

As I travel among the people of God around the world, I am touched in a sorrowful way by the weariness and anguish of the intercessors. In spite of prophetic promises stacked from floor to ceiling, their hearts are grieved by deferred hope. If they hear one more prophecy about the revival being "just around the corner," they will scream. Their eyes are focused primarily on the issues of the day that need to be set right and, make no mistake, the issues are real.

Like everyone else, I am aware of the political issues, the moral issues, the plight of our children, the influence of television and the Internet. But Beloved, *doesn't this sound even vaguely familiar?* The reason these issues are so overt is that we stand in the place of the widow. We have failed to consider our destiny! We have lost the sense of the passion of God for us as His people, and we approach Him as the widow approached the unjust judge—desperate, doubtful, certain that He is distant and not at all convinced that He even hears us.

We believe our anguish is travail, when in fact it is not travail, but instead a tragic and needless mourning over barrenness. Travail is by definition a fruit of intimacy, but it is not intimacy that is giving rise to most intercession today. I am speaking boldly, but I believe I am speaking truthfully. Beloved, let us consider our state before God!

The key is to see the parable as a contrast, not as a model. Jesus is saying that if this widow in her desperate situation can be effective with an unjust judge, how much more effective will God's chosen ones be as they call out to the One Whose heart burns with love for them? Jesus refers to *"the elect ones."* It is a direct reference to the majestic Servant Song of *Isaiah 42*, in which the pleasure and favor of God are announced as being upon the Servant, His *"Elect One, in Whom my soul delights"* (verse 1). We must see that God is delighted with His Elect One, and that in Him, by virtue of His work on the cross, we are likewise His delight.

God is no longer angry with His people, no longer venge-ful against them. He is no longer distanced; He has drawn near in the Person of His Son. The whole reality of the incar-nation of Jesus is that God has embraced human flesh and taken us into Himself, and the passion of His heart is to draw us to Himself in real intimacy and love. He is ready to move as never before in history, but He is waiting for the Bride to come to a place of confidence and delight that is borne of intimacy, so that she might pray with joy and faith—not in the doubtful and desperate mentality of the widow-woman.

## A HIGHER WAY OF PRAYER

In the parable of the persistent widow, Jesus leaves His followers with a sense that there is a higher way of prayer, a way of approaching the Lord in intercession that is more ef-fective than the model of the woman in the story. The key to understanding the parable in Luke 18 is presented in the form of a question asked of the disciples by the Lord Himself: *"When the Son of Man comes, will He find faith in the earth?"*

If the example of the woman in the story is the model of prayer the Lord is promoting, the obvious interpretation is this: When Jesus returns to earth, will He find individuals and groups of people who are in anguished prayer, beseech-ing the Lord day and night from the desperate perspective we examined in the previous chapter? Perhaps, though, there is a better definition of faith, one built on a God Who is not at all like the unjust judge. Based on the true character of God, I believe we should answer this question in a different way.

According to the Scriptures, in the mind and heart of God, all things have existed in a state of completion in the Person of Jesus Christ since before the foundation of the world.[10] Jesus is the living Word, and all other realities are lesser "words" subsequent and subordinate to the primary Word that is the Son. He alone knows the fullness of my identity and yours, and that of every human being who has ever lived or ever will live. In addition, every city, nation and culture is fully established in His heart, and He knows everything there is to know about each. Because of this, there is one reality, one opinion that fully defines and therefore fully expresses each living entity. That opinion belongs to the Lord Jesus Christ, and only He, in that relationship of intimacy with the Father by the Holy Spirit, has the power to unfold those definitions as He chooses.

Faith, then, is the matter of positioning oneself to hear from the Lord concerning His agenda, as Jesus did constantly,[11] and in the aftermath of hearing, to come to agreement with God's opinions concerning everything that has to do with my life and situation.

In his massive theological work, *The Glory Of The Lord*, Father Hans Urs Von Balthasar explains faith as "a participation in the vision of himself which God has."[12] To have faith is to stand in habitual agreement with God's perspective of reality and to live my life according to His principles. It means that I form my opinion of reality according to His view, not according to what seems evident. In order to come to that place of agreement, I must approach the Father from an intimacy in which the wounds of my heart have been healed and the voice of the enemy has been recognized for what it is. My heart must be able to hear and retain the things the Father says about me and the things that concern me. Only then am I able to approach intercession with serenity and confidence, even when things appear chaotic.

In *Isaiah 42*, the Servant of the Lord, because He is established in this reality, is able to go about His business of restoring justice to the whole earth without a lot of fanfare. He doesn't have to raise His voice in the streets, and He is able to be patient and at ease with those who are broken and weary. He is never discouraged, and He faithfully pursues His goal of restoring all things to the original design held in God's heart. He is able to do this *because* He is in full agreement with God's opinion of reality, and therefore can approach His ministry from a place of rest and not anxiety.

This is why, when the Servant came in the flesh as the

Man Christ Jesus, He was able to submit to the hand of the evil one without a word of objection. He understood the Father's purposes and ways.

That kind of confidence and certainty does not come amid the cacophony of soul that characterizes the widow's prayer.[13] Rather, it comes in the still and intimate places of the heart, where the knowledge of the Lord is revealed,[14] in the calm and quiet voice of the Lord Almighty tenderly wooing His Bride to Himself. This is where true travail is released, because from that intimate place arises a true birthing that brings forth the fruit of intimacy.

I do not mean to imply that all prayer has to be gentle and quiet. There is certainly an intensity to travailing prayer. Travail, the process of bringing something to birth, is often not gentle and quiet. *But it is rooted in the quiet spirit of intimacy, not anxiety.* That's the bottom line.

I have three children, and they were all born in travail. Believe me, there was intensity to it! I discovered dimensions of my wife's personality that I did not know existed. But the very reason she was in that condition was because there had been intimacy in our relationship. She was not in anguish because she was a widow, but precisely because she was a wife. Were there tension and anguish in the process? Yes, but they were rooted and grounded in wondrous joy, pleasure and anticipation.

The time has come for the Bride to be restored. Intercession is at the core of this restoration, but the agitated, fearful, problem-centered intercession of the widow will not suffice to accomplish what God has in mind. Only prayers of agreement with God's character, nature and agenda, brought to Him by a Bride in love, will accomplish His purposes.

In the next chapter, my goal is to provide a model that is much closer to what Jesus had in mind as He called His loved ones to pray.

CHAPTER 5

# BRIDAL INTERCESSION

## THE AUTHORITY OF INTIMACY

## AN ALLEGORY OF BRIDAL INTERCESSION

The Scriptures give us another story that I believe is a clear explication of the concept of Bridal Intercession. It is the Old Testament story of Esther, a series of historical events arranged to paint a marvelous picture of how God intends Bridal Intercession to work among His people. Jesus might very well have had this story in mind when He told the parable of *Luke 18,* because His central point was that in prayer the believer can fully presume upon God's delight in His Bride. Let's consider the story briefly.

Around the year 450 B.C., the high king of the Medes and Persians was a man named Ahasuerus (hereafter referred to as "the king" for obvious reasons). By most historical accounts, he was a pagan king, and as such was no doubt ungodly in many ways. But I believe he symbolizes the King of heaven, the glorious Bridegroom of the people of God, who are represented by the beautiful Queen Esther.

As the story begins, the king is hosting a huge celebration, a banquet for the lesser kings and national officials of the region. The purpose of the feast, according to chapter one, was *"to show the riches of his glorious kingdom and the splendor of his excellent majesty for many days, one hundred and eighty days in all."* This was a six-month feast to demonstrate this king's greatness and generosity!

Then on the tail end of that celebration, he hosted *another* seven-day affair for the denizens of the capitol city of Shushan, or Susa, which was even more lavish than the first one.

In the midst of that second celebration, the king decided to summon his wife, Queen Vashti. He wanted to exhibit her before the nobles and kings, that they might admire her beauty and thus hold the king in even higher esteem. It was common in the culture of that day for the beauty of the queen to be seen as a major enhancement of the glory of the king.

Many commentators believe the king was wrong to summon Vashti in this way, and even go so far as to laud her decision to refuse his summons as morally right. I am convinced that this position does not reflect the biblical understanding of this situation.

Throughout the Scriptures, the people of God are seen as the primary vehicle for the exhibition of His glory. In *Isaiah 62:3* we are told that God will hold His people as a crown of glory in His hand, with the express purpose of exhibiting their beauty as a testimony of His power and grace. *1 Corinthians 11* declares that the glory of a man is his wife, and that man is *"the glory of God."*

Furthermore, according to *Ephesians 3:10,* a day is coming when through the Church of Jesus Christ the wisdom and glory of God will be manifested to the principalities and powers in the heavenly places. In other words, God is going to exhibit the beauty and glory of His Bride, the Church, and the spiritual powers in heavenly places will fall down before the Bride and before her King, declaring His glory and power as His wisdom is vindicated for all to see.

What a picture of grace: the King of Kings, exhibiting His matchless glory as revealed through His Bride, the redeemed and sanctified Church!

This is the symbolic reality of the invitation the king extended to Vashti. He wanted to exhibit her beauty so that the officials of the land would honor his greatness and praise him even more. But the unthinkable happened. She refused to come. She was busy with her own party and didn't want to be interrupted, and to the horror of the king and his aides, without considering the impact of her decision, she declined the invitation.

By this act, Vashti incurred the wrath of the king and set the national advisors in turmoil. They got to work, and before the day was out, letters had been drafted and sent to the officials of the land censuring Vashti for her refusal to obey the king, and removing her from her place as queen.

I would suggest that this is a picture of the reluctant people of God, refusing to take the place of glory God has given them. Whether this applies to the nation of Israel for a season or to anyone in the same position of refusal is not the central point. The point is that the king desired to bring glory to his own name by exhibiting the beauty of his queen, and she refused, to her own demise.

Once the rage of the king had subsided, he began to rue the fact that he had no queen, and so a massive search project was undertaken to find a suitable replacement bride. A nationwide search was instigated, and all the beautiful young virgins were brought to the palace to be prepared in the harem for presentation to the king. This preparation, involving 12 months of bathing, perfuming and training, was overseen by Hegai, the chief eunuch over the king's harem. Each beauty, after her preparation, was presented in turn to the king, that he might choose the new queen. The book of *Esther* makes it clear that this young Jewish girl was more favored than anyone else and possessed great wisdom besides.

When the time came for a young woman to be presented to the king, she was allowed to take with her anything she thought might win the king's affection. In the wisdom of God that was upon Esther's life, she approached the king's man,

Hegai, and inquired of him what would please the king. Thus when she went in to Ahasuerus, she was prepared in a manner she knew would be pleasing to him.

I believe this is a picture of the Church's preparatory process of growing in holiness under the leading of the Holy Spirit. The Spirit of God, often operating through the ministry of the prophetic, instructs the Bride in her preparations, making sure she is washed and perfumed with the appropriate oils and scents, all of which have specific symbolic meaning.[1]

**The Bride Takes Her Place**

When the beautification process is completed and it is Esther's turn to go in to the king, she is fully prepared. She is adorned in the perfect garments, chosen by the king's counselor; she has the favor of God upon her; and she is a beauty! Of course, the king is stunned by her loveliness, his heart is captured in an instant and Esther becomes the queen of the Medes and Persians.

As time goes on, the king appoints an advisor by the name of Haman, an Agagite, to a significant place of authority in the kingdom. He is second in command to the king. An order is given that all people in the nation shall bow down to Haman, and he is honored in this way by everyone except a man named Mordecai, a Jew who happens to be Queen Esther's cousin and surrogate father. Mordecai is a righteous man, a God-fearer, and so refuses to bow in homage to another human being, especially an Agagite.[2]

Previously, Mordecai has uncovered a plot to kill the king, reported it to Esther and received written recognition for his heroic act. This is unknown to Haman, and when he sees that Mordecai will not honor him, the king's regent is thrown into a rage. His undisguised anti-Semitism rears up, and he conjures a plan to destroy Mordecai and all his people, not realizing that Queen Esther is implicated in his scheme.

Our story now begins to converge with the parable in *Luke 18.* Here is a woman who has a major need: She and her people are about to be slaughtered legally by an enemy. This is clearly symbolic of Satan's desire to bring destruction to the people of God, and there is much evidence in the Scriptures that his ruinous program is within the boundaries of God's authority.[3] Like God, the king has allowed a strategic threat to be set in place that will force the queen to take her place in the role of intercessor before the king.

Like many in the body of Christ today, Esther finds herself a reluctant participant in this story, but she is firmly reminded by her cousin Mordecai that *it is for this very reason—to intercede for the people of Israel— that she was brought to this place of intimate authority with the king.* I want to emphasize this point. God sets the Bride in a place of favored intimacy for the very purpose of intercession, that the human beings who are the focus of God's romantic passion may be delivered from their dilemma. The King is obviously the Deliverer, but the Lord has given the Bride an integral role in the deliverance through the ministry of intimate intercession.

It is here that the true model of Bridal Intercession begins to come into play. A loud and bitter cry is raised about the situation, but not by the queen. Mordecai, who is not part of the king's court but is outside the Holy Place and has no entrance, is one who mourns and cries bitterly over the situation. Like the widow, he stands outside of the context of intimacy, and is therefore gripped with anxiety and fear over the situation.

But Esther is in a completely different position. While the gravity of the circumstances does not elude her, she nevertheless prepares herself for a very different style of intercession, one that is based in and presumes upon a relationship of affection and intimacy with the king.

Esther instructs Mordecai to call all the Jews in Shushan for a three-day season of fasting and prayer over the situation. The queen and her handmaids join them in this, for they know that everything depends on Esther being received favorably by the king. Esther's fear of the king is appropriate, for she fully understands that he holds her very life in his hands.

As the day arrives, Esther dresses in her royal robes, the garments of righteousness she wore when she won the king's heart in the first place. She approaches the inner court and boldly enters his presence and, knowing that her life is forfeit, simply waits before the king. She doesn't shout. She doesn't raise her voice. She's not hysterical or weeping or anguished in any external way. She is presuming upon the king's favor and affection, and in that presumption is her only hope.

I can picture the situation. The king is engaged in the affairs of state, deeply involved in a session with his advisors. Haman may even be one of them. Suddenly, he hears an unexpected sound. The doors to the inner court are opening, but he has no appointment nor has there been a summons issued. As he raises his head, surprised at the interruption, the official of the court announces her presence: "May I present Esther, bride of King Ahasuerus, and queen of the Medes and the Persians."

Something happens to the king's countenance. Her fragrance fills the room. He hasn't seen her for a month, and she's even more lovely than he remembered. The favor of God is upon her and suddenly the king can't recall what he was doing. His eyes are transfixed, gazing only upon her, seeing and hearing nothing else. The policy meeting is over. With an absent-minded wave of the hand, the king dismisses his courtiers, reaches for his scepter without taking his eyes off his queen (what a woman!) and, with great drama, extends the scepter toward her, inviting her into the most powerful place in the land—the heart of the king.

## The Banquet of Wine

Esther walks forward in regal splendor and with every step her grip on the king's heart grows stronger. She touches the scepter and by the time she is standing before him, any resistance he might have had to her is gone. She is stunning! In a most significant statement, the king invites Esther to presume upon her positional authority. Everything at his disposal now belongs to her and he tells her so: *"What do you wish, Queen Esther? What is your request? It shall be given to you— up to half the kingdom!"*

Those are the king's opening remarks. He is ruined! His heart is on his sleeve. In an incredible stroke of wisdom, Esther responds, *not with her intercessory burden from her position as queen,* but with an invitation to a dinner to be given that night in the king's honor. Specifically, she invites him, along with his regent Haman, to a Banquet of Wine.[4]

In the culture of the Middle East, the Banquet of Wine was the style of the day. It was rooted in a most romantic tradition, namely, the engagement feast given upon the public announcement of the betrothal of a man to his prospective bride. In the *Song of Solomon,* when the Shulamite is taken by the king to his "Banqueting House," the literal translation is "the House of Wine."

The House of Wine, with its banner of love overarching all of the couple's interactions, was the formal setting for the betrothal feast. Subsequent Banquets of Wine were given to rehearse and celebrate the romance and intimacy of the days of first love.

During a Banquet of Wine, the prospective groom would at some point fill a glass with wine and set it on a table in plain view of the bride-to-be and everyone else. In so doing, the groom was saying, *"Here I am. This cup of wine represents everything I am and all that I own. I am pouring out my life for you at this moment as I propose marriage. Will you take me as your own?"*

It was a tremendously vulnerable and poignant moment, for the heart of the groom was on display for all to see, exposed and unprotected. At some later time in the evening the bride was expected to approach the table and take the cup in her hand to make a response. If she was a bit playful, she might lean toward the cup and then move away, sending the groom's heart into fibrillation. But finally she would take the cup in hand and drink it. By doing so she was saying, *"Yes, I will have you. My life is now sustained by yours, and you and I are one."* And the betrothal was formalized.

There is an immediate and powerful connection in this story for believers in the Lord Jesus Christ. The Lord's Supper, given at Passover, was just this kind of feast. The mingling of the symbols—the bread and meat from the Passover meal, the cup of wine from the betrothal banquet—was in fact the proposal of marriage from Jesus, the Eternal Bridegroom, to His disciples, who stood as the mystical Bride of Christ. *"This is my body and my blood, broken and shed for you. I will not eat of it again until I do so with you in my Father's House."*

Jesus was extending his heart to His people, with all the vulnerability and exposure of a groom at the Banquet of Wine, saying to you and to me, *"Will you have me? I long to have you as mine alone."* And when the disciples received the bread and wine and ate and drank, they said *"yes"* to His proposal, and the betrothal was formalized.

In the same way, when we as contemporary believers partake of the Lord's Supper, we are coming to Him as in a Banquet of Wine, recalling to our minds and His the romance and joy that drove Him to the cross on our behalf. It is the place of the marriage covenant where we renew our vows, and by so doing pledge our faithfulness again, looking forward to the day when we will eat and drink with Him in unmitigated pleasure in our heavenly home.

After the Banquet of Wine the groom would leave the bride for a season and return to his father's estate. There he would make a place ready for the bride, and would return to claim her and consummate the marriage—but only when his father said it was time to do so.[5]

Meanwhile, she also would prepare for the marriage, keeping herself pure and undefiled, all the while anticipating his return with great eagerness. Then one day, the shofar (ram's horn) would sound, and the voice of the bridegroom's friend would ring out through the land: *"The bridegroom is coming! Let all be made ready!"* The bride would go out to meet her beloved, the marriage ceremony would take place and the groom would take her away to her newly prepared home, there to live out their days together.

It's a profound picture, isn't it?

## Romancing the King

The Banquet of Wine that Queen Esther prepared for the king was rooted in this cultural understanding. She prepared a lavish dinner with the best of wine and presented it to the king that evening. The whole purpose of the dinner party was to stir up the romantic inclinations and emotions of the king. Esther was reminding him at every turn how much he loved her, how excited he had been at the prospect of their marriage, how thrilled he was at the prospect of giving himself to her and knowing her intimately.

Esther was standing before him in all her glory, not ashamed to be called his own, not hesitant to allow the nobles to see her beauty, thus bringing honor to the king's name. This was especially poignant in light of Queen Vashti's previous refusal to do so. Esther was saying to the king, in the presence of his nobles and attendants, *"I choose you again. I say 'yes' to you again, with the same passion and joy with which I said 'yes' the first time. You are my beloved and I am yours forever!"*

The king was pleased. His emotions were engaged, his sense of commitment and protection heightened. And Haman was there to see it all.

Esther had a problem to bring before the king, but she understood the higher place of adoration and romance. She ministered to him, served him and declared her affection for him to all who observed. His heart was stirred and during the course of the evening he once again invited Esther to presume upon her official standing: ***"What is your petition? It shall be granted you. What is your request, up to half the kingdom? It shall be done!"***

Now see this point: The king knows *exactly* what Esther is doing. He knows she needs to discuss something of major significance with him. He knows there's something on her heart. And he loves the approach she's taking! He's the king! He can give her what she needs, and he's glad to do so. He loves her, for she is his beauty, his bride and queen.

This is a picture of adoring worship as a necessary component of intercession. The essential place of the Bride of Christ ministering in adoration to her Bridegroom is such an integral reality in the matter of prayer. It is imperative that we understand that *the Lord Himself set it up this way!* This is how He likes it!

In the prophetic portrait called the book of *Esther,* He is inviting us to approach intercession through the doorway of romance, to dial up all His daring and passionate emotions, to tell Him all over again that we say "yes" to His proposals, that we choose Him again even as at the first. He wants us to presume upon His grace and mercy, to enter the Holy of Holies with confident boldness, knowing that His scepter of righteousness is extended toward us at all times because He is a King in love and we are His Bride!

In response to the king's inquiry about her petition, Esther does another remarkable thing. Once again, she restrains herself from interceding. Once again, she invites the king and Haman to come to a Banquet of Wine, and she promises that there she will make known to the king what is on her heart. She wants to worship more! She takes full advantage of her place of favor, her prerogative to stir the king's heart with her beauty. Her requests are secondary, for she is coming to understand that if the king's heart is ravished with her, he will deal with the issues that present themselves. And so the plans are made for the following night.

The night of the banquet, the king is restless. He gets up and asks for a reading of the Chronicles (the books of Chronicles were used back then as a sleeping aid, as they are today!), and discovers that nothing has been done to honor Mordecai for his heroic action on the king's behalf. So the next day, Haman is humiliated by being made to honor the very one he desires to murder. It is the beginning of the end for the king's regent.

At the banquet that evening, things progress as they should, until it is time for Esther to unveil her request. It is important for us to see that she is focused on speaking to the king about her issue. She never once speaks to Haman. She doesn't curse him, rebuke him or command him away from her. She doesn't bind him, consign him or have anything to do with him. She speaks to the king about what is on her heart, knowing that because of his love for her, *he will consider her issue as his own.*

Once again, the king asks what is troubling her, and she begins to reveal the plot of Haman to destroy her and her people. The wisdom of including Haman in the Banquets of Wine now becomes apparent, because up until this moment he has had no idea that Esther is Jewish! Haman has now had opportunity on two evenings to observe first-hand the affection and romance between the king and his queen, which now only serves to increase his sense of impending doom.

As the story unfolds, Esther does not reveal Haman's identity as her nemesis until the last moment. With incredible drama, the fury of the king grows hotter and hotter, until finally he can stand it no longer. *"Who is he, and where is he, who would dare presume in his heart to do such a thing?"* The enemy of the queen has become the personal adversary of the king! And Esther responds, *"The adversary and enemy is this wicked Haman!"* The text of *Esther 7* tells us that Haman is *terrified* before the king and queen.

Do we begin to understand the analogy? The queen ministers to the king in the presence of her enemy, and the enemy's heart is gripped with terror when she mentions his name to the king. This is precisely what God promises us in *Psalm 23* when the writer says, *"He prepares a table before me in the presence of my enemies."*

In the presence of the evil one, God sets up the banqueting table for the bridal feast, the place of worship, the Banquet

of Wine. It's provided specifically to reinforce the bridal relationship before the eyes of the enemy, so that he will become
terrified of the King and His Queen, the Bride.

Beloved, the enemy is not too impressed with our shouts
and protestations and sword rattling. That's his turf, and he's
an expert at it. But what strikes sheer terror into the heart of
Satan is the Bride ministering to King Jesus, singing the love
songs of the Lamb, agreeing with God concerning His opinions and His agenda, coming to a place of intimacy in which
her heart is at rest in the knowledge of God's love for her. In
that place, she is a formidable foe.

Haman was destroyed that day. His plan came back on
his own head. He was hanged on the gallows he had built
for Mordecai, and that righteous man was given the place of
authority in Haman's stead. The Jews were given the right to
defend themselves against the attempted slaughter. With the
king's blessing, tens of thousands of enemy warriors were
killed, and many of the citizens of Medo-Persia converted to
Judaism because of the fear of God and of His people.

My heart's cry is that we will come to know this type of
authority in the posture of intimacy. It is the place of rest and
peace. It is the place of confidence in God's sovereignty, the
place in which His power is released on behalf of His beloved Bride. We have been given this place. Let us stand in it
with joy and confidence.

## CHAPTER 6

# THE WARRING BRIDE

## THE BATTLE FOR THE
## STRONGHOLDS OF THE MIND

I t has been my pleasure to grow deeper in intimacy
with Jesus through prayer. Speaking and writing about
that topic are two of the joyous things I get to do. However, in the same way that one could not write a book about
Bridal Intercession without addressing issues of intimacy, one
also would be remiss to omit the topic of spiritual warfare.
There is perhaps no greater intercessory focus in the body of
Christ today than that of spiritual warfare, and my desire in
this chapter is to build a foundation of biblical truth and practical experience consistent with the paradigm of intimacy and
joy already introduced.

Historically, much intercession that could be termed spiritual warfare has been rooted in the posture of anxiety and
dis-ease discussed in Chapter 4 of this book, rather than in
confidence in the love and power of the Bridegroom God. I
believe this anxiety arises in the hearts of believers who focus
inordinately on the strategies of the evil one, on how much
is wrong and needs to be set right.

As the tactics of darkness find their expression in the apparent realities of day-to-day life, our eyes can be drawn away
from the beauty and majesty of the Lord Jesus to the squalor
and disorder of the present evil day. When that happens, we

experience the fight-or-flight emotions that are part of our
nature as fallen human beings, and we jump to the emotional conclusion that we must defend ourselves against the
intruding darkness. Our prayers begin to be driven by the
enormity of the situations before us rather than by the power
and glory of the Lord Who is our Warrior King. Eventually,
we find ourselves standing more in the anguished posture
of the widow of *Luke 18* than in the intimate authority of
Queen Esther.

The significant point to me is that the more clearly we
see Who God is, the more clearly we realize that the devil is
under His control, ever and always. I'm reminded of the delightful and fanciful portrayal of the sorcerer's apprentice in
the classic Disney movie "Fantasia." The apprentice, played
by Mickey Mouse, gets focused on conjuring up little demonic
entities that at first are fun to play with. Little by little, however, they get out of hand, until Mickey is overwhelmed by
their power and activity. He ends up totally out of control,
unable to manage a situation of his own making, facing the
massive and overpowering reality of Satan's very presence.
All seems headed for doom until, miraculously, help arrives
and normalcy is re-established.

It seems that while we have taken seriously the matter of
recognizing the devil and standing against him, the models
we have chosen by which to do that have tended to focus
more on the devil than on the majesty and power of God.
There is a short but powerful passage in *James 4* that speaks
significantly to this matter:

> **Therefore submit to God. Resist the devil and he will
> flee from you. Draw near to God and He will draw near
> to you. Cleanse your hands, you sinners; and purify
> your hearts, you double-minded.**
>
> **James 4:7-8**

The first thing we are commanded to do in this text is to
submit to the Lord Jesus. I believe this involves the *"drawing
near"* to God that James mentions in the next phrase. Sub-

mission to God is more than just sort of bowing one's head and obeying the teachings of the Bible the best we know how.

Submission to God involves understanding His character, His ways and His personality to the extent that He becomes the focus of our confidence and trust. It involves recognizing Him as the center of our lives and affections, allowing the majesty of the Lord and of His Christ to fill us with His glory. As we grow in the knowledge of the Lord's glory, submitting to His will and His ways becomes easier, and the task of resisting the devil takes its proper place in our lives.

## BEWARE OF NEGATIVE FAITH

I want to suggest that there is a *negative* application of faith that releases the work of the evil one even as positive and believing faith releases the power of God. When one comes into agreement with the agenda of the evil one in a given situation, a negative power is released. An example can be found in *2 Kings 3* when during the prophetic ministry of Elisha, five allied kings brought the nation of Moab under siege. The situation became so desperate that the Moabite king took his eldest son, his heir, and sacrificed him as a burnt offering on the wall of the besieged city.

The text says in verse 27 that there arose *"a great indignation"* against Israel, and so they (Israel) returned to their own land. There was such a power of demonic rage released through this horrible act that the entire nation of Israel was affected by it, and they ended their attack on the Moabite nation. When human beings set their hearts in agreement with the agenda of supernatural powers, there is authority released, whether it is authority from God or from the enemy.

In the *Gospel of Mark,* there is another intriguing account of how the unbelief of Jesus' own people hindered His activity. The text tells us that Jesus *"could do no mighty work there."* [1] The spiritual principle at work regarding faith is underscored in several other places as well. For example, in *Isaiah 59:1-2* the prophet declares that God's hand of salvation is not short, but that iniquity has kept the people of God from experiencing His salvation. In **Mark 9**, Jesus exhorts the father of a demonized boy that faith in God's Word and His power opens the doors of possibility to the release of God's power.

In the fourth chapter of **Hebrews**, the writer tells us that although there was a promise of rest, the power of God's Word was not realized by people because they did not *"mix the Word with faith."*[2] The point of all this is that faith-agreement with God's perception of reality is a potent weapon for the release of spiritual power.

When believers, in the name of doing spiritual warfare, become focused on Satan's power, the strength of the evil one begins to loom large before them. Then when we try to resist him, we find ourselves intimidated and on the way to defeat. I believe this negative focus can intensify the experience of warfare. We become what we behold, and in the gazing is the power of transformation. The chilling reality is spoken from the Lord's own mouth: *"if the light that is in you is darkness, then how great the darkness!"*[3] To become focused on the power of the evil one is to invite the dangerous possibility of becoming one's own worst enemy.

When my wife, Mary, was a young child, she had a recurring dream that troubled her greatly. Mary was raised on a farm in Nebraska, and one of the barns on the home place was the locus of this annoying dream. In her nightmare, Mary would find it necessary to enter that barn and would always be confronted by a large and fearsome "blackness" that would frighten her and drive her, crying, out into the yard. As she fled from this dark thing, the dream would end. This haunting experience disrupted her rest for some time until one night everything changed.

The dream began in the usual way, but this time as Mary turned to run from the specter, she realized she simply needed to turn around and face it. She stopped running and as she confronted the darkness head-on, it stopped and expired in front of her, collapsing like a billowing sheet from which the wind had been removed. She saw the darkness for what it was—nothing—and as she faced it, it disappeared and lost all its power.

When Mary saw the apparition for what it really was, something happened in her heart. She no longer believed that it had any power. It disappeared and she never had the dream again. She decided *not to have faith in unreality but to believe the truth,* and the unreal thing lost its ability to affect her mind and spirit. In the same way, faith that is focused on the beauty and power of God will enable us to see the darkness for what it is—nothing—and give us the joy of being untroubled by it.

I am convinced that the only way to resist the devil successfully is to have such a fresh and clear view of the majesty of God and of His power, which are *infinitely* greater than Satan's, that we are able to see the devil for what he is. And what is that? A defeated, rejected angel whose only power is the power of the lie, and who one day will be fully under not only the Lord's authority, but also ours in our identity as the Bride of Christ.

## APPROPRIATE FEAR

The Holy Spirit gives us perspective on our identity in a meaty little passage in *Luke 12*. Jesus is speaking about appropriate fear:

**And I say to you, My friends, do not be afraid of those who kill the body, and after that have no more that they can do. But I will show you whom you should fear: Fear Him who, after He has killed, has power to cast into hell; yes, I say to you, fear Him! Are not five sparrows sold for two copper coins? And not one of them is forgotten before God. But the very hairs of your head are all numbered. Do not fear therefore; you are of more value than many sparrows.**

**Luke 12:4-7**

Jesus implies that times are coming that may well involve bodily harm and even martyrdom for the disciples. They may lose their lives in this venture, even as Christ Himself was permitted to be killed. But Jesus enjoins His listeners to adopt an eternal perspective that only comes by submitting to the nature of God. We are not to fear those who can harm only our physical bodies. We are not to be nervous because the material stuff we own is threatened. Jesus lifts our gaze to eternal matters and lets us know that there are more important issues than physical life and death. The only one we are to fear is God, Who has the ability to enact eternal consequences.

Then, in a tender and surprising statement, Jesus tells us about the kind of God this fearsome Being is: He knows and cares about every sparrow and every hair on the heads of His Beloved! We are important to Him. When we see this God and focus on Him, our faith is settled and we experience peace.

It is important to understand that the faith necessary to release God's work on our behalf is rooted in two essential realities. First, we have the matter of "the Faith," which is the content of the body of doctrine we hold to be true. It is the human system of thought that agrees with God's systems of thought: that He is able and willing to do things for us that are above and beyond all we can imagine. This is essential, because our perception of reality influences to a great degree what we can hope to experience.

The second dimension of faith, which I call "faith of the heart," is the living process of holding something as true, the act of believing something to be so, possibly even in the face of contrary evidence. This act of faith is just as important as intellectual belief, for it is this dimension that releases us into the experience of God's objective goodness. It is through our exercising this heart-belief that God will do what He has promised. This faith of the heart is not a matter of intellectual assent (although it is rooted in the objective truth of God's nature), but it is a matter of relational intimacy. This faith is replete with confidence in His activity, rooted in the knowledge of His love and character.

The faith of the heart grows as our eyes are filled with the beauty of the Lord Jesus. A marvelous passage of Scripture underscores this principle:

> So . . . as they went out, Jehoshaphat stood and said, "Hear me, O Judah and you inhabitants of Jerusalem: *Believe in the LORD your God, and you shall be established; believe His prophets, and you shall prosper.*"
>
> And when he had consulted with the people, he appointed those who should sing to the LORD, and *who should praise the beauty of holiness,* as they went out before the army and were saying: "Praise the LORD, for His mercy endures forever."
>
> Now when they began to sing and to praise, *the LORD set ambushes* against the people of Ammon, Moab, and Mount Seir, who had come against Judah; and they were defeated. For the people of Ammon and Moab stood up against the inhabitants of Mount Seir to utterly kill and destroy them. And when they had made an end of the inhabitants of Seir, they helped to destroy one another.
>
> 2 Chronicles 20:20-23

We gaze upon Him, focusing upon the beauty of His holiness and meditating on His power. We receive His Word with faith, and the result is that our foundations are established in the truth. The Lord Himself begins to wage war on our behalf and little fear or insecurity can touch us. The enemy becomes confused because the hand of the Lord is set against him, and the powers of darkness move against one another instead of against the armies of the Lord.

If an individual's heart is not established in the agreement that comes through the intimate touch of God's Word upon the heart, that person cannot experience the full release of God's power in a given situation. This is the dynamic James refers to:

> **But let him ask in faith, with no doubting, for he who doubts is like a wave of the sea driven and tossed by the wind. For let not that man suppose that he will receive anything from the Lord; he is a double-minded man, unstable in all his ways.**
>
> **James 1:6-8**

The double-minded man, whose heart is not settled in the Father's goodness and love, will not see the hand of the Lord moving in his behalf. By the strategic reality of God's own choosing, His Word will not accomplish anything without the release of faith of the heart. But the good news is that in His great mercy, God will infuse into the human heart a "gift of faith," the supernatural ability to hear His Word and receive it, to believe against all odds that what God has said is true and trustworthy. The only thing that remains is for the individual to give assent to this revealed truth, to release the heartfelt "yes" that God is seeking as the appropriate response to His initiative.

Consider for example the magnificent message of *Psalm 91:*

> **He who dwells in the secret place of the**
> **Most High shall abide under the**
> **shadow of the Almighty.**
> **I will say of the LORD, "He is my refuge and my**
> **fortress; my God, in Him I will trust."**
>
> **Surely He shall deliver you from the snare of the**
> **fowler and from the perilous pestilence.**
> **He shall cover you with His feathers,**
> **and under His wings you shall take refuge;**
> **His truth shall be your shield and buckler.**
> **You shall not be afraid of the terror by night,**
> **Nor of the arrow that flies by day,**

nor of the pestilence that walks in darkness,
Nor of the destruction that lays
waste at noonday.

A thousand may fall at your side,
and ten thousand at your right hand;
But it shall not come near you.
Only with your eyes shall you look,
and see the reward of the wicked.

*Because you have made the LORD,*
*who is my refuge, even the Most High,*
*your dwelling place,*
No evil shall befall you,
nor shall any plague come near your dwelling;
For He shall give His angels charge over you,
to keep you in all your ways.
In their hands they shall bear you up,
lest you dash your foot against a stone.
You shall tread upon the lion and the cobra,
The young lion and the serpent
you shall trample underfoot.

*"Because he has set his love upon Me,*
*therefore I will deliver him;*
*I will set him on high,*
*because he has known My name.*
He shall call upon Me, and I will answer him;
I will be with him in trouble;
I will deliver him and honor him.
With long life I will satisfy him,
and show him My salvation."
Psalm 91:1-16, italics mine

As one reads through this wondrous passage, the clear
meaning is that protection is available for those whose hearts
are settled in the Person of God. The focus is not on what is
happening in the external situations of our lives that seem
out of control. We do not dwell on that. Rather, it is the Lord,
the Most High God Who is our "dwelling place." This is where

we plant ourselves day and night, reflecting on His beauty and majesty and allowing our hearts to be set ablaze with the knowledge of His goodness and power. In that place, no harm can come *to the part of us that really matters*—our eternal identity in Him.

## THE OBJECTIVE: COMPREHENDING GOD'S PURPOSES

For many who embrace the identity of intercessor, the expectation of God's activity in our lives often extends no further than resolving immediate external circumstances to conform to our perception of what is best in the matter for which we are interceding. Our engagement in spiritual warfare may focus on changing our circumstances to our definition of a more desirable state, even though the purposes of God in that situation may be very different. We become focused on the very matters Jesus told us not to be focused on.

The most obvious example of this is found in the response of the disciples to the horrors of the arrest, crucifixion and death of Jesus. From the external perspective, this seemed like the ultimate horror of the human experience, and yet Jesus was clear that He had come in order to drink that very cup,[4] and it is underscored in Luke's later assessment of the event that Christ's crucifixion had been the central plan of the Father all along.[5] The immediate resolution of external circumstances is not always what the Father has in mind for His children, and if we insist on bringing our situation to a place of comfort, we may not come to know the full joy of His plan, which is only revealed later.

It is my contention, therefore, that the chief objective of spiritual warfare is not the resolution of external circumstances, but rather the fullest comprehension possible of the Father's purpose in any given situation, and the conformity of our desires and pleasures to fit that purpose.

As I write this chapter, some dear friends of ours are wrestling with difficult circumstances. Ted and Debbie Perry left a comfortable and moderately affluent life in Texas a few years ago because they sensed that God was drawing them into a life of ministry rooted in greater intimacy with Him. They sold their belongings, moved themselves and their teen-age sons into a travel trailer and set out to follow the leading of the Holy Spirit. Their journeys took them from Texas to Arizona, and then to Kansas City, where they are now involved in the House of Prayer as full-time intercessory missionaries. As Mary and I have come to know and love them, we have seen that the deepest desire of their hearts is to love and serve Jesus as fully as they can, and to see His purposes released here and in the cities of the earth.

The Perrys recently went back to Texas to do some "friend-raising"[6] and while they were gone we experienced a December cold spell in Kansas City. Upon returning to Kansas City, Ted drove into the place where their unit was parked, and what he heard filled his heart with dread. It was the sound of running water. Sure enough, a pipe in the unit had burst, and for some 26-30 hours a full stream of water had flooded their home. As I spoke with Ted about it, he offered a magnificent and humble interpretation of the event. His words were something like this: *This little unit isn't much, but for the last period of time it has been our home. I'm not sure what we'll do now, but I guess God is expanding our comfort zone to fit whatever He desires.*

What a magnificent perspective! This family has made the Lord their dwelling place! Instead of seeing this event as a tragedy, Ted has made a choice to settle his emotions in line with God's promise that He would allow them a level of freedom and peace that is not tied to the external situations of their lives. What could be seen as a severe squeezing instead is being seen as a liberating reality. And although it does not entail matters of life and death, being thrust into such a condition demands a perspective rooted in grace and trust in the Lord's goodness.

Another friend at the House of Prayer whose name is Shelley Hundley is a vibrant, gifted young woman in her early

20s. Shelley joined the intern staff of the House of Prayer in the summer of 1999, only to be stricken with Crohn's disease the very day she entered the internship. During the past year and a half, Shelley has been on a roller coaster of hope and anguish, at one moment experiencing the excruciating pain and sickness of this disease's flare-ups, and at other times seemingly free from the symptoms. The sickness has wracked her body with pain, taking her from the thing she loves most—sitting in the House of Prayer and ministering to the Lord—and placing her in a posture of deep questioning and searching.

In the midst of this real suffering, which without question has its roots in spiritual battle, Shelley has gone deeper in her experience of the love of Christ. She has truly become a contemporary contemplative, and her perspective on the sufferings of Christ is profound beyond her years. For her, the primary battle is not focused on whether or not she gets healed, although she certainly longs to be healed, but the real battle has been in her mind, wrestling with the enemy's accusations against the goodness of God. And Shelley wins that battle day by day. She enjoys the Lord, loves Him, tells Him about her life and causes the rest of us to wonder at the glory on her countenance. She has taken her thoughts captive and focused her gaze on the beauty of the Lord instead of the rage of Satan. She can look you in the eye and echo the prophetically uttered words of Christ, *"It was the pleasure of the Lord to crush me."*[7]

Where does this kind of faith come from? How do human beings find the wherewithal to keep open hearts in the midst of difficulties that come as a direct result of being obedient to the Lord? The Perrys aren't in trouble because they've made mistakes; they're in difficulty precisely because they dared to risk following Jesus! Had they stayed in their comfortable surroundings in Houston, this would not be their plight. But they chose to leave everything to follow Jesus, and now the Lord has allowed the little they retained to be taken as well. And they are calling it "good."

Now I know Ted and Debby, and I know they are going through the normal processes of conflict and frustration as anyone would. I know Shelley Hundley. Her struggle is not with sickness that is a result of foolishness or sin. Her struggle is to accept the permissive purposes of God working something incredible in her inner being. These people are not superhuman. But the ultimate stance they are choosing is this one: Jesus is beautiful, He is worthy and His administration of our lives is perfect! How have they come to this place? I believe the answer lies in understanding the battle for the mind, the struggle to stay settled in the conviction of the goodness of God in the midst of difficult circumstances.

## THE PROBLEM OF FLESHLY WARFARE

Once again, the Scripture holds valuable information regarding the whole matter of spiritual warfare.

> **For though we walk in the flesh, we do not war according to the flesh. For the weapons of our warfare are not carnal but mighty in God for pulling down strongholds, casting down arguments and every high thing that exalts itself against the knowledge of God, bringing every thought into captivity to the obedience of Christ. . . .**
>
> **2 Corinthians 10:3-5**

Paul sets the battle squarely in the realm of controlling our thoughts. He refers to a carnal style of spiritual warfare, but opts for the one that is *"mighty in God for pulling down strongholds."* He then moves immediately to the definition of what those *"strongholds"* are, calling them *"arguments and every high thing that exalts itself against the knowledge of God."* Paul finishes the statement by asserting that spiritual warfare consists of bringing every thought into the glorious, liberated captivity of full agreement with Christ's obedience. This is the true exercise of spiritual warfare in the life of the believer. Let's look at these ideas more closely.

First of all, there is the matter of waging war according to the flesh, a way that is considered carnal by the apostle. I have observed over the years, and have participated to some degree, in a style of spiritual warfare focused on addressing spiritual powers directly, summoning them and calling them to account for their strategies and activities, and commanding them in no uncertain terms to cease and desist. This methodology is usually couched in aggressive language that is focused on the authority of the believer. It is energetic and, in our attempts to assert our positional authority as sons and daughters of the King, it is often frankly arrogant in its approach.

In my observation, the major characteristic of this kind of spiritual warfare is the engagement of the emotions of the one praying, with a stridency and pride that seem contrary to the nature of Jesus as revealed in the Gospels or in prophetic passages such as *Isaiah 42*. This kind of warfare excites what I call "the Braveheart syndrome" in the hearts and minds of believers, a level of human zeal that is "by God going to crush the devil and throw him out on his ear."

Now, I loved the movie "Braveheart." With certain cautions, it can be seen as a model for fervency in the Christian life. But I have observed that when the Braveheart syndrome takes over, it is often rooted in energized flesh, with vengeance against the devil as the motivating force. Whenever I hear someone engaging in this type of warfare, I am reminded of the admonitions stated in the epistle of *Jude*, written generally to the believers of the day.

In that little letter, Jude (who may well have been the physical brother of the Lord Jesus) speaks to the matter of addressing spiritual powers and authorities, "dignitaries" as he terms them.[8] Jude rebukes those who in their presumption speak evil of these "dignitaries" of the heavenly realm, and informs us that those who speak thus themselves become corrupt. He cites the example of Michael the archangel, who when arguing with Satan himself did not bring a reviling accusation, but instead enjoined him with the Lord's own rebuke. In other words, Jude is saying clearly that a protocol is needed for addressing evil powers lest we tread in arenas of authority and power unknown to us, resulting in our own condemnation.

I believe this speaks directly to the common approach to spiritual warfare today. Those who have authority don't need to posture themselves as authoritative. They *are* authoritative. Successful spiritual warfare is not a matter of decibels and energy, power-packed phrases and prophetic gestures. Successful spiritual warfare is rooted solely and completely in our position of influence with Jesus Christ. And that position of influence comes only in the secret place of intimacy by receiving the Word of God implanted in the human heart.

Mike Bickle, the director of the International House of Prayer in Kansas City, attended the annual convention of the Italian Charismatic Catholic Network in May 2001. While there, he was privileged to observe a ministry session led by Father Mateo, an elderly priest. Father Mateo has been walking intimately with God for nearly 80 years, and Mike was struck by the simplicity and effectiveness of his prayers.

Father Mateo simply sat on the platform and in a relaxed, almost monotone voice, asked Jesus to come and deliver people from demonic oppression and heal their sicknesses. There were no theatrics, no dynamic presentation, no fancy prayers. Instead, this friend of God quietly said "Jesus, come deliver your people. Jesus, come heal the sick." Mike's testimony is that many people in the crowd of more than 30,000 began to cry out as the demons left them and as their bodies were healed of disease and affliction. The power of God was released not because Father Mateo was dynamic, but because he knows his God and has full confidence in His willingness to loose His power and help those in need.

I believe this intimate authority is much less attractive to our way of thinking precisely because it is a posture of humility and quietness, not the aggression and loud sound effects Westerners tend to admire. We somehow feel as though we have really meant business and touched heaven if we release much emotional energy in the guise of warring. That is not necessarily so. The kind of warfare referred to in the Scriptures has little or nothing to do with the level of outward energy evidenced in make-believe battles in the midst of a prayer meeting. It has much more to do with assertively believing the truth and living in the gentle, undiscouraged character of Jesus in the face of contrary opinion.

For the Perrys, spiritual warfare has little to do with God's ability to protect them against some nefarious scheme of the devil to steal their material belongings. For Shelley Hundley, it is of only secondary significance whether her body is well or not. Rather, the warfare she wages has everything to do with her ability to perceive God as good, generous and kind in the face of contrary evidence.

When these people choose to worship Him and love and trust Him even more in the midst of physical difficulty, the battle is won. The enemy doesn't want their physical stuff; he wants their minds and hearts to become discouraged about the nature of God and His trustworthiness. The devil doesn't care whether they live in a trailer or a mansion. He wants their trust undermined, and he doesn't care how it happens. When I look in Ted's eyes and see the tears come as he speaks of the goodness of the Lord Jesus in the midst of a lousy situation, I know the battle has been won.

When I am struggling because of my external circumstances, it's all I can do not to complain or become critical or seek to resolve my horizontal issues to set my soul at rest. *But it isn't about those things!* It's about my own heart's confidence before the One Who says He is the Lover of my soul. And when in the midst of those kinds of struggles I can stand and worship, when I can love Jesus and agree that His administration of my life is wise and good, when I can live graciously in relationship to my family and the others around me—then the enemy has nothing in me and the battle is won. Then I can stand and say with Jesus, *"the ruler of this world is coming, and he has nothing in me!"*[9] It is then that the Father can turn to the evil one and speak what He spoke over Job and over all those who stand in the heritage of trusting God in the face of mountainous difficulty: *"I will accept (my servant Job), for (he has) spoken of me what is right."*[10] Lord Jesus, let this be the testimony of my life!

## DEFEATING STRONGHOLDS

If the first step of spiritual warfare, according to Paul, is realizing that we can't wage war according to the flesh, the second step is *"pulling down strongholds,"* which he defines as the casting down of arguments that are exalted against the knowledge of God. Strongholds are demonic systems of thought that argue against the character and beauty of God. The Greek word used here is also translated *"castle,"* implying a structured argument that provides a dwelling place for spiritual influence.[11] Though the word "strongholds" is also used in the Scriptures in a positive way, in the sense of providing a place of defense or protection, in this context they are seen as negative. We are told in the very next verse that these strongholds are false things that exalt themselves against the knowledge of God, "defending" individuals against the purposes of God being realized in their life. As such, these structured arguments must be dismantled one thought at a time.

We grow up with all sorts of untrue messages implanted in our hearts, spoken by those with spiritual authority— parents, teachers, pastors and doctors, to name a few. Some patterns are seeded by the enemy himself. We develop thought processes that seem right in our own eyes but on further examination are found untrue in their testimony of who God is and who we are in relationship to Him. Ways of thinking don't change overnight. What is required is the systematic ingestion of the Word of God, taken deep into our hearts by the ministry of the Holy Spirit.

The apostle Paul tells us in *Ephesians 5* that we can be filled with God's Spirit through singing, speaking and sharing God's Word, especially by *"making melody in your hearts to the Lord."* Melodies of the heart. As the truth of God's Word is internalized, there is a stabilizing, a filling *of the heart* with confidence that comes in the sense of His presence, and we become settled in the truth.

A marvelous example of this kind of spiritual warfare is found in the well-known parable of the prodigal son in *Luke 15:11-24.* The younger son of a wealthy man comes to ask for his inheritance and then proceeds to a far country where he squanders that inheritance in wild living. In his wisdom, the father allows the boy to experience the full consequences of his wrong choices, and the boy ends up slopping hogs in a feed lot, eventually yearning to fill his own belly with the food the unclean animals eat.

When he hits bottom (and for a Jewish young man, feeding pigs would be the bottom!), the text tells us that *"he came to his senses."* That phrase means "he saw things as they actually were." He is no longer under any illusions about life; rather, he is totally disillusioned and thus ready to receive the truth. He decides to return home.

The young man's decision is based on the understanding that his father is a generous man, and that his father's servants are eating at the father's table and enjoying his good graces, while he, the son, is stuck in a pigpen. It occurs to him how stupid he has been, and so he devises a plan. The first thing he comes up with is repentance: *"Father, forgive me. I have sinned against heaven and against you."*

So far, so good. Nothing wrong, nothing untrue there. But in the next phrase, we see that in his assessment of his own value, the prodigal has now crossed over to the opinion of the evil one and has lost his perspective as a son. His next statement is, *"I am no longer worthy to be called your son. Make me as one of the hired servants."* He no longer has his father's perspective of the truth, and therefore cannot anticipate that restoration is available to him. But he is desperate enough for food, shelter and some sense of wholeness, so he heads home anyway. Better a servant in the father's house than a free man anywhere else.

When he gets home, he is dumbfounded by the welcome he receives from the father himself. Not used to the running, wildly embracing heart of the father, the boy sort of pushes himself away so that he can give his speech. He begins with the first phrase and receives no argument from the father. He has sinned, and his sin was against both the father and God Himself. It is serious and true. But then the boy tries to go to the second phrase, speaking out of his current self-assessment instead of from an understanding of the father's heart. When he begins to talk about his unworthiness to be called a son, the father *immediately* interrupts him, and doesn't allow him to finish! Why? Because the father sees that the son has presumed to understand the father's assessment of the situation, and has presumed to know the father's attitude concerning him. The central foundation of the young man's identity has been destroyed, and a new stronghold of fear and separation has been built.

The father stops the speech, not allowing his son to speak the lie even once more, and calls immediately for the servants to come. He commands them to dress the young man in the robe of family identity (I assume he had a thorough bath, symbolizing the washing of the water of the Word), to put the shoes of ownership on his feet and the ring of authority on his hand. In effect the father is shouting aloud for all to hear, *"This is my son! He lost his mind for a moment and fraternized with pigs, but he's home now. Get him dressed right, do it now and don't let him out of your sight until he remembers who he is. Servants, I'm holding you accountable! Treat my son according to who I say he is, not according to what seems to be the case. He'll get the point sooner or later. Now, let's party!"*

This father was not interested in what the enemy had to say. He knew the power of his own words and embrace, and they were what mattered. He didn't rebuke the boy. He trusted the power of a loving heart to penetrate the barriers of guilt and shame and re-ignite the heart of sonship and intimacy. He didn't curse the pig smell. He didn't bind the spirit of the city. He didn't rail against those who cooperated with his son's demise. He simply spoke truth over his son and commanded his servants to do the same. The boy was restored through the tearing down of an old and evil stronghold and the rebuilding of a new and holy one. His positional liberty was restored in a moment, and his existential liberty would be restored as he set his mind and heart once again in full agreement with his father's correct perspective of reality.

To push the story a little further, it would be essential for the lad to continue to accept the father's opinion as the right and true one. The thing that got him in trouble in the first place was that he began to believe the enemy's false report concerning where fulfillment could be found. He constructed the strongholds of thought long before he left the father's house, and once he got into a new setting, the demons were all too glad to take up residence and bring destruction. Now that he was home, he would need to forsake that line of reasoning and embrace again his father's perspective. He would also need to embrace his father's heart relationally in order to heal the emotional damage caused by meeting his own needs illicitly. His new system of thought would be reinforced with new experiences of love, and the power of the enemy would be forever defeated. No demons could drag him away again. He could, however, choose to believe the lie and subject himself to their influence again, and that would be tragic.

## BUILDING RIGHTEOUS STRONGHOLDS

Jesus tells another parable in *Luke 11:23-27* showing that demonic spirits can inhabit structures of thought, here pictured as "houses." These are the strongholds spoken of in *2 Corinthians 10.* The point Jesus makes is that when evil spirits are driven out of a stronghold, it is essential to fill the stronghold with something else lest the enemy return with greater force than before. This is a reference to the need for building new systems of thought to replace the old ones, which were inhabited by the influences of darkness. Without ingesting the Word of God both systematically and experientially, the individual remains susceptible to a renewed attack from the evil one.

The implications for our prayer lives are immediate and clear. My task is not to rebuke demons, bind spirits and command principalities and powers to leave my loved ones and me alone. Jesus never bound the spirits over any of the cities in which He ministered. He cast demons out of individuals, but that is the extent of His activity in addressing the realm of the demonic.

My task is to do ministry the way Jesus did. Over my family, for example, my job is to go before the Lord, hear His heart concerning them and then speak that loving truth over their lives. I must set parameters to help them walk out the truth and love them affectionately and unconditionally until they get it straight in their hearts. As they embrace that process, they will see the nature of God in it. In due time, I will freely give them over to the Heavenly Father and He will assume the same functions in an infinitely greater way, using the Word of God, the leading of the Holy Spirit and the counsel of mature brothers and sisters in the body of Christ.

My task of intercession over my city does not consist of rebuking enemy activity by addressing the demonic powers and their agenda. There is not one biblical example of that strategy being employed. Now make no mistake: I am fully aware that these powers are real and that they have an agenda. I simply want no part of their agenda. My task as an intercessor is to determine what is in the Lord's heart and mind regarding Kansas City and to come to agreement with what He has said He intends to do.

My friend Jon Petersen has made it his task to research the blessing heritage that God has spoken over cities since their founding. As he has lived in various cities over the years, he has developed a pattern of research that enables him to trace the strategies of God during a city's history. He then brings these realities to the pastors of the city, and they begin to pray, agree with and bless God's agenda. For example, there is a region south of Houston, Texas, that is called Brazosport. Consisting of several small communities in close proximity, Brazosport is in an area where a certain waterway splits into two forks before it empties into the Gulf of Mexico. The Cajun name for these two forks means "the arms of God," and refers to the sense that one of the founders had that God was watching over this place with tender care. A positive way of interceding over this community would be to focus on this dimension of the Father's heart revealed, asking that His care would be realized among the people of the area.

When Jon and his wife, Mindy, moved to Kansas City in the fall of 1999, he gave himself energetically to discovering the spiritual heritage of this place. He is deeply involved with several pastors' prayer groups here, which are focused on declaring the Lord's agenda over this place. Jesus has a plan for my city. His plan is to love my city, to nurture the people in it and bring blessing to it. I'm going to wage war over the city by agreeing with the heart of Jesus and then cooperating with the strategies to walk out the heart of God street by street, neighborhood by neighborhood, person by person.

This is how spiritual warfare ought to be done—from a place of confidence and partnership, not from fear and anxiety. If the Holy Spirit speaks to us about something the enemy is planning, we should take note of it, but never to the extent that the enemy's agenda becomes the focus of our energy. Let's allow the agenda of the Lord to become and remain the center of our attention.

This reality is powerfully stated in *Isaiah 42*. There is a marvelous pattern here of how Jesus brings justice to the ends of the earth. *Justice is the full restoration of all things according to the original design held in the mind of God from the foundation of the world.* In the first four verses of this passage, the Servant is pictured as confidently and calmly going through the streets of the city, gently restoring the broken. He is not discouraged as He embraces the task of restoring justice in the earth.

How can Jesus not be discouraged when He sees the craziness of the human dilemma? He walked the streets as a man, divested of the prerogatives of divinity. He lived by the power of the Holy Spirit just as He intends you and me to do. He never rebuked a principality over a city. Rather, He spoke blessing over the lives of individuals, saw them with heavenly eyes and called them to live according to their identity in God. I am convinced that Jesus' ministry was not focused on overcoming darkness, but on bringing light. He called Himself the Light of the world, not the defeater of darkness. Darkness is a nonentity. It is the absence of something. It is not something to be overpowered, but rather something that will be dissipated as the Word of God illuminates the hearts of human beings.

I believe that when Jesus walked the streets of Jerusalem, His focus was on hearing from the Father concerning the identity of those He met. We are told in *John 5:19* that He never did anything but what He saw the Father doing, and in *John 8:28* that He only spoke as the Father taught Him. When Jesus ministered healing or deliverance, resurrection or natural miracles, it was because He was focused on what God was doing in that situation. He didn't come against starvation; He blessed bread and fish and gave the people food to eat. When He did speak a curse, in the example of the fig tree in *Mark 11*, it was as an object lesson illustrating the devastation that would come upon the nation for refusing to cooperate with the Word of God Who had been living among them. Those who refuse the Word experience the devastation of the curse.

In the second section of *Isaiah 42,* in verses five through nine, the Heavenly Father puts His stamp of approval on the activity of this Servant and pledges His sustaining power. To verify His abilities, He cites the fact that He sustains the created universe and declares that He Who gives breath to the peoples of the earth will not allow the Servant to be adversely affected by the powers of darkness. God will sustain His servants who go about His business in His way.

In response to His keeping power, the peoples and the nations of the earth praise the Lord with unrestrained joy.[12] They exalt His Name and minister with great gladness to the King of the universe. The result? In verse 13, the Lord of the armies of heaven rouses Himself to hear and asserts Himself to answer the praises of His people with deliverance, for the enemies of His people have become His personal enemies. The intimate authority of Esther in the place of worship has now become the national paradigm for waging war.

## BRIDAL INTIMACY AND WARFARE

In conclusion, how do we as bridal intercessors exercise spiritual warfare? I believe we embrace that task with a joyful and positive approach. We first of all come to know the heart of Jesus for ourselves, our friends and loved ones, our cities and the nations of the earth. We do this by listening to His heart in the context of worship, and by studying the prayers that the Holy Spirit inspired the writers of Scripture to pray over the cities in which they were ministering. The apostolic prayers of the New Testament are unfailingly positive and inspirational in their revelation of the heart of God for the cities of the earth. His heart is still the same for our cities. The Word of God does not change, and neither does His opinion of what He wants to do with human beings. He loves people and wants them redeemed by the power of the living Word released among them.

When we pray over individuals, we find out from the Lord who they are in His heart, and then like the servants of the father in *Luke 15,* we relate to them on that basis. There is such power in relating to individuals according to the Lord's definition of their identity, for when we speak words to people that are in agreement with His truth, those words touch His image, which dwells deep in the heart of every human being. As that truth is addressed, grace is released in their hearts and they are given the strength to respond to the drawing of the truth. The choice is theirs, but the power from the Lord is there to make that choice. This is why Paul tells us in *2 Corinthians 5* to relate no longer to one another according to the flesh, but according to the Spirit. We are to see one another according to the Father's opinion, then draw one another up into that identity.

When I was a teen-ager, every time I left the house, my father would say to me, *"Son, remember who you are."* While it bugged me at the time, I now see the genius of what my dad was doing. Rather than trying to enumerate all the problems I could get into and trying to convince me to avoid those situations, he instead spoke over me what I knew in my heart to be true: *I have an identity from the Lord that is rooted deep inside my own immature being, and if I take the time to get in touch with it, that knowledge will lead me according the ways of the Lord.* I knew that then, and I know it now. It hasn't always kept me from making the wrong choices, but I have never made those wrong choices out of ignorance. When people around me have taken the time to see that reality in my heart and to speak over me according to that reality, it has always drawn me forward into the truth.

This is how Jesus did what He did, and it's how He intends us to walk as His partners today as well.

## CHAPTER 7

# THE WISDOM AND POWER OF INTIMACY

## THE STORY OF MARY OF BETHANY

I n the late 1980s the Lord began to stir my heart toward prayer in a significant way. At the time, it seemed as though what was going on inside me was nothing more than a jumbled confusion of thoughts and feelings rooted in my pastoral ministry experience, which was coming upon difficult times.[1] I was beginning to feel drawn into a more focused and intimate place of prayer and it was very unsettling to me because I knew of no context of ministry in which this type of prayer could happen in more than a marginal way.

During that season, the Lord began to draw me toward the writings of historical contemplatives such as St. John of the Cross, Teresa of Avila, Jeanne Guyon and others. It was also during this season that I began hearing the whispers of the Holy Spirit concerning "Marys of Bethany," people who would someday join the ministry to which I was being called. I really had no idea who these people were or why they would come. This impression seemed like nothing more than a vague breath of information from the Spirit, about which I could do nothing.

In the short years since 1999, during which the International House of Prayer has been established in Kansas City,

I have come to understand to a greater degree these faint murmurings of the Spirit of God. The Marys of Bethany have started to come, and a significant group of intercessory worshippers has gathered in Kansas City to spend their lives ministering to the Lord and coming to agreement concerning His agenda for our city and for the cities and nations of the earth. These individuals are male and female, married and single, old and young. Their hearts burn with one primary passion—to love the Lord their God with all their heart, soul, mind and strength. With a fiery zeal they want to love what He loves and pray for the salvation of human beings all over the world.

This may sound very exciting, especially to those who have a similar sense of vocation smoldering in their breast. But in the contemporary evangelical church of our day, it is difficult for those whose hearts pulsate with this sense of calling to feel like anything but square pegs trying to fit in round holes. The reason for this, I believe, is that today's Church in the Western world is consumed with activism. We adhere to a "go" doctrine, rooted in the expectation of effective performance and results-oriented ministry activity. Therefore, the idea of giving oneself vocationally to a place of contemplation that may not yield short-term, immediate results is a concept that often meets with skepticism at best and outright rejection at worst. My hope is to face this mind-set head-on in this chapter and the next, and attempt to bring validation and understanding regarding the ministry of extravagant lovers of God.

## THE WISDOM OF EXTRAVAGANT PRAYER

Near the end of Jesus' public ministry, He told a parable that holds significant meaning for us today. It is the parable of the 10 virgins:

> **"Then the kingdom of heaven shall be likened to ten virgins who took their lamps and went out to meet the bridegroom. Now five of them were wise, and five were**

**foolish. Those who were foolish took their lamps and took no oil with them, but the wise took oil in their vessels with their lamps.**

**But while the bridegroom was delayed, they all slumbered and slept. And at midnight a cry was heard: 'Behold, the bridegroom is coming; go out to meet him!' Then all those virgins arose and trimmed their lamps.**

**And the foolish said to the wise, 'Give us some of your oil, for our lamps are going out.' But the wise answered, saying, 'No, lest there should not be enough for us and you; but go rather to those who sell, and buy for yourselves.'**

**And while they went to buy, the bridegroom came, and those who were ready went in with him to the wedding; and the door was shut. Afterward the other virgins came also, saying, 'Lord, Lord, open to us!'**

**But he answered and said, 'Assuredly, I say to you, I do not know you.' Watch therefore, for you know neither the day nor the hour in which the Son of Man is coming."**
**Matthew 25:1-13**

This story instructs us in several ways concerning extravagantly pursuing intimacy with Jesus through prayer. First of all, it is one of the final public words Jesus spoke, given only a few days before His crucifixion and death. We can presume that if Jesus knew He was coming to the end of his life, He would speak about the things closest to His heart. In this case, Jesus speaks from the bridal paradigm, and His topic is the marriage celebration of the Bridegroom and the Bride! He likens the Kingdom of Heaven to the expected return of the groom to claim his wife, and builds this parable around the events associated with that return.

Secondly, it is important to notice that Jesus is speaking here about an important contrast: the difference between the "wise" and the "foolish" virgins. The virgins in the story are the wedding party attendants. They are fully focused on the return of the bridegroom, and they speak to us in symbolic fashion of individuals or churches who have understood the message of the coming of the Lord, and of His passionate love for His Bride. They have heard the call of the Holy Spirit, their hearts are turned toward the Lord and they are eagerly awaiting His return.

Each attendant carries a lamp, which may be interpreted as referring to the ministry each virgin represents. In the book of *Revelation*, the Lord Jesus speaks to John the apostle about the lamps of the Churches, and about what the Churches must do to have their lamps, their effective ministries, restored to full authority and influence. Collectively, these virgins make up the Bride of Christ, and they are called individually to know the depth of that identity.

It is important to see that this is not a parable that builds a contrast between those who are saved at the end of the age, and those who are cast out of the Kingdom of God. The contrast is not between "holy" and "wicked" people, but between those who are "wise" and "foolish," and the difference between the two groups is not their doctrine or their methodology. The contrast consists of one essential thing: At the crucial moment of the story, when the call goes out that the bridegroom is coming, five of the virgins have oil for their lamps and five of them do not.

The "oil" in this parable speaks to us of the fuel for ministry, which causes the light of the Gospel to burn brightly before the eyes of the watching world. That fuel is the combustible reality of a fresh and intimate relationship with Jesus Christ through the ministry of the Holy Spirit. Consider this brief reference from *The New Unger's Bible Dictionary*:

> **Oil was a fitting symbol of the Spirit or spiritual principle of life, by virtue of its power to sustain and fortify the vital energy; and the anointing oil, which was prepared according to divine instructions, was therefore a symbol of the Spirit of God, as the principle of spiri-**

**tual life that proceeds from God and fills the natural being of the creature with the powers of divine life. Anointing with oil, therefore, was a symbol of endowment with the Spirit of God for the duties of the office to which a person was consecrated.[2]**

When the story begins, all 10 virgins have enough oil in their lamps to meet the normal expectation of the day. The bridegroom is scheduled to come, the call has gone forth and the preparations have been made. The lamps are all burning brightly and the atmosphere is festive with gleeful anticipation. Then a significant factor is introduced into the story. It is the matter of *strategic delay*. The bridegroom does not come when he is expected. As a matter of fact, by the expectations of the wedding party, he is very late, so late that all the members of the wedding party become weary and fall asleep.

In my experience in Christian ministry, one of the most surprising realities of the Christian experience and one for which most Christians are not well prepared, is that of strategic delay as a tool in the hand of God. Human beings, especially those of us who live in the Western world of the Day Timer and the Palm Pilot, expect the events of our lives to occur according to a certain timetable.

Almost nothing makes us more nervous than not having a clear sense of when something is going to happen. When God decides to introduce a strategic delay into the equations of our lives, it can be disorienting and disturbing. While we Westerners are more prone to this sort of confusion than our Eastern brothers and sisters, this parable makes it clear that the virgins, too, had an expectation of the timing of this event. The fact is clear that the bridegroom's delay was much longer than any of them had projected, and only half of them had prepared adequately for such an eventuality.

The five virgins called "wise" are so designated by Jesus because they have taken the time to collect extra oil. I don't know whether they did so because they mysteriously anticipated the delay, or because they just felt more comfortable having extra oil with them. Regardless, these five represent those in the body of Christ who are enamored of the Person of Jesus not so much because He will strengthen their ministry, but because they are in love with *Him*. In the symbolic interpretation of this text, the wise group has taken the time to cultivate a deeper relationship of intimacy with the Lord beyond the day-to-day function of their ministries. They have established the pattern of developing intimacy with Jesus *as an end in itself,* rather than as the means to effective ministry. Regardless of their external circumstances, this internal reward is the motivating factor of their lives.

Those who are "foolish" have only taken time to fill their lamps for the expected activities of the day, without provision for an unexpected delay. It is my conviction that this "foolish virgin" pattern of operating is one of the chief weaknesses of people in vocational ministry today. In spite of an awareness that the ministry cannot go forward without the blessing and anointing of the Holy Spirit, the goal still is not intimacy with Jesus, but rather achieving ministry success. We become "brokers" of the word and the Spirit, men and women who study the Scriptures and pray, *not* because of a passion for intimacy with the Man Christ Jesus, but because we have to preach a sermon or teach a lesson or prepare for a discipleship group. In the language of the parable, we have oil enough for our lamps to burn, but nothing in reserve to sustain us during an unexpected delay. Again, please note that this is not about wickedness, but about foolishness as opposed to wisdom.

The coming of the Bridegroom is delayed without regard for the relative level of preparation. The day stretches into the evening . . . and then into late evening. All the virgins become weary of waiting, and fall asleep. Suddenly, at midnight, the cry rings out: *"The bridegroom is coming!"* Everyone scrambles to alertness, bustling about to get ready for the celebration of His joyous arrival.

This is when the foolish virgins make a terrifying discovery: Their lamps have run out of oil. They realize with horror that they cannot participate in the festivities without oil in their lamps. Their first thought is to go to the wise virgins and borrow some oil. They are flatly refused and told to get their own from the merchants.

This seems quite a harsh posture on the part of the wise women, but it is eminently understandable as we grasp the meaning of what is being said. The truth is simply that one individual cannot give to another the relationship of intimacy that has been cultivated with Jesus over weeks, months and years. There is nothing more personal than one's own place of intimacy with one's beloved, and try as we might, we cannot "borrow" from someone else's depth of relationship. I might look with envy at the life of one of these people and desire to emulate their pattern of cultivating relationship with Christ, but I cannot have their life in God. I must cultivate that on my own.

The foolish five are faced with this reality and they become aware that the only course of action is for them to go to the merchants and buy their own oil. In other words, they must go and invest the time and energy necessary to cultivate intimacy for its own sake.

Why is this critical? I believe that during the "strategic delay" in which the body of Christ finds itself at this moment, there is an increasing influence of darkness and trouble that will try the very foundations of our faith in God. Evil is rampant and the darkness is getting darker. The Lord of hosts is preparing to become involved in a significant way in bringing justice to the earth in the form of His temporal judgments, and these judgments will be terrible in their force and their effectiveness. Judgment is rooted in the jealous heart of the Bridegroom God and has as its purpose the removal of all barriers to bridal love.

But the sober reality is that the judgments of God will affect many believers as well as unbelievers in negative ways. Everyone will experience the coming troubling circumstances—natural disasters, weather situations, wars, diseases and human violence. All of these things will be used in the sovereign power of God to work justice in the earth and to defeat the powers of darkness that hinder the people of God from loving Him as He deserves.

I know many intercessors who have grown weary in the waiting, skeptical that the promises will be fulfilled, because their eyes are focused on the resolution of issues rather than on the Person of Jesus. Their goal is the realization of prophetic promises instead of deepening intimacy with Jesus, and thus their reward remains external. When the fulfillment of their dreams and promises is delayed, discouragement and weariness take their toll.

By contrast, those whose hearts are rooted and grounded in the love of the Lord and whose relationship is one of intimate friendship, have the resources to stand strong. They can discern the ways of the Lord and become His partners in the activity of loosing judgment on the earth. Their focus is not on the realization of an external promise. They know experientially that He is the fullness of every promise, and in His sweet kiss upon the heart their joy is made full.

The Lord, in the time of strategic delay, will bring the peoples of the earth to the point at which His intervention is absolutely necessary, and He will orchestrate the timing of that intervention to bring maximum glory to His own Name. Those who have oil in abundance, who have cultivated intimacy with Jesus by the Holy Spirit, will understand with a much greater degree of peace and rest what His strategies are, and will find the grace to cooperate with them.

Those who have only enough oil for the day-to-day function of their ministries may find themselves in a dry state, having lost their effectiveness. Their lamps will go out, and they will miss the celebration enjoyed by those who have entered the intimate place. This is what I believe the parable means when, at the very end, the foolish virgins are turned away at the door. I do not believe this speaks of eternal judgment, but rather of being turned away from sharing as partners with Christ in the celebration of the Bridegroom's joyful activity at the end of the age.

## THE WISDOM OF INTIMACY

Once again, in the goodness of God, He has given us a real-life story in which the people involved live out this reality before our eyes. I began this chapter by speaking of the "Marys of Bethany" who today are being drawn by the Holy Spirit, and it is the story of Mary of Bethany and her siblings, Martha and Lazarus, that provides the context for understanding Jesus' parable. We can learn much from this story if we have ears to hear.

The story begins with the familiar recounting of Jesus' visit to Martha's home:

**Now it happened as they went that He entered a certain village; and a certain woman named Martha welcomed Him into her house. And she had a sister called Mary, who also sat at Jesus' feet and heard His word.**

**But Martha was distracted with much serving, and she approached Him and said, "Lord, do You not care that my sister has left me to serve alone? Therefore tell her to help me."**

**And Jesus answered and said to her, "Martha, Martha, you are worried and troubled about many things. "But one thing is needed, and Mary has chosen that good part, which will not be taken away from her."**
**Luke 10:38-42**

At the beginning of the narrative, we notice a couple of things. The house belonged to the elder sister, Martha, and was probably her inheritance from her parents, who are not mentioned in the story. Since it would be culturally unusual for a single woman to own a home if her parents were still alive, this is the likely scenario.[3] Lazarus, in all likelihood, is the younger brother of the sisters.

Jesus comes to visit their home and it is evident that He enjoys their company. Martha, who is dearly loved by Jesus, is the one who lives the life of ministry and service. She is so engaged in serving that she is "distracted" by it. Mary, on the other hand, gives herself to sitting at the feet of Jesus, hearing His word. From a human standpoint, there is much to be done. There is much serving, *"preparations that had to be made"*[4] and Martha is giving herself to those tasks with her customary vigor. Mary is not being helpful to her sister, but rather is focused on what Jesus has to say.

One must have a certain perspective in order to comprehend the import of what is going on here. The living God is sitting in the living room of this little family, on a real day in history. He is encountering real people, just as He comes by the Spirit to encounter you and me today. *The eternal Word of the Father, the Word of God made flesh, is in the front room, and He is in the mood to talk!*

That is a staggering reality! We have become so inured, so accustomed to this kind statement in the Bible that we tend to miss the power of it. The incarnate Christ is encountering human beings. Because of the eternal nature of His word, He is also encountering me if I will turn aside and listen. The bush is still burning, and God Himself will speak to those who come and see. One of those people has the wisdom to sit at His feet and listen to what God is saying to her, while the other has too much to do. Martha is distracted from true wisdom by doing things for God, while Mary makes the choice to hear Him and be drawn into His life.

It's important for us to see that, in Martha's eyes, Mary is the foolish one in the beginning of this story. Those who take the time to cultivate intimacy are at first seen as the foolish, the distracted, the unrealistic. They are viewed as those who have lost their grip on reality. "What do you *do,* after all? You mean, you just sit in this House of Prayer and think about God?"

I am struck by how often the question comes: "What results have you seen in the community since you began the House of Prayer?" Now, I understand this question, because there is a focus on prayer for revival in our city. But the first commandment must come to hold first place in our hearts if anything is going to be established in the truth of the Kingdom. I must settle in my own heart that Jesus is worthy of my love and affection, of my extravagant ministry to Him, *just because He is worthy!*

Make no mistake, there will be community impact, but it is because *He loves the community,* not solely because we are praying that He will do things. The evangelization of our cities is not the first order of business—worship is! John Piper makes this claim so boldly: ". . . the Church does not exist to do missions. The Church exists to worship the Lord Jesus Christ. Missions exists because worship does not."

The horizontal effect of prayer is not the first thing on the heart of God! Loving and glorifying His Son is the first order, and without that, nothing else counts!

The Marys of Bethany still are seen as foolish in the eyes of many, but I tell you, it is they who are wise. The Psalmist wrote a powerful song that speaks to this reality:

> **Now therefore, be wise, O kings;**
> **be instructed, you judges of the earth.**
> **Serve the LORD with fear,**
> **and rejoice with trembling.**
> **Kiss the Son, lest He be angry,**
> **and you perish in the way,**
> **when His wrath is kindled but a little.**
> **Blessed are all those who put their trust in Him.**
> **Psalm 2:10-12**

*Be wise, peoples of the earth, and rejoice with trembling. Kiss the Son, lest He be angry and you perish in the day of the kindling of His wrath!* It is wisdom to kiss the Son of God, to sit before Him and gaze upon His beauty, to hear Him and gain His perspective on what is right and true. He is worthy, He is lovely and in His presence there is fullness of joy forever.

Martha doesn't understand. She is focused on her ministry. She has enough oil for the day, enough energy to do her ministry, and she is mostly satisfied (although she would like a little more help!). Mary's heart burns for more than that, and Jesus' response to Martha's indignation is that Mary has chosen the better part, and it will not be taken from her.

With this the story seems to end, leaving us with a rather unresolved feeling. Those who are like Mary find in this story a good deal of vindication, and those who are more like Martha feel rebuked but don't know how to bring closure to the issues. It has been helpful to me to not look at the story in too much of an individualized fashion, but to see it in a holistic way. In other words, this is not so much about being a Mary or a Martha. Rather, in the household of faith there are those like Mary, and those like her sister, and we must understand the importance of doing first things first so that the secondary things can be done with effectiveness and joy. Jesus was not telling Martha that her ministry was invalid. He was saying that there is a first thing without which the second things will burn us out. I don't think Martha understood that yet, but the story was not complete.

Although Luke's Gospel goes on to different events, in the eleventh chapter of John's record, Jesus' involvement with Martha and Mary picks up again. The text is lengthy so it is not included here, but I will summarize the story as it unfolds. Jesus receives word from Mary and Martha that Lazarus, the younger brother of the sisters, is sick. Implicit in the message is the expectation that Jesus will come and heal him.

At this point, God's "strategic delay" is introduced into this real-life situation. The sisters need help, and they need it now. Their brother is sick and dying, and they need the Lord to come, now. They don't need a sermon or a prayer. They need an intervention by God Almighty, and upon hearing the request, Jesus does the absolutely unthinkable thing— *nothing!* He decides to do nothing for a couple of days, and that decision embodies the dramatic dilemma of the strategic delay. Everything in the realm of common sense points to the logic of an immediate intervention—He loves these people, He is within walking distance, He has the power to speak from anywhere and bring healing, they are begging Him to come. He does none of it. He just waits.

Why? My soul feels the tension of this as I write it. *Oh, God, why?!! Where are You? I need You now, not tomorrow! Why don't you hear my cry?* All of these emotions and more must be going on in the hearts of Martha and Mary, their friends and the disciples. What is Jesus doing? Why is He not doing anything? There seemingly are no answers available, *because in fact the true answer lies outside of the realm of human possibility!* God is getting ready to do something at the end of the strategic delay that will absolutely rock their world, that will set in motion cataclysmic events, that will turn a village upside-down and bring infinitely more glory to the Name of Jesus than would a mere healing. His plan is so outrageous that the human mind cannot conceive of it.

One is reminded of the story of Abraham and Isaac in **Genesis 22.** God tells Abraham to take Isaac, his only son, *whom he loves,* and offer him as a burnt offering to the Lord. Abraham is willing to do this, but the only reason he can give for his willingness is that apparently God is going to raise Isaac from the dead, which in a figurative sense is what happened.[5] His only conclusion is that God is going to do something outside the parameters of normal activity. His obedience therefore makes sense.

Like most of the folks around Jesus, Mary and Martha in that day did not have the same depth of relationship with God that Abraham had, and so were not at that place of quietness and rest. When Jesus made His decision to go to Bethany *more than four days late* in the view of the sisters, the worst-case scenario had in fact happened. Lazarus was dead.

The text in *John 11* tells us that as Jesus enters the town, Martha comes to meet Him but Mary stays in the house. Here is already a picture of the comparative peace resting upon the two women. Martha, in her busyness and anxiety, at least knows where to go. She is, in this story, like the widow of *Luke 18.* She is precious to God but her soul is disquieted and confused. Seeking some understanding, she goes to the Lord and brings, as a prayer, a very simple statement: *"Lord, if You had been here, my brother would not have died."* Her level of intimacy with Jesus, her depth of comprehension regarding His ways, is limited, and therefore all she can conceive of as real is what seems obvious. Lazarus has died; therefore the story is over. That's all there is.

One can only pause for a moment to feel the human anguish of that scene, the confusion and accusation that must have been in her heart as she faced the One Who had the power to change things, and had chosen not to do so. Do you know that place of near madness? How do we stand in such a place with any kind of faith? A God Who can do something and does not. It is a major dilemma.

Jesus responds to her with tenderness and begins to comfort her with words of truth about the situation. He promises her that Lazarus will be raised from the dead, but all she can think of is right doctrine, and she refers to the resurrection at the end of the age. But Jesus responds with unimaginable words: *"I am the resurrection and the life. He who believes in me, though he may die, he shall live."*

Jesus personalizes the doctrine and announces to Martha that its fulfillment is standing in front of her. And she still doesn't get it! You see, she still has not taken the time to get past the doctrine to the Person Who fulfills the doctrine, the living Word of God. The Resurrection is standing in front of her and she does not recognize Him because she has not cultivated eyes to see. I imagine the eyes of Jesus boring into Martha's soul at that moment, searching for the light of faith that will quicken something inside His heart and release Him to do what He longs to do. But He does not find it in her. Martha's lamp has gone out. Jesus turns from her, leaving her standing at the door, a foolish virgin with no oil in a time of darkness. She will have no immediate partnership in what He is about to do.

Jesus asks for Mary. She is in the house, in a place of rest and peace knowing in the midst of her grief that her Beloved will come when it is time. Her quietness is supra-rational, not something she can easily explain, but in the midst of all the pain and confusion, Mary is at rest! Anxiety does not rule the day with her, because she has come to know the Man Christ Jesus, and she has confidence that in His time He will come and do what needs to be done. Her lamp burns brightly *in the midst of God's strategic delay,* and her faith is not shaken. Is there tension and confusion in her heart? Of course there is! She's a human being with all the passionate emotions that anyone would have in such a circumstance. But she has successfully waged the violent war of chosen trust in a Savior Whose character is worthy of her trust, even when she can't understand what He's doing.

When Jesus calls for her, she goes to meet Him and *utters the exact prayer that Martha has spoken moments earlier.* This seems so significant to me. Mary's prayer and Martha's are exactly the same, but the power is not in the words spoken; rather, it is in the depth of relationship behind the words.

Today, many who are caught in the widow's mentality of intercession are focused on praying exactly the right way, binding this, loosing that, and Beloved, I tell you it is not about that![6] It's about the authority of intimacy. Mary understood that fact, and the prayer of her *heart* did the loosing that was necessary, unlocking the power of God in a way that no one except Jesus could anticipate.

*John 11* tells us that when Mary speaks those words, Jesus sees her weeping, and something is released in His inner Being. He groans in His Spirit and is troubled or agitated. His Spirit begins to roll and tumble, brooding over the chaos of the moment, waiting for the right time to utter the word of power. Then He asks for information concerning the location of Lazarus' tomb and goes to do the impossible.

What is so gripping to me about this story is that *it was the prayer of Jesus' intimate friend that loosed resurrection power from His Spirit.* I have mused upon this scenario and the different ways the scene could have unfolded. If I were the Messiah, I might have come into Bethany with a fanfare of trumpets blazing forth as I strode down the path to where Lazarus was, doing my best Charlton Heston impersonation. After all, this is God in the flesh, coming to do the impossible. What a scene! The papers would have loved it, and the fame of His Name would have spread through the land!

Jesus' mode of operation, though, is not to show off, but to call His friend, His bridal partner, one with whom He has shared the secrets of His heart, to His side. He has given *her* the authority to stir His heart to do the work that needs to be done. He will not do it on His own. He will not do it without His friend. So when Mary prays, when the wise virgin comes to the Bridegroom, when the Queen serves up the Banquet of Wine and whispers her request, the door is opened, all the power of heaven comes to bear upon the issue of the day and resurrection power is released. The voice of God thunders into the nether regions, the gates of death are shattered by the sound, the breath of God enters once more into a human frame that has been held in the grip of the enemy, and life comes forth from death.

This is *all* released by the power and authority of intimacy. *Bridal Intercession!* There is no authority like it in heaven or on the earth.

At the end of the day, the one who seemed foolish at the beginning was found to be wise. And please understand, Martha was blessed as well! She was not sent off in shame to lament her lack of intimacy. She received her brother back as well. But what she missed was the celebration of partnership, the exhilaration of touching the heart of God with her prayers and seeing Him do in partnership with her what only He can do.

Beloved, I believe with all my heart that God intends to release a ministry of power in the earth in these last days. The Lazarus generations will be brought forth from the dead through the power of prayer, but that power cannot be released in full measure to the widow-like intercessors whose hearts are filled with right doctrine but who know little intimacy, who have the right lexicon of prayer but whose hearts are weary because they lack a fresh and vital friendship with the Beloved. God is showing Himself to be nearby, not far off. The Bridegroom is in the land, and He has brought His redemption with Him. He has come to Martha's house and He is in the mood to talk, to reveal His ways and means.

Jesus invites you who stand in the place of that precious sister to come aside for a moment and put first things first, to allow the issues and agendas of the day to be set aside for a moment. I am utterly convinced that those who draw near to love Him will find themselves on the receiving end of the earth-shaking power of the living Word, for He cares about the issues and agendas of the day in an infinitely greater way than we do. God talks to His friends so that they might be established in faith, that in the time of delay their hearts will not be shaken and that they might stir the very heart of God with their prayers. They are the wise virgins. What they have chosen will not be taken from them.

## CHAPTER 8

# VISION IN OUR HEARTS
## AGREEMENT WITH GOD'S AGENDA
### FOR OUR LIVES

I n this chapter I want to address the relationship of intercession to vision and leadership, from the perspective of what has become for me one of the most exhilarating stories in the entire Bible. This narrative, found in *2 Samuel 6 and 7,* in which King David brings the Ark of the Covenant up to Jerusalem and establishes the Tabernacle of David, documents a tremendously fulfilling time for the king and sets the stage for one of David's most powerful encounters with God.

The story is rooted in a desire that had been resident in David's heart for many years. Working in his youth as a shepherd in his father's fields, David had begun to respond to God's initiative in cultivating an affectionate friendship with his Maker.

As he walked through the open fields focusing on the grandeur of the created order, the "eyes and ears" of David's heart were continually open, taking in the wonders hidden in the stark design of the Judean hillsides. He saw the works of art that make up the created realm and recognized the passionate Artist behind what was made. His poetic gift was honed in the exhilarating monotony of days and nights spent in the open air, with little to do other than contemplate the wonder of what was there.

It was during this time, as David began to experience the beauty and wonder of the Person of God, that he began to get a sense of his life's destiny. When he needed strength to repel the lion and the bear, the power of God came upon David, convincing him of God's trustworthiness in times of battle. It was a confidence he would need in future days, before and during his reign as king.

I believe it was in these days that God began to show Himself to the future king in deeper realms of His beauty and majesty in order to establish an assurance in David's heart that God would be true to His Word. To those who receive from the Lord with thankfulness and gladness of heart, more is given, and it is obvious from even a cursory reading of the *Psalms* that David's heart consistently responded out of exhilaration with the initiatives of his God.

Believers all over the earth are discovering what David knew—that when we come into the presence of the Lord, as we do night and day in the House of Prayer in Kansas City, with open and hungry hearts, the Spirit of the Lord is most gracious to reveal Himself in a personal way to the human soul. The surprise is that He seems always willing to give more than we can embrace, and we come face to face with our own limited ability to comprehend His beauty and love. Yet there comes in those times an increasing hunger and thirst for the Lord's presence and we find ourselves more and more eager to be with Him and draw our life from His.

As David grew in these kinds of experiences, there came a cataclysmic event in which the beauty of the Lord was revealed to him in such power and majesty that he made a vow to the Lord, a vow that is articulated in poetic fashion in *Psalm 132:*

**LORD, remember David and all his afflictions;**
**How he swore to the LORD,**
**and vowed to the Mighty One of Jacob:**
**"Surely I will not go into the**
**chamber of my house,**

or go up to the comfort of my bed;
I will not give sleep to my eyes
or slumber to my eyelids,
Until I find a place for the LORD,
a dwelling place for the Mighty One of Jacob."

Behold, we heard of it in Ephrathah;
we found it in the fields of the woods.
Let us go into His tabernacle;
let us worship at His footstool.
Arise, O LORD, to Your resting place,
you and the ark of Your strength.
Let Your priests be clothed with righteousness,
and let Your saints shout for joy.
For Your servant David's sake,
do not turn away the face of Your Anointed.

The LORD has sworn in truth to David;
he will not turn from it:
"I will set upon your throne
the fruit of your body.
If your sons will keep
My covenant and My testimony
which I shall teach them,
their sons also shall sit
upon your throne forevermore."

For the LORD has chosen Zion;
he has desired it for His dwelling place:
"This is My resting place forever;
here I will dwell, for I have desired it.
I will abundantly bless her provision;
I will satisfy her poor with bread.
I will also clothe her priests with salvation,
and her saints shall shout aloud for joy.
There I will make the horn of David grow;
I will prepare a lamp for My Anointed.
His enemies I will clothe with shame,
but upon Himself His crown shall flourish."
Psalm 132:1-18

David makes this vow to the Lord in the context of the revelation of God's majestic plan for David's life, and it forms a foundation, a platform from which everything else in his life will find its focus and meaning. Key to our understanding of this is that *David's vow is made in cooperation with God's initiative concerning David's life.*

Through the course of his youth, David had come to an embryonic awareness of his place in God's design for human history. The plans in the heart of the Father were so astonishing that the supernatural "planting" of these truths in the heart of this young man would be a necessity.

The fact of the matter is that the same is true for every human being. What believer has not taken comfort in Jeremiah's marvelous words as he declared the reality of God's intentions?

> **For I know the thoughts that I think toward you,**
> **says the LORD,**
> **thoughts of peace and not of evil,**
> **to give you a future and a hope.**
> **Jeremiah 29:11**

David was beginning to come to grips with the massive truth that God had designed his life for a specific purpose and that, in the genius of His sovereignty, He would invite David into a partnership that involved real choices yet was settled in the bedrock of certain fulfillment.

Compared with what David could dream, God's plans were infinitely greater, and the same is true for each of us. Paul writes to the Corinthian believers that their eyes, ears and imaginations cannot begin to conceive of what He has planned for us who love Him,[1] and therefore the only way we can realize His plan is to hear His voice in the place of prayer and come into agreement with it. My hope is that through this chapter you will come to a greater awareness that God's magnificent plan involves you, and that He will cause your heart to believe and agree with His agenda for you.

It is important to understand that although I am focusing on leadership in this chapter, the same realities apply to every individual in the body of Christ, for we all yearn to realize the dreams of our lives. These dreams include the internal awareness in every human being that we are destined for significance, that we are designed for intimacy and that we ought to be taken seriously. Though we may not be apostles to the nations, the Lord's Word to Paul is His Word to us, that He wants us to fully *"lay hold of that for which Christ Jesus has also laid hold of me."*[2] Therefore this chapter is not exclusively applicable to leaders, but to all who desire to *"press toward the goal of the upward call of God in Christ Jesus."*[3]

## BUILDING SOMETHING FOR GOD

In *Psalm 132*, three things are happening. In the first section, David cries out to the Lord for permission to build the house of the Lord, a longing that would eventually find its fulfillment in the establishment of the Tabernacle of David. Secondly, God gives voice once again to His incredible desire to make His dwelling place among human beings. Finally, He makes personal promises to David regarding his kingly lineage, which will be established as the Tabernacle is set in place.

Notice that long before the fulfillment of these promises, God plants in David's heart the seeds of a vision so colossal that it either has to be from God, or it is the mad ramblings of a megalomaniac. One is reminded of the dreams given to the immature Joseph and how, though he was young and did not have the favor of his brothers, he was precious in the eyes of his father and would be established by God as a ruler over all of them. It was a vision so sensational that only God could perform it.

What is true of these two biblical leaders is also true of us regarding the vision God has seeded in our hearts. The plans God has for us seem, upon first hearing, so extraordinary that in order for these promises to become reality we need a season in which the brooding presence of the Holy Spirit can move these ideas and plans from the shaky place of mere intellectual perception to the heart conviction that God is actually going to do what He has said.

In the meantime, between the seeding of the vision and the fruit of it, we tend to be seduced by the siren song of human endeavor. In my observation and experience, there is a universal human misperception that causes us no small degree of pain and difficulty. This misperception is the belief that, once I have received a vision for my life, the *fulfillment of that vision depends on me and my efforts.* I need to do something for God. I need to build my business for God and it's my job to generate the business plan. I need to take my city for God, and the strategies are up to me. I have to raise my children for God, because how else will they know Him unless I lead them to Him? I need to go to the mission field for God's sake because, after all, I owe Him my life.

I have observed situations in which those kinds of statements were made in the attempt to stir up human fervor for a specific task or outreach program. Even if our theology tells us that our relationship with God is not based on our performance at any level, the practical reality, what I call our "heart-theology," in fact tells us something else. Our heart-theology is often very different from our doctrinal positions. And, very simply, our heart-theology controls what we experience.

Out of this dichotomy of what we know intellectually and what we believe in our hearts comes a great difficulty that I can best describe as "aggressive striving."[4] Aggressive striving is the attempt by a Christian with an unbelieving heart to produce by the energy of human zeal what God has promised to give by His grace. I have had a deep struggle with this over the course of my life, and want to share my pilgrimage with you.

## STRIVING FROM UNCERTAINTY

Like every person with some sense of vision and purpose imparted by the Lord, I have had a growing awareness that God has a place of significant spiritual leadership for me. I was raised in the context of ministry, my father being a pastor in a small evangelical denomination, and I knew early that I was "called" into a similar role. Over the years this sense grew, and like many others I went through college and seminary preparing to serve in the body of Christ.

I was completely unaware of the nature and amount of personal baggage that I brought with me into ministry. Coming through adolescence and young adulthood with all the typical woundings of human existence—fathering issues, intimacy issues, insecurity issues—I approached leadership in the same way I have observed as common among people like me: I used statements of vision and the goals for attaining those visions as a means for self-validation and self-actualization. I didn't mean to do that. I longed to be pleasing to the Lord and effective in His Kingdom. But I did not have the *heart understanding* of His goodness and love that would allow me to minister to others from a secure place of personal freedom.

I am convinced that this is the common dilemma of human beings and not only leadership folks. One of the fundamental results of humanity's fallen nature is the brokenness of our relationship with the only Father Who can truly affirm our identity. Without that affirmation, it is simply impossible to function in a right and healthy way. And so we strive aggressively to bring to reality the vision we hold in our hearts, knowing deeply that those things are real but not understanding that the grace of God will bring them about in His timing and His ways.

Somehow I knew a real dimension of my calling was that I would someday stand in a place of influence that was broader than one local congregation. Spiritually, I wanted everyone to know what I know and get excited about the things that get me excited. Therefore, much of my life in ministry has been characterized by striving to be heard, straining to have a platform from which to declare the truth I've been shown, and meeting the resistance of God and people in trying to do the thing I was created to do.

My outward goal was to bless the body of Christ, but the underlying objective was the self-validation that comes from getting insights from the Holy Spirit.

You see, the point of difficulty for me was the subconscious and erroneous belief that it was up to me to build the platform from which I would have the influence that I longed for. In the church systems I knew, there was only one kind of platform, namely a growing and successful local church (or at least one that had the appearance of growth and success). And so ministry in the local church became a means to an end and touching the lives of human beings became the pathway to fulfillment.

Much good fruit from that season endures to this day. There was also a corresponding holocaust, though—a destructive trail of burned out and wounded people who got caught in my process of working out my vision, and who were set aside or ignored when I no longer felt they were helping the cause. Because the reward I was seeking was the establishment of something external—a successful ministry of being "influential" in the larger body of Christ—the internal reward of the affections of Jesus was not established as the motivation of my heart.

I am convinced today that all of that difficulty, spanning a number of years, which caused so much pain in my life and in the lives of my family and many others, was due to the fact that I *did not believe in my heart that what the Lord had spoken to me, He would also perform*. I was convinced it was up to me to produce it in order to please the Lord and bring release to what burned inside of me.

The pursuit of the dream became, in itself, a nightmare. It was not until the Lord began to establish me, through no doing of my own, in the House of Prayer in Kansas City, that

I began to understand these realities at a heart level and therefore to come to the place where aggressive striving could begin to die down, if not cease altogether.

At the same time, I also came to see that even in the midst of my own striving and failure, God knew that in the depths of my heart I longed to be fervent and faithful to His will for my life. The Lord had placed something inside my heart, and what I was striving for was to realize the vision He had set within me. God looks upon the motivations of our hearts, and sees the longing deep inside to be obedient sons and daughters, and to serve Him with effectiveness and zeal.

While this reality neither justifies nor qualifies us, God is pleased when our hearts desire His ways. He is quite willing to wait until our human zeal is dealt with, either burning itself out in the place of failure, or being addressed in the sweetness of His gentle encounters so that He can demonstrate His love for us when we have nothing to present to Him that would justify His affection and care. It is upon realizing that God loves us passionately and completely in the midst of our deepest failures that our hearts finally begin to receive His love. It is then that He can release the enabling power in us that fulfills His vision for our lives, a vision that can never be realized by our efforts, but only by His grace. Only then can we begin to minister to others out of the mercy and grace He has shown to us.

## SETTING OUT TO BUILD GOD'S HOUSE

I believe this kind of dynamic was also happening in David's life as he sought to establish the Tabernacle in *2 Samuel 6 and 7.* An overwhelming sense of destiny had been burning in his heart and mind for years, and the Lord had already taken him through an incredible process to bring much of that vision to pass.[5]

There was one dimension of the vision, however, that had not yet been settled, and that had to do with the eternal nature of David's kingdom. David's heart still did not believe this final element of God's plan, and the only setting in which it would be established was the house of the Lord. But there was a process through which David would have to be taken in order for this final dimension to be fulfilled.

At the beginning of *2 Samuel 7*, we see King David in a place of contentment and rest, having been given victory over all the enemies of his kingdom. One day, David is sitting in his cedar home and he begins to consider the possibility of building a temple for the presence of the Lord. David has an experience I believe is common among leaders in the body of Christ. He has the idea of doing something great for God. God has made His presence known in the Ark of the Covenant for several hundred years. David has taken note of the house in which he himself lives, and because of its relative opulence, it occurs to him that the Almighty may be weary of His simple dwelling place.

I believe that in the matter of vision and destiny, we as leaders often get things turned upside-down, making the assumption that God is looking for a people who will do something for Him, and that in the performance of that thing will come the fulfillment of our own longings for destiny and significance. The relationship God has with His people, though, has never been built on what they can do for Him, but rather on what He will do for them. Any activity on our part is the living out of a partnership with God in establishing His purposes in the earth.

The truth expressed in *2 Chronicles 20:17* has always been the standard for the people of God:

**'You will not need to fight in this battle. Position yourselves, stand still and see the salvation of the LORD, who is with you, O Judah and Jerusalem!' Do not fear or be dismayed; tomorrow go out against them, for the LORD is with you.**

**2 Chronicles 20:17**

The clear message of this verse is that it is the Lord Who is the Actor with regard to the well being of His people. He is not looking for people to defend Him or support Him or work for Him.

In the same tone of benevolent and affectionate sovereignty, we are instructed in *Psalm 50* that our worship is pleasing to the Lord not because of all the things we do or bring, but because our heart attitude is one of thanksgiving and trust. Consider the passage:

> **"If I were hungry, I would not tell you;**
> **for the world is Mine, and all its fullness.**
> **Will I eat the flesh of bulls,**
> **or drink the blood of goats?**
> **Offer to God thanksgiving,**
> **and pay your vows to the Most High.**
> **Call upon Me in the day of trouble;**
> **I will deliver you, and you shall glorify Me."**
> **Psalm 50:12-15**

God is saying to His people in this psalm that it is not because He is hungry that we bring sacrifices. In fact, He goes so far as to say that if He were hungry, He wouldn't bother to inform humans, because there is nothing we could do to satisfy that hunger. The earth belongs to Him. He doesn't need our gifts. Rather, He desires offerings of thanksgiving, expressions of a grateful heart and a willingness to ask for help again in the times of our need. *"Tell me 'thank You,' and ask Me for help again!"* That's a rather startling truth to us as performance-oriented believers, but it has been the basis of relationship with God from the beginning.

David shares with his prophetic counselor, Nathan, his idea of doing something for God, and receives the prophet's blessing to pursue the project. But no sooner has Nathan given his approval than the Spirit of God encounters him and gives him a very different perspective of what is in the heart of God concerning the matter. For all practical purposes, God says to Nathan, *"You know, this temple project David has in mind is a very nice idea, but it isn't My idea. The temple will happen in My timing and by the hand of another, but I have in mind at*

*this time not that David would build Me a house, but that I'm go-*
*ing to build him a house!"*

In other words, the Lord says to Nathan that He's not
interested in David doing something for God. Instead, God
is going to do something for David so that the reign of this
earthly king will become an eternal partnership of intimacy
with a God Whose heart is gripped with love for His people.

In fact, in this chapter, the Lord goes so far as to funda-
mentally say, *"Actually, Nathan, tell David that I really like living*
*in this tent. I've been in the tent now for several hundred years and*
*I'm not in a hurry to leave it. I would much rather focus on estab-*
*lishing him in the place I have for him, that we might share the place*
*of glory forever."*

What a statement of humility by the God of the universe!
He's a God Who is not concerned about external trappings
but is focused on the joy of the heart. The external expression will come in time and it will be glorious, but for now the
priority is the establishment of David's identity and purpose.

An important passage parallels the longings of David's
heart to build an adequate temple for the Lord. David had
his focus on an earthly building. In *2 Corinthians 5,* Paul the
apostle speaks of the inner longing of the believer to be
clothed in the heavenly habitation instead of the earthly
"tent" that is our physical body. We long for this fulfillment,
eagerly awaiting the establishment of the true heavenly
dwelling place and groaning at the delay with anticipation.

I believe the Spirit is saying in these passages together
that God is not in a big hurry to have us abandon the fleshly
tabernacle. His higher desire is that we come to a greater
degree of conviction that He really enjoys us in our physical
habitations. He has made an earthly tabernacle called the human body in which He has clothed *Himself* for all eternity,
and I believe His desire is that we enjoy the beauty and majesty of the physical body, limited as it may be.

The comparison of our bodies with the ones we *will* have
is like the comparison of a leather tent with Solomon's Temple
in all its glory.[6] But it was a *body* that the Father prepared for

the Son, in which He would live out obedience and intimacy—the Word made flesh, dwelling physically on the earth. It is enjoyable to Him when we live in faithfulness even though clothed in inadequate stuff, and He's in no hurry to be done with that. He says to us, *"Don't be overly concerned about the limitations of your physical being. I understand what it is to live in an earthly tent, and I enjoy you in that limitation more than you can know."*

## God's Unexpected Promise

God goes on to speak to the prophet about His desire to establish the house of David in the most amazing way. What the Lord has in store for the king is the permanent establishment of his heritage, the promise of the favor of God on His household and an unthinkable pledge regarding the blessing that will surround his kingdom: The Messiah Himself will come through the lineage of David! The king's heart is gripped with the enormity of the prophetic word and he is overwhelmed. And here is the key: *David is fully conscious that there is no way he can produce by human effort what God is imparting.* The only thing he knows to do is to take this promise into the house of the Lord and wait upon God for the confirmation of it.

I believe the key here is that David had heard this word before, at the time of the writing of *Psalm 132,* but what had gripped his heart in the first hearing was the passionate desire to build a physical Tabernacle and establish a locale for the the Lord's presence in the nation.

The second part of the promise, that there the Lord would *"make the horn of David grow, (and) prepare a lamp for (His) anointed"[7]* had perhaps not yet been fully formed in the heart of David. And now the enormity of the whole matter was getting hold of David's heart. The only thing he could do with it was to sit before the Lord until the revelation of the beauty and power of God became sufficient to settle the personal vision as a reality in his inner being.

We can observe David's process of digesting this word in the text of *2 Samuel 7:*

**Then King David went in and sat before the LORD; and he said: "Who am I, O Lord GOD? And what is my house, that You have brought me this far? "And yet this was a small thing in Your sight, O Lord GOD; and You have also spoken of Your servant's house for a great while to come. Is this the manner of man, O Lord GOD?**

**2 Samuel 7:18-19**

This is the center of what I am hoping to communicate in this chapter—the need to take the promises of God, bring them before the Lord and sit before Him until our perception of His beauty and power is great enough to believe that He will bring about these promises for His own glory.

This is not an easy thing for us in the Western world. We are addicted to activity. We often think that the moment we get a vision from God we are accountable to produce the effects of that vision in order to please Him. But there is a greater need: the need for a level of intimacy with the Lord that will characterize all that we do in the expression of our vision. The need for depth of intimacy is profound in the Church of the Western world, but we are so compulsive in our need to *do* something that we find it difficult to sit still long enough for God to reveal His greatness and settle in our hearts His vision for our lives.

Again and again I hear laments from pastors and worship leaders that go something like this: "I came to Kansas City and saw what you guys are doing in the House of Prayer and I loved it, but when I went home and *tried to get the worship team and the people to do it,* they just didn't get it."

There is little concept of waiting upon the Lord, of going deep in the presence of the Lord and allowing the ministry and the model to be birthed in the ways and the timing of the Holy Spirit. We are so eager to do the new thing that we try to put even intimacy on the fast track of the "next hot new program," and it simply doesn't work. We must develop the willingness to wait on the Lord personally until the fire in our hearts burns brightly and He brings release to the "doing" of the ministry.

I'm so grateful to God for the years of plowing and sowing that went into the House of Prayer in Kansas City. I want to honor Mike Bickle and the team there for their wisdom in approaching the promises. Mike took it deep before he tried to take it wide, and the nations of the earth are the beneficiaries of his patience and wisdom. Marvelous things were spoken to Mike, and had he tried to produce the fruit of these words earlier, his actions would have given rise to difficulty.[8] As a result of his patience, the House of Prayer is now emerging as a significant influence in the body of Christ and Mike's role as an intercessory leader among the nations is a settled reality.

You see, it is in sitting before the Lord, gazing upon His beauty, meditating on the wonder of Jesus Christ and hearing His heart concerning these promises that we develop the kind of faith that bears eternal fruit. In the secret place of the Most High we hear Him speaking to us about ourselves, our neighbors, our children, our cities and our world. Until we hear His living Word we will not find the faith to bring forth what He has spoken.

I have recently been touched powerfully by *Psalm 39:3:*

**My heart was hot within me;**
**While I was musing, the fire burned.**
**Then I spoke with my tongue.**

It is in the "musing," the meditation upon the living Word of God—the Man Christ Jesus revealed in the Scriptures—that the fire of His love gets ignited. Then we begin to have something to say, to offer to Him in the public place. The "fire" John the Baptist spoke of is not merely the emotional stirrings of the public worship time, but the deep burning of

God's Spirit that is kindled in the secret places of personal intimacy with Him. That is where the fragrance is added, the pleasing, aromatic incense of laying a life at His feet, attending to Him and doing His business.

My heart is thrilled as I continue to meet precious and gifted people who are longing to come into His presence, to be about the business of the Father. But I ache with the desire that they would not try to move too quickly to the programming of their vision, be it night-and-day prayer or any other expression of the Kingdom of God. To move to action too quickly is to miss the essential thing, the "one needful thing," the ongoing contemplation of the Man with whom we are in love. We must not be so eager to have a program of intercession that we forget to intercede over God's ways and means.

## Three Revelations

In *2 Samuel 7,* we find that as David sat before the Lord, he was gripped by three things. First, he was struck by his own smallness in comparison with the plan of God. In our striving for significance, we can miss the requisite humility by moving too quickly to action. The soul's deep need for true humility then fails to be established. True humility comes only through the revelation of the Lord's beauty. In His presence alone we say, *"Who am I that You would love me like this, that You would do this for me?"*

There is a false humility that sounds like the real thing. In saying, *"Who am I?"* in fact we are saying, *"It's about time. I've deserved this sense of promotion and recognition for some time now, and it's finally here. Now I can afford the humble posture. Who am I?"* Inside, our soul quivers with excitement in anticipation of the affirmation of our peers. We congratulate ourselves again on having formulated the hot plan. We believe we're God's man or woman of power for the final hour.

In the revelation of the beauty of the Lord, though, there is true humility as we become lost in the overwhelming wonder of the Person of God, and fully acknowledge that we are in no way deserving of His love and favor. In that place, as He ministers to our spirits, we are granted the humility that knows we are fully established only by His loving grace, and understands there is no reason for Him to grant it to us except that He loves us.

Our attention now shifts automatically to the second point of David's focus: *"Who are You, Lord, that You would make such promises to one like me? You must be very great, and this must be a small thing to You."* In the process of becoming aware of his smallness, David becomes overwhelmed with the greatness of God, and realizes that *this* Sovereign can do anything He pleases! More on this in a moment.

The third point of focus for David is the startling realization of the ways of God. David wrote at one point **"Show me Your ways, O God, teach me Your paths."**[9] The ways of God are radically different from our ways as human beings, and to discover those ways with understanding is a marvelous thing. Suddenly, in *2 Samuel 7:19,* a powerful awareness grips David in the form of a question to God: **"Is this the manner of man, O Lord God?"** The word "manner" here translates the Hebrew word "torah," which in this context means "the customary way of dealing with human beings." The *"torah"* is the law, and it refers to God's patterns of operating in relationships.

David is saying here, *"God, is this the normal way You deal with people, that You do not ask them to do something for You, but commit Yourself to do something magnificent for them?"* And the wonderful answer is "Yes! That's the way it is!" God is much more concerned with establishing us in the place of our calling and ministry than we can imagine, because it is through doing so that, in the long term, the greatest glory will come to Him. He is focused on the beautification of His sons and daughters in their places of ministry and service so that He will be able to present to His Son a Bride who is fully formed in His likeness, able to move with Him in bridal partnership without fear or compromise.

As David comes to realize this in his heart, he breaks forth in the following verses of *2 Samuel 7* in a marvelous hymn of praise and thanksgiving to God. As one considers verses 20-26 of this chapter, it is easy to see that David's full focus now is the majesty of God, the wonder of His plan and the all-encompassing nature of His agenda for humanity in general and for his life in particular. The glory of God released through David's realizing his true place of identity, leadership and authority, gives David the liberty to pray big prayers over his own life without a sense of inappropriateness.

Until I am settled in God's perspective of my identity and purpose, I will never find the courage to pray big prayers over my own life with the humility of true faith. Either I will pray presumptuously in an attempt to convince my own heart of what is true, or I will hesitate to pray assertively for fear of seeming proud.

But one who has stood in the councils of the Most High, and in that place become soberly convinced of His opinion of one's life and destiny—that person can pray with a humble certainty borne out of agreement with the opinions of God. There is no arrogance; what emerges is only the confidence and patience that come from knowing the will of God and understanding He is certain to keep His Word.

## Released to Action

Out of the certainty of his identity, David sought the counsel of the Lord about when to proceed to horizontal activity. In *2 Samuel 8,* we find David conquering all of the neighboring nations and bringing them to submit to the Lord's authority. And though David was involved in the activity of having his name established,[10] in reality it was the Lord Who preserved him in all of his activity.[11]

As the Lord establishes us in His purposes, there is activity, to be sure. But it is *derivative* activity, born out of the place of confidence and identity that are already established in God, rather than in the place of striving to be "someone" in God's presence and in the presence of others.

Next time you find yourself saying, *"Lord, we want to do something for You. We want to take our cities for God. We want to build a ministry to honor the Lord,"* remember that the promise in fact is from the Lord to us: *"I'm going to establish your ministry, I'm going to give you your city, so that you may present it to me as a trophy of my grace."*

You see, the cities and nations of the earth already belong to the Lord. *Psalm 24:1* tells us, *"The earth is the Lord's, and all its fullness."* He owns the nations and will give them to us as a part of our inheritance with which to bless Him. Did He not command us to ask of Him, that in response to our asking He would give to us the nations of the earth as our inheritance?[12]

Of course, we know that this is primarily a Messianic Psalm, but in relationship with Jesus as His joint heirs, we are the recipients of the same promises. We become established in the Father's goodness, confident in His love and purposes. As we ask for the nations, He gives them to us to bring glory to His own Son.[13]

I believe with all my heart that God intends to establish His vision in the hearts of His people, but He desires to take it deeper than merely the revelation that comes to our minds, where we interpret it as something we are supposed to do for Him. Rather, He longs to root us and ground us in the experiential knowledge of His beauty, power and affection for us. From that place, He wants to convince us that it is He Who will be the Actor in the situation, establishing our house, our ministries and our lives for His own glory and honor.

## CHAPTER 9

# THE FELLOWSHIP OF THE SUFFERING SERVANT

## BRIDAL PARTNERSHIP IN THE SUFFERINGS OF CHRIST

Since the spring of 1998, God has allowed me to come into increasing awareness, intimacy and depth in my relationship with Jesus as the Lover of my soul, my Bridegroom. It has been a sometimes frightening journey, because I've found that if one wants to go deep in the understanding of the passionate love of Jesus, one also must be willing to explore the pain in one's life. This is not particularly fun, but I believe by faith and am *experiencing* that it is worth it.

Some surprising things happen when we start thinking about getting to know Jesus and His passionate love for us as our Bridegroom. I don't know about you, but I had sort of a romantic expectation that He would come and speak tenderly and woo me and tell me how cool and nice I am and how much He enjoys various aspects of my life. Have you had that kind of expectation? And then all of a sudden He did a very surprising thing: In my process of exploring the reality and depth of His love for me, He took me to *Isaiah 52 and 53* and began to teach me about His passion on the cross, and what the cross of Jesus has to do with His love for me as an ardent Bridegroom.

I began to find myself wrestling with some of the difficult, paradoxical and contradictory realities of what it is to live as a bride. We are passionately loved by an all-powerful God. Yet at the same time, we must live as real people in a broken world, in the midst of fallen circumstances and difficulties, with the irresolvable conflicts we experience from time to time.

## THE GOD WHO IS ABLE TO SAVE BUT DOES NOT

There come to us, face to face, uncomfortable nagging questions of why God does not do the things He is powerful to do. When Jesus was ministering to the disciples of John the Baptist, He said, *"Blessed are those who are not offended because of Me."*[1] I believe in the context of that teaching Jesus was saying to them something they would come to understand later: *"You are in for a surprise because your leader, John, the one who is the epitome of the burning and shining light, is at death's door and I am not going to rescue him; he is going to lose his life."*
Sometimes the Word of the Lord comes to us and says, *"You are not going to be so much offended by what I do but what I do not do."* It is the difficulty of facing what God *refrains* from doing that gives us the most trouble, perplexes us and causes us to wonder at a deep level about His goodness and grace.
Until we begin to understand that He related to His own Son in the very same way, that He allowed His Son to go through the shame and confusion and perplexity of the cross, we cannot gain perspective on our sufferings. We are forced, in gazing upon the sufferings of Jesus, to deal with the massive contradiction of history: a loving God and Father Who is *pleased* to cause His Son to suffer pain.[2]
So I found myself in the disturbing and distressing place of experiencing the increasing love of a Bridegroom God and then having to wrestle through the reality of difficult situations. For example, there are friends in the House of Prayer in Kansas City who are deathly ill, some of whom are not

being delivered out of illness, even as we proclaim the power of God to heal and to save.

We hear of other tragedies daily, some too close for comfort. Two couples who were very dear friends were involved in the leadership of the congregation in Aurora, Colorado, where Mary and I ministered with our family for a number of years before we moved to Kansas City in 1996.

The young worship leader and his wife had been praying for years for a child to be born into their home. Yet the wife had repeated miscarriages, including one that occurred while she was attending a "Women in the Prophetic" conference in Kansas City. It was a devastating and difficult time for her.

The young woman had surgery for severe endometriosis. She conceived again and gave birth to a beautiful daughter in April 1999. We went out to see them that July on our vacation and rejoiced with them over their delightful daughter, the joy of this couple's life. Three days later we were in Wyoming when late one night we got a phone call. Our friends had put the baby to bed that evening, and when they had gone up an hour later to check on her, she was dead from Sudden Infant Death Syndrome.

A few days later we sat and wept with them, held them and said, "God, how do we reconcile this?" How do we wrestle through the anguish of living in a broken world and yet worshipping a God who loves us passionately and is all powerful—how do we do that?

In that same little fellowship, another friend was at that time the leader of the intercessory group. In the early fall of 1999, his vibrant young wife, 42 years old, an athletic, healthy, joyful woman, came into her husband's office one evening and said, "I feel very strange. My left side has gone numb." He took her to the hospital and found that she was in the midst of a massive stroke. By morning she was dead. Like that! In the midst of this trauma they believed God, and they prayed and called out for resurrection *and it did not happen.* We find ourselves grappling with those kinds of issues. How do we handle those kinds of contradictions and paradoxes, at the same time believing in a God Who is powerful and loving?[3]

Beyond these situations, as trying as they are, lies the much darker reality of the suffering endured by those who undergo abuse. The self-centered cruelty of human beings toward one another is a terrible thing, perhaps the most difficult kind of situation to grapple with. Even if we have not experienced the trauma of physical or sexual abuse, most of us have experienced some level of undeserved rejection. The statements others make about our identity are powerful— from the parent who criticizes our intelligence or physique, to the spouse who rejects us for not measuring up to some arbitrary or culturally influenced standard. Even the insensitive brashness of children and teachers during our formative years can have a devastating impact on how we see ourselves.

How does one who has suffered physical and/or emotional abuse at the hands of another cope with the fact that an all-powerful and perfectly loving God *could have* prevented the abuse, but did not? Where is God in those kinds of situations?

In the wake of such circumstances, beyond the immediate question of our emotional condition, how do we maintain a faithful posture of confident intercession? It is one thing if the God you believe in is distant and cold, One Who has removed His presence and power from the equation. But we do not believe in that kind of God! We sing praises to a God Who is nearby, Who cares passionately, Who loves, Who intervenes, a God Whose power is made manifest. We rejoice in the testimonies of those He has touched in a dramatic way, and then it seems that *when we need Him the most,* He does not act. What do we do?

I don't know about you, but these kinds of questions give me pause. I find myself wrestling with disturbing issues: What part does the cross of Christ play in all this romance language? What part does suffering play in this emerging theology of a glad Bridegroom God? And what does this theology have to say to people who are struggling with the tragedy of human existence in a broken world?

I have been wrestling with how to handle these kinds of situations as His bridal partners. And I believe the answers are found in the naked reality of the cross of Jesus Christ.

## THE SERVANT BRIDEGROOM

The prophet Isaiah's four Servant Songs, including the well-loved passage in *Isaiah 52 and 53,* speak of "the Servant of the Lord." These prophecies initially are fulfilled in the nation of Israel but ultimately and obviously in the Person of Jesus Christ. The prophecies are fulfilled secondarily in relationship to us, the Bride of the Servant, the servant community. In this chapter, we will consider the Servant's high place. We will look at the paradox of His exaltation and devastation. We will examine the Servant's reward and finally how He involves us as His bridal partners.

### The Servant's High Place

In order to understand the devastation of the Servant, we must first understand His high position in the created order and in the eyes of His Father. We get a glimpse of His exalted position in one of the most familiar of Isaiah's Servant Songs, which is found in Chapter 42.

> **Behold! My Servant whom I uphold,**
> **My Elect One in whom My soul delights!**
> **I have put My Spirit upon Him;**
> **He will bring forth justice to the Gentiles.**
> **He will not cry out, nor raise His voice,**
> **Nor cause His voice to be heard in the street.**
> **A bruised reed He will not break,**
> **And smoking flax He will not quench;**
> **He will bring forth justice for truth.**
> **He will not fail nor be discouraged,**

**Till He has established justice in the earth;
And the coastlands shall wait for His law.
Isaiah 42:1-4**

The first thing mentioned about the Servant is that *He is exalted in the delight of the Father.* In our way of thinking, delight and devastation are far separated. When someone is delightful to us we will go to every length to protect that person from devastation. The expectation in our culture is that if God is really with us and for us, He will protect us from difficulty.

When the Lord says, *"I delight in this Servant Son of Mine, He is lovely,"* we are comforted knowing that as God delights in the Son, so He delights in us.

He says secondly, *"He will accomplish justice, He will set things right."* In His exalted position, He is going to restore all things to their proper place and set things in order according to the Father's design and purpose.

Even though He is exalted, this passage speaks about His humility. He does not call out loudly in the streets. He does not bring attention to His own name. He deals gently with broken people. He does not break off the reed that is bent and He does not snuff out a dimly burning candle. He is a humble God. What a concept: humility in the Son of God!

Finally, this song talks about His effectiveness. Because of His exalted identity, He will not be discouraged until His mission is accomplished in the earth. I tell you, that is good news, isn't it? Aren't you glad to hear that God is not discouraged with you? He is not worried about how things will turn out in the end. He has your life in hand and will complete His work until the day of salvation.

**The Devastation of the Servant**

Three of the four Servant Songs speak of Messiah's promised glorification, yet almost in the same breath prophesy His devastation.

The second Servant Song, in *Isaiah 49*, describes the Servant's high place, then hints of the difficulty in store for Him:

> Listen, O coastlands, to Me,
> And take heed, you peoples from afar!
> The LORD has called Me from the womb;
> From the matrix of My mother
> He has made mention of My name.
> And He has made My mouth like a sharp sword;
> In the shadow of His hand He has hidden Me,
> And made Me a polished shaft;
> In His quiver He has hidden Me.
>
> And He said to me,
> "You are My servant, O Israel,
> In whom I will be glorified."
> Then I said, "I have labored in vain,
> I have spent my strength for nothing and in vain;
> Yet surely my just reward is with the LORD,
> And my work with my God."
> **Isaiah 49:1-4**

This is a passage that has been precious to me over the past 20 years, and perhaps to you as well. The first couple of verses speak of the perfect preparation of the Servant. He is the bright and shining sword in the hand of the Father. The Father has hidden Him and prepared Him like an arrow, a polished sword in the hand of the Father. But then verses 3 and 4 forecast His seeming ineffectiveness:

> **"I have labored in vain. I have spent my strength for nothing and in vain and yet surely my just reward is with the Lord and my work with my God."**

Here we are introduced to the idea that among the servants of the Lord there are periods of seeming ineffectiveness. We have spent ourselves seemingly for nothing. We have given it our best shot and there is no fruit, no permanence. We find ourselves wrestling with the sense that everything we try to build seems to come to naught.

What surprises us is that this was also true in the life of Christ. Although God had promised Him glory, He had to suffer ineffectiveness, at least by all appearances, in the short term. But in verses 5 and 6, where He is commissioned to the nations, we find that the fulfillment of God's promises is not thwarted by seeming failure. In verses 7-13 the ultimate success of the Servant's ministry is prophesied and we rejoice in the Servant. He is high and lifted up. He is exalted. God's purposes are fulfilled. The devastation was temporal and temporary.

The next Servant Song, in *Isaiah 50:4-11,* speaks of the cruel abuse of the Messiah at the hands of His tormentors:

> **I gave My back to those who struck Me,**
> **And My cheeks to those**
> **who plucked out the beard;**
> **I did not hide My face from shame and spitting.**
> **For the Lord GOD will help Me;**
> **Therefore I will not be disgraced;**
> **Therefore I have set My face like a flint,**
> **And I know that I will not be ashamed.**
> **Isaiah 50:6-7**

What grips me about this passage is that the Servant is pictured as totally innocent of any wrongdoing. In fact, He is presented as one who is perfectly obedient and responsive to the will of God, and yet is forced to undergo the torturous abuse of men who despised Him.

Although the physical anguish inflicted on Jesus was motivated by religious issues, the fact is that self-centered and hateful human beings violently abused the only completely innocent person Who ever lived.[4] Jesus endured physical abuse that was completely undeserved, simply because depraved people wanted their own way. Because He experienced this kind of abuse, He understands the cry of those who suffer similar torment.

The fourth Servant Song, which begins in *Isaiah 52:13* and continues through *Isaiah 53,* sets the stage for the Servant's exaltation, then turns immediately to His devastation. *Isaiah 53* speaks of the uncharacteristic identity the Servant adopts for a season. What is this uncharacteristic identity? *He is vulnerable!*

> **Who has believed our report?**
> **And to whom has the arm**
> **of the Lord been revealed?**
> **For He shall grow up**
> **before Him as a tender plant**
> **and as a root out of dry ground.**
>
> **He has no form or comeliness**
> **and when we see Him**
> **there is no beauty that we should desire Him.**
> **He is despised and rejected by men.**
> **A man of sorrows and acquainted**
> **with grief and we hid, as it were,**
> **our faces from Him.**
>
> **He was despised and we did not esteem Him.**
> **Surely He has borne**
> **our grief and carried our sorrows**
> **and yet we esteemed Him**
> **stricken and smitten by God and afflicted.**
>
> **But He was wounded for our transgressions.**
> **He was bruised for our iniquities**
> **and the chastisement**
> **for our peace was upon Him**
> **and by His stripes we are healed.**
>
> **All we like sheep have gone astray,**
> **we have turned everyone to his own way**
> **and the Lord has laid on**
> **Him the iniquity of us all.**

He was oppressed and He was afflicted,
yet He opened not His mouth.
He was led as a lamb to the slaughter
and as a sheep before its shearers is silent
so He opened not His mouth.

He was taken from prison, from judgment,
who will declare His generation?
For He was cut off from the land of the living
for the transgressions of my people.

He was stricken and they made
His grave with the wicked
but with the rich at His death
because He had done no violence,
nor was any deceit in His mouth.
Isaiah 53:1-9

This is the King of heaven! This is the same Son of God Who in *Proverbs 8* swirled in that creative dance with the Father and the worlds spun off from their celebration together! It was the joyous celebration of Father, Son and Holy Spirit. The universes came out of His very thought processes. He spoke and it was! And suddenly, the Son of God, the *Genesis 1* Creator, is a tender plant growing up out of dry ground, the vulnerable God.

What a massive paradox. It is difficult to grasp what it means for the Creator God to be vulnerable, tender and defenseless, but that's what is clearly implied here.

He also is "uncomely." What an inexpressible concept that the One who is the Beautiful Branch should be "uncomely." Isaiah himself prophesied in *Isaiah 4*, *"In that day, the Branch of the Lord will be beautiful in all the earth."* David sat before the presence of the Lord in the Tabernacle, and said, *"Oh, that I may gaze on your beauty,"* yet this verse says that for a season He takes on the stigma of uncomeliness. He had no beauty that He should be desired.

He was despised and rejected, the One who is called the Desire of all the nations. This is the Man Christ Jesus, the

One in whom all human desire ultimately will find its culmination. And when we see Him, we will fall before Him and say, "You are what I have always wanted!" And *this One* becomes despised and rejected for a season. Why would He do it?

Perhaps the most deeply gripping aspect of His devastation is that His Name becomes "the Man of Sorrows." *Psalm 45* talks about the Messiah as One who is anointed with the oil of gladness above His brothers because He loves righteousness. Jesus is the happiest man in the universe and yet for a season He becomes a man of sorrows and acquainted with grief.

The devastation of the Servant is not merely emotional devastation. He is physically devastated. Verses 4-9 speak about this: *"He was wounded and smitten and bruised."* A little phrase in *Isaiah 52:14* says, *"His visage was marred more than any man."*

The commentators agree that the little Hebrew phrase means His person was bruised beyond human recognition. It is not just that He appeared to be a beaten man; it is that when people walked by, their response was, "Is this thing human?!"

We have a very antiseptic view of the cross today. We have cleaned it up through Christian art and through our lovely songs, and they should be lovely. We delight in the cross. The cross and the resurrection are the centerpieces of Christian joy. But I tell you, the cross was a devastating thing.

Once when I had preached on this topic, someone came to me who has ministered in Hispanic countries and said that when *Isaiah 52:14* says, *"He was marred beyond human recognition,"* the phrase in Spanish means, *"to be ground up like meat." That was the condition of the King of heaven!* He was physically devastated. He was bruised beyond recognition.

Yet He was silent in His suffering. He did not say anything to those who had wounded Him. In Gethsemane, He spoke only to the Father. *Hebrews 5:7* and following tells us that in the garden He cried out vehemently with tears to the One who was *able to save and did not.*

That is the paradox, is it not? We come in full confidence to God, convinced of His love, and then we discover that sometimes He is One *who is able to save and does not.* And *that* is the anguish. It would be less anguishing if He were a God who could not. Somehow it would even seem less anguishing to me if He did not care enough to intervene in human situations. But the fact that *He wants to*, the fact that He loves us and *the fact that He can and does not*—that is the place that makes us crazy, isn't it? That is the place of confusion and paradox in the life of the believer.

I want you to know that Jesus was in the same place. He cried out to the Father. In His humanity, Jesus did not just accept His circumstances. He knew what was ahead. He said yes to it but it was an anguished, considered yes because He knew what it was going to cost Him. And beyond all that, even though it was only a brief *earthly* time, in *eternal* terms, beyond time and space, He was separated from the Father, Who was His very life.

We are told in ***Revelation 13:8*** that Jesus embraced the cross from the foundation of the world. In other words, from before the beginning of time Jesus had already embraced the reality of separation from the Father. In His earthly testimony, He said, "I do nothing apart from the Father," yet He was separated from Him in His death. He was cut off from His inheritance.

He apparently had no descendents. (How could His detractors know He would have multitudes of adopted descendants?) They looked at Him and said, "Ugh! He is smitten of God!" They said, "Nothing like that could happen to someone who was cared for by God!" And He went through the anguish of being on the cross and being tormented by the evil one through the voices of His captors, who said, "If you are the Son of God, come down from there!" And yet Jesus chose not to come down.

Can we not relate to that? Have we not been harassed by our own thoughts that say, "If God were really with me, wouldn't I be able to get out of this circumstance?" Have you not been in a place where the enemy has come to you in your brokenness or difficulty or devastation and said to you, "If God loved you, if you were His favorite as He says, would He not rescue you from your harsh circumstances?" And we find ourselves wrestling through the very thing Jesus wrestled with on the cross. We find ourselves in that place where in the heat of the moment our correct theology abandons us. We are overwhelmed by the emotion of the experience and we cry out, "MY GOD, WHERE ARE YOU?!" Just as He did.

He knew ahead of time that He was going to be resurrected, did He not? Obviously, He knew after the fact that the resurrection had happened, but in the depths of the moment *He did not know*. He could not find the Father anywhere. The one time in the life of Jesus that He called His Father "My God" was when their relationship was broken on the cross. We ask, "Why did this happen?" And the startling answer comes when we get to *Isaiah 53:10*. We read the first phrase and it staggers our sensibilities. Verse 10 says, *"Yet it was the pleasure of the Father to crush Him."*

What kind of God are we dealing with here? What kind of Father does that to His beloved Son? The only answer that we have from Scripture is the most astonishing answer of all: It was out of the passionate heart of a Bridegroom God, who said, *"The deepest longing of my soul is to have a Bride for my Son who is like Him, who is worthy of Him. And so, My Son, You must take her place. You must suffer in her stead, personally experiencing and making payment for every dimension of human suffering so that she might indeed be Yours."* It was *His pleasure* to crush the Son so that we would be His.

Unbelievable! As I face this and wrestle through it, I realize that He did it so He could know me. He did it for you. He endured what He endured so that He could rescue you and me as His Beloved. We are His reward.

## The Servant's Reward

The bridal love of Jesus Christ: *"It pleased the Lord to crush Him."* His blood was the purchase price of the Bride. In *Matthew 13:45-46*, there is the beautiful parable of the Kingdom about the "pearl of great price." Through my youth I was always taught that the pearl of great price was the Kingdom of God and that the merchant was a picture of the Christian. In the story, we Christians sold everything we had and turned away from everything else in order to obtain the pearl, the Kingdom of God.

I no longer believe that is fully the right interpretation. It may be a valid application of truth, but the pearl of great price, in reality, is you and me. And the Merchant is Jesus. It was He Who laid the whole thing down; He sold everything, giving up His dignity at every level, that He might have you and me. He paid the price for the Bride. The transaction is made and His suffering, according to *Isaiah 53:10*, is accounted as payment for sin.

Read *Isaiah 53:10* again: *"It pleased the Lord to crush Him. He has put Him to grief."* God was behind this breaking, this crushing of the Messiah. And then comes the interpretation of the previous statement: *"When you make His soul an offering for sin, He shall see His seed. He shall prolong His days and the pleasure of the Lord will prosper in His hand."* And once more we have the inexplicable pleasure and crushing that become congruent, side by side. The pleasure of the Lord is revealed through the brokenness of the Servant.

Because He *"was numbered with the transgressors. . . . (and) He bore the sin of many, and made intercession for the transgressors"* (verse 12), His suffering is rewarded. Notice: His suffering is labeled as "intercession." He interceded, stood in the gap for me, in the place I could not stand.

Part of His reward is that He will see the redemption of His seed, the Bride. Jesus is the true Kinsman-Redeemer, this God Who in pictorial fashion in *Ezekiel 16* goes through the countryside and finds this bloodied and abandoned little naked child in the street. His heart breaks, not out of impotent pity, but with the passion of a Bridegroom God Who says, *"I am going to take that little bruised and broken and neglected one, nurture her as a Father would, and make her my wife. I am going to take her and give her beauty for ashes and the oil of joy for her mourning!"*

He raises her and nurtures her and brings her up. He makes her His Bride. He has paid the price. He is the Kinsman-Redeemer and His pleasure now prospers. He has His prize, the Bride. And He looks at us as we will be and He says, *"Ohhh, it was worth it!"* My God, He is satisfied, satisfied!

The longing of the heart of Jesus is satisfied with you. He has done what was necessary for you to be won. He has interceded effectively. Therefore He is accounted as great in the eyes of God and man.

There has always been a place in the human heart for the story of the heroic lover. It has been the stuff of tragic drama and poetry all through human history: The king whose bride is stolen goes through enormous difficulty and danger to get her back. He sails the oceans, fights the dragons, wins the wars—does whatever it takes! He goes through countless struggles to get his wife back, his bride, his queen. We exult in that sort of story as the great romance of history.

The startling reality is that the "story" is true and it is the Gospel as lived out through Jesus Christ on the cross. He went through it for LOVE! For the love of a woman called the Church! He takes it beyond the corporate thing and makes it deeply and intensely personal. He comes to you and me and says, *"Yes, I love the Church but I love you like that! I interceded for you!"*

When the emotional heart of the Bridegroom God grips our hearts, everything changes. We discover that He enjoys us, He delights in us, He would do it again. But it is not necessary to do it again. His sacrifice was enough. He gladly did what we were powerless to do. No wonder the songwriter says:

'Man of Sorrows', what a name
For the Son of God who came,
Ruined sinners to reclaim,
Hallelujah! What a Savior!

What a Savior.

## The Servant's Bridal Partners

Now one question remains: "What does this have to do with us as the Servant's bridal partners?" The promise of the Scripture is that we are going to be like Him, that we are going to be fully conformed to His image. It is this understanding that begins to give us perspective for the ruined and devastated places of our own lives. The cross gives us a handle. The understanding that we will be conformed to His image gives us a template for interpreting our own difficult experiences.

There is a longing in the heart of the Bride to know Him. Paul wrote it in *Philippians 3:10* and following, *"That I might know Him and the power of His resurrection."* Most of us would like the verse to end there, but the rest of it says, *"and the fellowship of His sufferings, being made conformable to His death that we might know the power of His resurrection."* Suffering is a reality that cannot be skipped. If we are going to look like Jesus, we are going to look like Him completely. And the Lord will allow in our lives the same kinds of experiences He has allowed in the life of His own Son.

And we must—if we are going to have a theology of Bridegroom love that is adequate for the world at the end of the age—*we must have a theology of redemptive suffering.* It is the only thing that will work. It is the only thing that will allow us to preach a glad Gospel to a real world.

God has a mysterious accounting system. He employs it in *Isaiah 53.* When He says, *"When you make His soul an offering for sin,"* something mysterious happens. He takes the physical and emotional and spiritual devastation that happens to His Son, and He says, *"I am going to account that as salvation for the many."*

The many, you and me. All we have to do is come and put our faith in what happened at the cross. It is a substitutionary atonement. And as we believe this applies to us, God will account it to us for righteousness. But then He comes to you and me and says, *"Now I will take your sufferings and I will account them exactly the same way."*

He illustrates this in some startling passages like **Colossians 1:24,** where Paul writes to the Colossian church and says, *"I now rejoice in my sufferings for you."* Paul is going through all kinds of difficulties. He is getting beaten, stoned, left for dead. He is abandoned, he is dumped out into the ocean. He is beaten with 39 stripes; 40 would kill a person, so they stop one short. And he endures it again *and again.* Why!? Because he understands the cross, you see, and he understands his partnership with Jesus. He understands that somehow, in the mysterious economy of God, *his brokenness is for them.* God will take the trouble he endures and translate it to salvation for the people who hear the message, just as He did for Jesus. It is astonishing.

He goes on to say, *"I fill up in my flesh what is lacking in the afflictions of Christ."* What is lacking in the afflictions of Christ? Theologically nothing, except that God in His mystery, in His bridal partnership, says to you and me, *"I am going to give you meaning for the brokenness! I am going to take the difficulties and count them as partnership in the cross of Jesus!"* And we become conformed.

The key is to *learn how to interpret our lives* in the light of His Word, in order to understand that when God does not do what He is capable of doing, He is doing a bigger thing. He is doing a more meaningful thing, that there might be more people in the company of the redeemed He calls His Bride. It is for the sake of His body, the Church. Consider this passage:

**We have this treasure in earthen vessels that the excellence of the power may be of God and not of us. We are hard-pressed on every side, yet not crushed, we are perplexed but not in despair. Persecuted but not forsaken. Struck down but not destroyed.**

**2 Corinthians 4:7**

We sing that! It is a happy tune we often sing in our worship services. *"I'm trading my sorrows. . . . I'm pressed but not crushed, persecuted not abandoned. . . . "* In some ways it seems that we know hardly anything about that reality, doesn't it? But I would venture to say that there is not a single believer reading this who has not gone through some kind of pressing situation, some kind of circumstance in which the enemy has come to you, as he did to Jesus on the cross, and said, *"If you are God's favorite, why is this happening? If you are the child of God, come down from there."* And we cry out to the God *who is able to save and does not.*

There is only one way to understand this dilemma, and it is in understanding the way of the cross. We must understand that He is allowing us the awesome privilege of becoming conformed to the image of Christ through what we suffer. I carry about in my body the death of Jesus! Do you see how Paul interpreted his sufferings? It was not just his own struggle apart from the Gospel. It was the death of Jesus that was working in him. Therefore, the Gospel would be advanced. He interpreted and understood his own difficulties from that perspective.

We who live are always delivered to death for Jesus' sake. That is an awesome thought. *"We who live are always delivered to death for the sake of Jesus, that the life of Jesus also may be manifested in our mortal flesh, so then death works in us but life in you."* He takes the broken places, the devastations of our lives and works salvation in those around us through it. We say, well that is fine for Paul. He's noble; I mean, he is suffering for the Gospel. He's giving himself out there on the front lines. But God uses *all* our suffering—

-whether it results from religious persecution, abuse or down-right foolishness—for His ends.

## GOD'S AMAZING ACCOUNTING SYSTEM

Frankly, I look at my own life and most of the suffering I have endured in my life is not because of noble self-sacrifice, but because I have been stupid. I have never been persecuted for the Gospel, at least not as far as I am aware. Even if I have, it is nothing like Paul's experience.

The uncomfortable reality is that persecution is starting to happen in our culture and our nation. We are going to know more of this. But the Word of God becomes even more startling when we realize that *not only does He count the noble suffering in that kind of way,* **He also takes the stupid suffering**—the suffering we bring on ourselves by our own sinful choices—and translates even that into the power of the Gospel.

Consider *Hosea 2:1-16.* It is the story of Israel, the Bride of God, and her devastation. The child He rescued in *Ezekiel 16* grows up into a beautiful young woman, *"the most desirable young woman."* God's intentions are to marry her but she turns away. She gives herself repeatedly to foreign gods. She is not seduced; *she becomes the seducer!* How many of us understand that the Scriptures sometimes use language that is simply not permissible in church? The Old Testament talks about Israel running after foreign gods, not being pursued by foreign gods, but running after them in the most lewd and vulgar ways imaginable.

That is how God described the attitude of His people. They ran after every god, they prostituted themselves under every tree. They gave themselves to false idols. The imagery the Lord uses again and again is sexual immorality to describe the unfaithfulness of the nation of Israel. In *Hosea 2* we find the picture of the aftermath of the whole thing: The Bride is devastated, ruined. She has been so used up by these false lovers that this passage pictures her as standing there in her shame with her dress pulled up over her head, fully exposed in her dishonor and devastation, and her false lovers look at her in that condition and say with disdain, *"Oh . . . I am not interested anymore."*

And they walk away and abandon her and in that place, then the Lord comes. He says, *"Now I will allure you. Even as you stand in the results of your own foolish, stupid sin, I will draw you. I will take you to the wilderness and speak tenderly to you and give you what you need to reinterpret your story. Your place of trouble will become a doorway of hope for the nations. And in the end you will not call Me 'my master' anymore. You will call me 'my Husband.'"* It is the love of a Bridegroom that takes even the stupid sin of His people and dares to interpret it in the same way as the precious sacrifice of His holy Son.

He takes our foolishness, and treats it the same as the noble sacrifice of the apostle Paul, who called himself the "chiefest of sinners." He knew what it was to have his stupid sin transformed.

Jesus takes the foolish sin that we can perhaps identify with, more than noble suffering. He takes the suffering we have brought on ourselves, the suffering that results from living in a broken condition and He says, *"If you will entrust it to me, if you will account this the way I account it, I will enable you to see that this too, is about redemption. If you will trust Me, if you will put your story in My hands, I will tell it in a different way. I will give you a story of redemption. I will give you a story of rescue. I will give you a prophetic history of a God who loves you! You will declare it and it will become a doorway of hope to countless others just like you."*

Finally there comes the powerful truth that in His suffering, Jesus also carries the pain of those who suffer abuse at the cruel hands of others. We are told in *Isaiah 53:4* that He *"bore our griefs and carried our sorrows."* What could be more grievous and sorrowful than the condition of being physically, sexually and emotionally abused by another human being, particularly if that person stands in the role of one who ought to be able to be trusted?

Behind the abusive behavior of human beings is found the raging hatred of Satan, who intends not only to harm us in physical and emotional ways, but tempts us to become embittered against God and thereby miss the message of His redeeming love. In fact, it is Satan's rage that is expressed through abuse, and his goal is our spiritual death. The enemy of our souls desires that none should receive the blessings of God's redemption.

When Jesus experienced the cross, He took upon Himself the full hatred of the enemy, and carried not only the pain that one individual might know, but the *cumulative* sorrow of every abused human being for all time. Because He became sin itself,[5] He experienced the full weight of shame, abandonment and rejection that are tasted by all who endure abuse, and received into Himself the full wrath and judgment of God upon that sin. In addition, the Father poured out on His own Son the full measure of His righteous indignation against the perpetrators of the abuse, so that the sin itself might be judged along with its damaging effects.

With this understanding, we begin to see that even in the most extreme circumstances, we have not been left in the lurch. In Christ, we have as our Role Model the perfect, sinless Man who in the face of indescribable pain chose to trust the Father's love for Him. Because of this, He is able to understand the anguish of the abused, share that experience with them and stand alongside them in creating a testimony of hope in the face of terrible fear and shame.

This testimony becomes a doorway of hope[6] for many who stand in the same place, and whose lives are transformed as they encounter the preserving love of Jesus in the place of pain. If we are able to bear this thought, He even invites us to count our personal suffering as a partnership in His sufferings for the entire human race, thereby conferring a dignity on our grief similar to what is bestowed upon a soldier who is wounded in battle for the sake of his country. Jesus is the one who suffered fully, and in His grace He invites us to count our sufferings as one with His.

Thus our stories are transformed. Our suffering and brokenness and tragedy are transformed into the image of Jesus. He redeems others through our experiences. It increases His joy and ours to do so. We see those who come to the knowledge of the King's love because of our story and their glorification on the last day becomes a crown for us that we lay at His feet. He accepts this gift and adorns Himself with it. The stunning reality is that for eternity Jesus will be a Man in heaven with scars in His hands and a hole in His side, but those have been transformed from devastation to glory. And we stand as His partners. Is that not incredible? Who could think of it except God?

So He transforms our sufferings into gladness. He gives us the oil of joy for mourning, He lets us trade our sorrows, but not the way we thought He would. He does not obliterate the sorrows and suffering. He transforms them. He takes the ashes of lives the enemy thought could be destroyed, and exchanges them for a crown of beauty that is a testimony to His grace. The Lord adorns the head of the broken ones with love and affection, heals their griefs, and calls them His Beloved. God not only redeems crushed individuals, but turns their tales of woe into stories of triumphant love, gateways through which other shattered lives may pass on their way to restoration.

The greatest miracle may well be that in the end, as we stand with Christ before the throne of God, we will see the faces of those who are in the presence of the Father, redeemed and holy, who entered in the wake of our healing. We will see the pleasure on the face of our Beloved as He receives them to Himself, and we will realize that our story of suffering, transformed by grace to a testimony of victory, was the vehicle of their healing. On that day, as we share in the joy of the Lamb, the scars that once were reminders of the painful suffering in our lives will be the beauty marks of the Bride, and we will agree that though the pain was horrible, it was all worth it.

# THE RESTORATION OF FERVENCY 10

## FAILURE AND RESTORATION IN THE CONTEXT OF BRIDAL LOVE

I n 1981, the unpretentious "Chariots of Fire" won the Academy Award for best picture by addressing the theme of human zeal. The film focused on the contrasting fires that burned within the breasts of two athletes of the 1920s, one named Harold Abrahams and the other Eric Liddell. Abrahams was Jewish, and what fed his fire was the fear generated by his being born and raised in a society in which anti-Semitism was widespread and overt. The passion for excellence and the anticipation of acceptance that would result from winning drove Harold Abrahams to succeed at any cost, and when he tasted defeat it was a crushing blow to his person, his very right to exist. Abrahams' validity was tied to external success, and the only acceptable reward was the triumphant designation of "World's Fastest Human."

Eric Liddell, on the other hand, was a Scotsman, a strong believer in Jesus Christ who had given his life to evangelism and missions in China. Liddell later gave his life for the Gospel in that nation, being finally conformed to the image of his beloved Savior through the grace of martyrdom.

In the story of the film, though, he is a runner driven by passion, a "chariot of fire" ablaze with a different kind of fervency, one borne not of fear but of pleasure. In one scene,

Liddell is conversing with his sister, who is concerned that in the pursuit of an Olympic medal Eric has lost his sense of direction and focus on the mission to which God has called them. As he explains his running to her, Liddell speaks one of the movie's great lines, which summarizes what it means to be driven by joy. He says to his sister, *"Jenny, God has made me fast, and when I run, I feel His pleasure!"*

Oh, Beloved, that's it! God has made us for the passion and fervency that are rooted in His pleasure, and when we live by them His joy touches our hearts with the delight and liberty we were created to know. We were never intended to be motivated solely by duty, by the crushing weight of fear or "ought-ness."

Human life is designed to be lived with passionate liberty, running at top speed (within the parameters of the personality God has given each individual) and feeling His pleasure in it—a confident passion, the liberated reality of the sons and daughters of the King of the universe, the *"glorious liberty of the children of God,"* in anticipation of which the very creation groans with eager expectancy.[1]

We are enjoined to exhibit this kind of liberty when we come to God in prayer. In his letter to the Ephesian believers, Paul the apostle calls us to this:

> . . . to make all see what is the fellowship of the mystery, which from the beginning of the ages has been hidden in God who created all things through Jesus Christ;
>
> to the intent that now the manifold wisdom of God might be made known by the church to the principalities and powers in the heavenly places,
>
> according to the eternal purpose which He accomplished in Christ Jesus our Lord, in whom we have boldness and access with confidence through faith in Him.
>
> **Ephesians 3:9-12**

This little paragraph is so crammed with magnificent truth that I stand in awe at the gift of God upon Paul to articulate it so concisely! The *"fellowship of the mystery,"* which is God's eternal plan to have a human Bride for His Son, shall be declared *through the Church* to the very spiritual powers of the heavenly realm. By the power of what was accomplished in the sufferings of Jesus upon the cross, we have been given, in Him, *"boldness and access with confidence"* to the very throne of God.

This term "boldness" is a wonderful word. Translated from the Greek word *parrhesia,* it literally means the confidence of full self-disclosure without fear, the freedom to speak one's heart and mind that is rooted in the full acceptance of the One listening.[2]

As used in the Ephesian passage in combination with the Greek term *peitho,* translated as "confidence" in this text, it literally means *"coming with the boldness of full self-disclosure into the presence of God, fully confident that He can be trusted to accept us just as we are because of Jesus."*

It is the exact opposite of the contemporary kind of defiant, in-your-face boldness that discloses everything, but without a shred of vulnerability: *"Here I am. Deal with it!"* The boldness Paul speaks of is that of a dearly loved child coming to his father, knowing he is accepted as he is. The child also knows that the grace and power are present to become everything he is intended to be. Thus he has the freedom to give full expression to everything that is inside him.

This word *parrhesia* is used in the Greek translation of the Hebrew Old Testament (called the Septuagint) to describe the self-disclosing activity of God:

**The Mighty One, God the LORD,**
**has spoken and called the earth**
**from the rising of the sun to its going down.**
**Out of Zion, the perfection of beauty,**
**God will *shine forth.***
**Psalm 50:1-2, italics mine**

We are told here that God has spoken, and that out of the perfection of Zion's beauty, which is a euphemism for the glorious people of God revealed in their full maturity at the end of the age, God will *"shine forth."* This term is rendered *parrhesia* in the Septuagint, showing that God's passion is rooted in this confidence, this free willingness to say it all, to fully disclose Himself so that we might know Him exactly as He is.

In the incarnation, the Word of God is made flesh so that we might see God as He is. In His activity and in His methods of relationship with His friends and with the people of Israel, God is saying *"Here I am! Look at me! This is Who I am, and I am here for you!"*

The culmination of this confident, fervent self-disclosure is the cross of Jesus Christ. His sacrifice is known as His *passion* for the very reason that on the cross Jesus was fully and gladly disclosing everything about Himself. Behold the Lamb of God! Here He is, the exact representation of the divine nature of God.[3] This is your Sovereign—One Who hangs naked and unashamed so that He might call me His own. What a Savior! He is the personification of fervent passion based in confident joy, not ashamed to call me His Beloved.

And we are invited, no, *commanded* to come into His Presence with this same kind of confident boldness, fully self-disclosing, not having to pretend about anything anymore. This confidence is based in the shed blood of Jesus, Who in an unashamed way took all our sin upon Himself and paid the price for our full disclosure. He speaks the Father's heart to us: *"I know you as you really are. I took all your sin into Myself on the cross. I know you and I love you with an unquenchable zeal! Come to me confidently. I have made the way open."*

This is our inheritance. This is our confidence. We can with absolute freedom and joy come to God's presence exactly as we are, for He has declared us accepted in His beloved Son, and we are welcome.

Unfortunately, only a very few know the freedom of approaching God in that kind of liberty. Most of us come in a different way, with a fervency that is more akin to that of Harold Abrahams than that of Eric Liddell. There is a fire that burns in many to be fervent for God, to be the most committed, the most radical, and thereby to win the affections of the heart of Christ. Like Abrahams, they find themselves motivated more by fear than by love, driven to earn the love they have already been given from the joyful heart of God.

But I am suggesting that much of this fervency is rooted in the fear that we are not fully loved by the Lord. We come from a position of no confidence unless we are somehow able to prove ourselves to Him. And this radically affects our ability to live joyfully and intercede effectively. We are required to come in faith, in full agreement with His opinion concerning us, in order to receive what we ask of Him.[4]

## THE EXAMPLE OF PETER

I believe there is no better example of one in Scripture who comes to this place of true fervency rooted in confidence before the Lord than that of Jesus' wonderful disciple, Peter. He is perhaps my favorite character in all the Scriptures. Though not technically one of the "sons of thunder,"[5] Peter was the third member of Jesus' inner circle, and seemed to bear the same sort of fiery personality that gave rise to that designation. As such, Peter becomes for me a great example of a disciple who stumbles heavenward strictly by the grace of God. On the way to maturity, he runs into himself again and again, sometimes causing minimal effect, and sometimes resulting in major catastrophe in his own life and the lives of those around him.

I love Peter's example, probably because I see so much of myself in him, and therefore can see in Jesus' friendship with Peter a place of safety and hope for one like me. As I consider Peter's fervent life, I encounter the One Who sets the pattern for unrestrained fervency and passion. Jesus is the true Burning Heart, the passionate Lover and Seeker of my soul, and my desire, as Peter's, is to love Him in the way He deserves, to be fervent for Him with all my heart, soul, mind and strength.

Let's look at a few snapshots of Peter in the Gospels to observe how Peter attempts to show himself fervent, and how the Lord brings him to the end of his confidence in his own attempts to be passionate enough, finally setting him in the place of true confidence rooted in the unutterable love of Christ.

We begin to see Peter's outspoken ways in the very first encounter between Jesus and His newfound friend, recorded in *Luke 5*. Jesus comes to the shoreline where Peter and Andrew, along with James and John, are mending and cleaning their nets after a night of fishing *during which they have caught nothing.*

Now, I am admittedly using my imagination here, but I cannot believe that when Jesus approaches Peter after a long night of fruitless work and asks Peter if he would mind letting Jesus use his boat as a speaker's dais, that Peter is all that thrilled about it. Remember that Peter and the other recruits are just young men, probably in their late teens or early 20s— Jesus Himself is only 30 at this time—and that they are not yet formed in any kind of way into His character.

Jesus chooses these guys for what He sees they will become, not for what they are at the beginning. So even though Peter relents, it is easy to imagine that the attitude in his heart of hearts is anything but cheerful.

As if that is not enough, at the end of the sermon (did Peter doze off during the teaching?), Jesus turns and says to Peter *"Launch out into the deep and let down your nets for a catch."* Again, the Scripture text reports a polite, submissive response by Peter, but I can hardly believe the attitude behind the words is all that nice.

I think Peter's internal response was probably something like this: *"Y'know, Sir, You really are a pretty good teacher and all that, but I'm the fisherman, and we've been out here all night, and nothing's worked. I'm tired and I wish You'd just let me go home and sleep."* What came out of his mouth was, *"Nevertheless, at Your Word I will let down the nets."*

Peter doesn't realize he is speaking to the One Who created the fish in the first place, and Who has been on the shore all night speaking quietly to the fish, saying, *'Don't go there!"* every time they came close to Peter's nets.

So Peter obeys, reluctantly, and suddenly *all the fish in the world come and jump into his net!* The nets break, and the men signal frantically to the guys in the other boat to come help. *There are so many fish that both boats sink!* You see, Jesus is demonstrating to Peter that the Son of Man is the authority over Peter's own area of expertise, and he uses the fishing profession to accomplish that task. Peter's response is beautiful. He sinks to his knees before Jesus, and says, *"Depart from me, for I am a sinful man, O Lord."*

In that sentence we see the true heart of Peter, the fact that he is painfully aware of his own shortcomings, and doesn't want the Lord to see or know him as he actually is. This is the opposite of *parrhesia*, confidence. This is shame brought suddenly to the surface by an inexplicable encounter, and the miracle is that Jesus does not depart, but rather summons Peter, Andrew, James and John to follow Him, because He has plans for them that are eternal in nature.

Jesus knows what Peter will become by the power of His grace. Peter will one day catch men for the Kingdom of God in numbers that far surpass the number of fish caught that day, and in that role as a fisher of men, he is going to need to be able to trust Jesus for his sustenance and provision. Peter's double-mindedness does not bother Jesus in the least. But it does bother Peter.

## An Incident of Carnal Fervency

My interpretation of the second encounter, found in *Luke 9*, again is based partly on conjecture. It involves Jesus, James and John. Although Peter's name is not mentioned, I am utterly convinced he is close by, agreeing with every word of the conversation.

Jesus has sent the disciples out as messengers to the villages, to prepare the way for His ministry in the area. But when they approach the citizens of a certain Samaritan village, the people refuse to welcome Jesus into their town.

Now, imagine that the disciples have been studying the Old Testament story of the reprobate King of Israel, Ahab. Ahab sent messengers to search for and retrieve the prophet, Elijah.[6] As they approached where Elijah was staying, he called down fire from heaven on them (actually, on three groups of 50 men!), and the fear of the Lord was established by fire. Maybe the disciples have been reading about that. In any case, they have the same idea. *"Lord, do You want us to command fire to come down from heaven and consume them, just as Elijah did?"* They want to nuke this village, and not with love! But Jesus rebukes them, telling them that the spirit from which they are speaking is not the Holy Spirit!

I want you to feel the sting of these rebukes. Have you ever felt fervent about something, only to discover your fervency was not holy, but carnal and self-serving? Your intentions may have been good, but your spirit was wrong, and you got rebuked in front of others for your attitude. Or perhaps it was a situation in which you blundered, and the silent awkwardness was just as condemning as any spoken word.

We run smack into ourselves on the way to holiness, and the encounter is painful. If that kind of encounter happens often enough, eventually we stop being quite so fervent! We begin to back off *just a little,* partly because we grow in wisdom, but mostly because we begin to fear that if we really go for it (whatever *it* is), our boldness will result in another rebuke.

I remember hearing about a scientist, an entomologist, who was studying the behavior of fleas. He knew that fleas can jump hundreds of times their own height, and he wanted to test their ability to adapt to a negative environment. So he placed a large number of fleas in a jar and put the lid on the jar.

As the fleas began to jump, they would hit the lid, and after a time the scientist noticed that they were *not jumping as high!* The fleas adapted to the pain that resulted from the full expression of their fervency, if you will, and backed off in their attempts. After a while, the scientist was able to take the lid off the jar, and *not one flea jumped out of the jar*, although they were fully capable of doing so.

Have you ever "hit the lid" in your attempts to be bold for God? Repeatedly? Have you ever been corrected, and afterward felt your own heart shrink back *just a little?* Next time, partly from wisdom, mostly from fear, you backed off a bit.

The complicating factor is that we don't want people to see that we're backing off, so we retain the language of fervent and passionate commitment, even though the full expression of it is not there. We begin to choose a way that is just a bit safer, but that still allows us to appear fully committed. This false representation of fervent passion is called "a religious spirit," and it can come upon us almost unnoticed through these kinds of painful circumstances.

Our responses would be easier to deal with if they were black and white—if we were either totally and righteously fervent, or totally phony in our passion. But there is usually a mixture, and the mixture is hard to measure. Peter was in that place. His fervency was not mature and completely holy, but he wanted it to be. In that immature place, God continued to give him powerful understanding and insight.

## A Right Revelation, a Wrong Application

In *Matthew 16*, Peter has one of the greatest revelatory moments that has ever come to a human being:

**When Jesus came into the region of Caesarea Philippi, He asked His disciples, saying, "Who do men say that I, the Son of Man, am?"**

**So they said, "Some say John the Baptist, some Elijah, and others Jeremiah or one of the prophets." He said to them, "But who do you say that I am?"**

**Simon Peter answered and said, "You are the Christ, the Son of the living God."**

**Jesus answered and said to him, "Blessed are you, Simon Bar-Jonah, for flesh and blood has not revealed this to you, but My Father who is in heaven."**
**Matthew 16:13-17**

The very Spirit of God has declared to Peter the truth of Jesus' identity as the Messiah. Jesus' answer to him is clear and profound: This kind of understanding does not come by human intellect, but by the revelation of the Spirit of the Father. It is a wondrous revelation, and Jesus follows these statements with a magnificent prophecy of Peter's true identity as one who would stand in a foundational place of authority in the Church of Jesus Christ from that day forward.

Now the dynamic of this is that Jesus has been waiting for this revelation to strike the hearts of the disciples so that He can begin to instruct them about His passion and death, which are on the horizon. Jesus knows that until the *hearts* of His friends have become convinced by the Holy Spirit that He is the Christ, they will not be able to understand the necessity of His suffering. The paradigm is too radically different from what they expect.

The text tells us that from that time, Jesus begins to instruct them that He is about to suffer and be crucified in order to complete the Father's purposes for His life. When Peter hears what Jesus is saying, he reacts strongly, and not in the grace of the Holy Spirit:

**Then Peter took Him aside and began to rebuke Him, saying, "Far be it from You, Lord; this shall not happen to You!"**
**Matthew 16:22**

Here is such a powerful example of that mixture of mature revelation and immature, impure fervency. Peter takes Jesus aside *and begins to rebuke Him!* Peter is thinking, *"I've got the insight now, I know Jesus is the Messiah, and Messiahs don't suffer, they conquer!"* He assumes that because he has received a revelation, he has the full understanding of all of its implications. He speaks fervently, but with error and presumption. He pays for it:

**But He turned and said to Peter, "Get behind Me, Satan! You are an offense to Me, for you are not mindful of the things of God, but the things of men."**
**Matthew 16:23**

Now that's a rebuke! Do you feel it? In the space of a couple of minutes, Peter has gone from having one of the greatest revelations and prophecies that comes to anyone in the Gospels, and *Jesus is calling him "Satan" in front of all his friends!* Once again, Peter slams into the lid of his own personality, and is faced with the pain of correction.

I know that Jesus is addressing the evil spirit speaking through Peter, but the text says that He says these words *"to Peter."* Peter has spoken out of the mixture of his maturity and immaturity, fueled by his misguided passion, and once again it gets him in trouble. The result is that true and pure passion receives another damaging blow, and the only alternative is either to shrink back completely, or to crank up the human zeal, the religious spirit that comes forth in those kinds of situations.

### Misguided Desire for Acceptance

This pattern of behavior in Peter's life continued to be expressed in his behavior and conversation. And the other disciples were not immune to it, either. I am convinced that all the arguments about which disciple was the greatest[7] were rooted in this kind of false fervency—the desire to be seen by Jesus and by one another as the most passionate, the best disciple, the greatest follower. For Peter, the issue came to its climax as the time of the arrest and crucifixion of Jesus drew nearer.

On the final night before His crucifixion, Jesus is meeting with the disciples. They have the Passover meal together, Jesus shares communion with them (the Banquet of Wine, which in essence is Jesus' marriage proposal to the disciples as representatives of the whole Bride of Christ), and then He begins to speak to them of His death. He tells them He must go somewhere that they cannot follow. Peter protests:

> **Peter said to Him, "Even if all are made to stumble, yet I will not be."**
>
> **Jesus said to him, "Assuredly, I say to you that today, even this night, before the rooster crows twice, you will deny Me three times."**
>
> **But he spoke more vehemently, "If I have to die with You, I will not deny You!" And they all said likewise.**
>
> **Mark 14:29-31**

I am fully convinced that Peter is sincere in his protest, that he really wants to follow Jesus, even to the death. He really wants to be the most fervent, and probably even believes that he is. And so his claim is, *"No one loves You the way I do! I love You better, Jesus, with a greater and more perfect love than any of these! I will not fail!"*

But in the midst of Peter's passionate protest, Jesus interrupts him with the sober truth: *"O Peter, not only will you stumble, your failure will be the worst of all of them, for you shall publicly deny, three times, that you ever even knew Me!"* What a horrible statement to come from the lips of Jesus! Imagine the humiliation!

Yet Peter's response is even more passionate! He responds with *"vehemence,"* attempting to refute Jesus' statement. *"Even if I have to die, I will not fail You, I will not deny You!"* This term is also used in *Ephesians 3:20* to describe the super-abundant ability of God to do more than we can ask or think. Peter was saying *"not only am I more committed than these guys, I am **super-abundantly** more committed."*

Peter is so convinced he has to be the best for Jesus that he is totally out of touch with his own level of commitment and passion. His human zeal will not be enough to take him through the night, and in his false fervency, he cannot see it.

Have you ever been in the place where your human zeal was about to explode in your face, and you were so committed to your course of action that you couldn't see the warning signs? I have been in that place. I have exercised leadership with the immature passion of a fearful zealot, trying to prove my superior faithfulness. Yet I was deaf and blind to the signs of impending disaster as the brick wall loomed nearer and nearer. Many were hurt in the resulting crash. A church died, and a tremendous battle with shame and failure was the result.

Like Peter, my fervency exploded in my face and I was left nearly alone, except for my family and a few faithful friends who, in the midst of the disaster, saw the grace of God on my life and chose to walk it out with me to the end. They will never know the place they hold in my heart, though I try my best to communicate it.

It is essential that we understand the fuller meaning of Jesus' prophetic statement about Peter's failure. In Chapter 5 of this book, I explained the significance of the Banquet of Wine as the cultural context of the Lord's Supper. Likewise, this interaction between Peter and Jesus, in which Peter's failure is spoken by the Lord as a certain thing, happens in the context of the Bridegroom's agenda being fulfilled.

In His role at the Lord's Supper, Jesus has just invited the disciples to the place of bridal intimacy and they have said "yes." The banqueting table of the Lord is now the dwelling place of the disciples, and according to *Song of Solomon 2:4*, the banner that now flies over all their interactions is one of romantic love. Again, I am aware that the bridal imagery is somewhat unsettling for those who are men, but I remind you that the disciples are representatives of the whole Church here, which is the mystical Bride.

Jesus' sobering prophecy of Peter's denial is spoken in the wake of Peter's acceptance of Jesus' invitation to permanent intimacy. They are betrothed, along with the rest of the disciples (and in their acceptance is included yours and mine!). The prophecy is spoken with certainty at the end of *John 13*, and then a wondrous thing occurs. Although in our Bibles there is a chapter division at this point, the statements made to Peter in the first part of *John 14* complete the contextual setting of Jesus' prophecy to him:

> **"Let not your heart be troubled; you believe in God, believe also in Me. In My Father's house are many mansions; if it were not so, I would have told you. I go to prepare a place for you. And if I go and prepare a place for you, I will come again and receive you to Myself; that where I am, there you may be also. And where I go you know, and the way you know."**
>
> **John 14:1-4**

With these incredible words, the truth of Jesus' all-conquering love is spoken into the heart of Peter, and his failure is fully and firmly set in the context of the Bridegroom's love for him. Jesus says, *"Peter, you are going to fail more miserably than you can even imagine, but don't let your heart be troubled by this. Have faith in My love! I am your Bridegroom, and I'm going to prepare your place even now, so that when the Father gives me permission, I can come to receive you to Myself."*

Jesus sets the certainty of Peter's failure firmly in the center of His grace and assures Peter that the ultimate outcome of the whole situation is positive and certain. This is stunning when we relate it to our own lives. Although Peter didn't comprehend what was being spoken at the time, and though he would go through the darkest season of his life during the following hours, his restoration was already settled, fully encompassed in the grace of God.

Jesus had invited this man into the most intimate place of relationship, fully knowing who he was and what was about to happen to him. He had already made provision for his failure and his restoration, and it was just a matter of walking them out in real space and time. The obedience that had been set in place from before the foundations of the world now was being enacted by the Man Christ Jesus, and the outcome was certain, though the process would be excruciating.

Even though over the next hours Peter would deny Jesus with cursing, Jesus was on His way to get the bridal mansion ready for him. What kind of love is this! O, Jesus, help us see it!

## The Inevitable Confrontation

The disciples follow Jesus to the garden to wait for the inevitable. Here, yet another surprising encounter between Jesus and Peter takes place. Matthew's Gospel tells us that the men reach the Garden of Gethsemane and Jesus goes to a secluded place to pray, to seek the grace of God for what is about to come.

He invites Peter, James and John to accompany Him and informs them that they should "watch" with Him. This is, simply stated, an exhortation for them to pray during this time, to enter into the intercession that will strengthen them for the events of the night and prepare them for what is ahead. They are invited into an incredible place of partnership with Jesus. Instead, they fall asleep.

Jesus returns from His first encounter with the Father in agonizing prayer, and finds the three asleep. Matthew records Jesus' statement, made specifically to Peter:

**Then He came to the disciples and found them asleep, and said to Peter, "What? Could you not watch with Me one hour? Watch and pray, lest you enter into temptation. The spirit indeed is willing, but the flesh is weak."**
**Matthew 26:40-41**

Take note of the second phrase spoken to Peter: *"Watch and pray, lest you enter into temptation. The spirit indeed is willing, but the flesh is weak."* What is the temptation Peter is about to face? I believe that Jesus is offering Peter the way to escape the very thing that Jesus Himself prophesied was about to happen to him. *"If you will pray, Peter; if you will watch with me, your spirit will receive the grace to stand in this moment. You are willing, but you are weak and if you pray, I will give you strength to endure the test."*

Jesus has seen the real and pure desire of Peter's heart to be faithful in his fervency, and He loves him for it. But He also knows that human zeal alone will not withstand the pressure that is coming. Fully knowing that Peter will fail, Jesus nevertheless offers him the way out. *It is prayer that is offered to Peter!* The place of watching, of waiting upon the Lord, even as Jesus Himself is doing, will prepare him for the battle, enabling him to stand in the midst of the terror.

Peter can't do it. He falls asleep again, only to be startled into wakefulness by the approaching army. Judas approaches Jesus to do his part, and as the soldiers move to arrest Jesus, all the passion and zeal pent up in Peter's heart explode to the surface. This is his time! This is how he will demonstrate his loyalty to Jesus and be vindicated! All those embarrassing situations of rebuke and correction—he will show them. He loves Jesus most and best, and now is the time to prove it. So he whips out his sword (never give a fisherman a sword!) and attacks the Roman army. All he can do is hack the ear off a servant—but bless God, he is going for it!

Peter will not be denied in his quest for fervent commitment, and is about to lay down his life, when Jesus stops him. *"Put away your sword, Peter. Shall I not drink the cup that has been given to me?"* And Jesus bends down, picks up the severed ear of the Roman slave *and heals him,* then goes quietly with the soldiers to face His death! What a staggering moment!

Put yourself in Peter's place. He has laid it on the line, risking life and limb, and one more time, Jesus rebukes him.

He fixes the damage Peter caused, and leaves him standing there, dumbly, with his sword in his hand, able to do exactly nothing. Dazed and confused, all he can do is follow at a distance, feeling horrified and perplexed, baffled at the turn of events and clueless about what to do next.

He ends up in the courtyard of the high priest, standing by a fire to warm himself, fully undone by what has just happened. At this moment, a servant girl approaches to ask the question that brings Peter's demise. What the Roman cohort couldn't accomplish, this little girl does in the swift stroke of a few words: *"Aren't you one of them?"* He denies once, then twice, then three times. And the rooster crows.

And hell descends on Peter's head, for the naked truth of his own collapsed commitment now stares him fully in the face. He has done the unthinkable, and it is fully exposed. He has denied his Lord. He goes out and weeps bitterly.

Have you touched that place? That place where everything is on the line, and in the moment of truth you bail out and say *"NO, I'm not who you say I am"*? In the moment of reckoning, with the judicial scales set in place, you are weighed and found too light. I know that place. I have been where Peter was. There is no darkness like it.

And the worst part of it for Peter is that in the place of his failure, the One Who has been his Comfort and Friend for the past three years is nowhere to be found. Jesus is walking in the opposite direction, to His own suffering and death, and Peter is left standing alone, abandoned, emasculated by his own choices, naked and ashamed before God and man.

For us as 21st century believers, the reality of the cross of Christ is difficult to grasp. Viewed with 20 centuries of perspective, we revere the cross; it has become the very symbol of victory and grace. We look back through the lens of time, from the perspective of the resurrection, and the cross seems like a moment in time. We find it difficult to touch the horror the disciples experienced during those 40 hours between Friday afternoon and Sunday morning.

The Lord helps us with this by allowing you and me, in the crucible of our own failures, to be unable to find the presence of the Lord in the moment of our deepest need. Have you ever been in that situation? Have you ever really needed God to be there for you, and in the place of your deepest crisis, He was nowhere to be found? He might as well be dead, we may find ourselves thinking, for all the help He gives in those moments.

This was Peter's experience. In the time he needed Jesus the most, the Son of God was dying! Unavailable! Not hearing, not seeing Peter's dilemma, focused on some greater work. What Peter couldn't know then was that in reality Jesus was carrying him and all his failure in His broken body on the tree. In the moment that seemed like the greatest abandonment, Jesus was in fact carrying out the ultimate intercession. And in that place, He took Peter's failure, his very real shame and guilt, into Himself. Jesus bore the penalty for it, dying in Peter's place. Though Peter would touch the emotion of that moment, he would never have to pay the full price, for it was paid in full by the blood of the Lamb, shed at the height of His unfailing passion.

Peter endured what must have been the worst weekend of his life. We can dial up the memory of our worst moments, and in those memories we can taste the bitterness that encompassed Peter during that time. All perspective is gone. The promises are shattered. The things He said, the hope He instilled—all gone! All Peter could do was survive. And that's the Word of the Lord to us in those kinds of places: *"You don't know the end of this thing, but I do. Don't die. Just endure, and you will see the glory of the Lord."*

## The Terror of Restoration

It's Sunday morning. Suddenly, incredibly, the voice of Mary Magdalene pierces the isolation of Peter's pain. *"Peter! He's alive! I've seen Him, and He told me specifically to tell you that He wants to see you."* It's unimaginable, and yet something in Peter's heart knows it's true. And Peter is at once faced with the best and the second-worst day of his life. Do we understand that Peter's deepest joy and his greatest fear are at this moment the same thing? He is going to see the risen Lord! *"O God, yes! The miracle has happened! The promises are not gone. Death has not won the day. O God, no! What will I say? I'm so ashamed."*

The restoration happens in an unexpected way. In the wake of that disastrous weekend, Peter has gone back to fishing, convinced that his little foray into glory was only a sham, and that he would always and only be a fisher of fish. And so he's back in his boat with the others, and they haven't caught a thing all night. Sound familiar? I can only imagine Peter's frustration, because not only is his life vision in the dumpster, but he can't even make it in his old vocation.

Suddenly, a voice calls from the shore: *"Hey! Did you catch anything? Throw your net on the right side of the boat, and you will!"* Peter turns to Andrew and says, *"Man, is this* déjà vu *or what?"* And something compels them to obey. At that moment, the Creator of the universe, the Living Word of God standing on the shore as the Son of Man, releases all the fish in the sea to jump into the nets of the fishermen. Only this time their nets do not break and their boats do not sink. Peter sees it with his natural eyes and the eyes of his heart are opened as well. *"It's the Lord!"* he exclaims, and in his over-the-top zeal, he strips off his garments and dives into the water, this time to draw near to the Lord, not to beg Him to leave.

Jesus is waiting for them on the beach, having already cooked breakfast on a campfire. The disciples join Peter, and there is a wonderful, awkward renewal of relationship. The Lord knows that Peter needs something deep and personal. He knows that Peter's humiliation has been painfully public, and so He ministers restoration to him in the presence of his friends. It begins in the form of a question: *"So Simon, son of Jonah, do you love Me more than these guys do?"*

The query pierces to the center of Peter's heart, because Jesus uses the word *agape* in His question. *Agape* is the highest kind of love, the permanent, never-failing kind of love known only to the heart of God and to those to whom He grants the grace to stand. It has been Peter's testimony of himself that he loves Jesus more than these others do, that his love is unfailing and strong, yet his testimony has been proved hollow and empty. And so when Jesus asks Peter about this, it scores a direct hit on the pain pulsing in Peter's heart.

In the light of his failure, all he can do is say, *"Yes, Lord, You know that I love You."* But he uses a different word. He uses the Greek word *phileo*, which means "affection, brotherly love or friendship." In other words, Peter is acknowledging his less-than-perfect commitment. In effect, he is saying *"Lord, You know my heart. You know that my heart burns with love for you, with affection and adoration. But is it perfect love, never-failing love? No, it's not, Jesus. I wish it were, but friendly affection is all I can muster. I'm sorry Lord, but that's about it."*

I'm convinced beyond all doubt that this is a moment of crushing humiliation for Peter. The truth is out, and in front of his friends it is being addressed. What will Jesus say? He holds every option. He can smite Peter with the breath of His mouth. One word of judgment and Peter will be done for. Peter is here, fully exposed, naked and still ashamed, and completely at the mercy of Jesus. And in that place, the absolute best place to be, the Lord speaks the most incredible thing: *"Peter, feed My lambs."*

Now this may seem like a simple statement, but it is anything but simple. Jesus, the Bread of Heaven, the One Whose life was given as real food and real drink, is the only sustenance for His lambs, His beloved children who will become His Bride. And in this statement, Jesus says to *Peter*, this failed man, that *he, Peter*, is one who will break the bread of life to that flock. In so doing, Jesus elevates Peter from the place of shame back to his true identity as a partner in the Gospel, as one who stands in the very place of Jesus to speak the truth. And in Peter's heart, the reality explodes: Who he is in his flesh is not what matters. The reality of Christ's life within him is all that matters.

Jesus asks Peter about the quality of his love again, using the same terminology. Again, Peter responds with the confession of a love that is of lesser quality, but more in touch with the reality of his heart. And once again, Jesus allows him to see into His heart, and to experience the wondrous truth that if we will come in humble honesty about ourselves, God will open to us *His* perspective of who we are, and elevate us to the place of partnership with Him. But it is in the third question that the power of this situation becomes thoroughly focused.

The third time Jesus asks Peter about his love, He doesn't use the term *agape*. Rather, Jesus uses Peter's term, *phileo*, and in so doing, grieves the heart of Peter. In essence, Jesus says something like this: *"So, Peter. I know that agape is not part of what's in you now. So do you love me as much as you can? Are you affectionate toward me? Is your heart toward me, even though it is mixed? Is that about it? Where are you, Peter?"* And Peter responds in his grief, *"Lord, You know all things. You know that I feel affectionate toward You."*

Once again, Peter touches the anguish of his own lack of fervency. And again, Jesus responds with His incredible statement of restoration, assigning to Peter the responsibility to feed the very flock of God.

Jesus helps Peter to see that for the first time in their relationship, Jesus and Peter are in agreement concerning Peter's level of commitment. Jesus has always known where Peter was, and He has loved him fully in that place. Jesus knew that Peter didn't have what was necessary—he couldn't! Neither can we, outside of the grace of God.

Peter has never been able to stand in that *parrhesia*, that confidence that he could be who he truly is and still be cherished and still function as the partner of Jesus in the ministry of reconciliation. Only now, in the aftermath of his terrible failure, can Peter finally perceive that Jesus' love for him is not conditioned on Peter's fervency, but on his willingness to say "yes" to the Lord. For the first time, Jesus and Peter have a common understanding concerning Peter's level of commitment.

Jesus' message to Peter is that it was never about Peter's fervency, but about the Lord's. *"It's not about you, Peter! It's about Me! It's always been about Me, and it always will be. I'm the only hero, Peter. You couldn't stand in that place of perfect love. Only I could walk that road. I had to go it alone. Even though your love was flawed, it was precious to me, and my commitment to you was to purify that love. Therefore, your failure was certain, for without it, you would not need Me. But now, you are a testimony of My grace, and now I will exhibit you and empower you to be fruitful in ministry once again, but in a very different way from before. Now you will come to rest and to trust in My love for you, for it has been proven in the crucible of your failure. And out of the overflow of that confidence, you will feed my lambs with the living Word that I will release through you."*

The Lord comes to us in the place of our deepest failure, and there He speaks to our hearts of His perfect love and grace. And for the first time, we truly believe that He loves us unconditionally. It is only when our hands are completely empty of any self-validating success that we can really believe that we haven't earned His affection.

I will never forget the moment when, in the midst of the rubble of a shattered ministry, the Lord came to me and touched my heart with His affection and love, and spoke this truth to my heart. For the first time, I saw that my identity and value were settled in the heart of God. I saw that my fervent obedience was not the operative factor, because what I had done in my fervency lay shattered in pieces. And in that place, the Lord spoke to me again that I would be His partner, that I would be one who would feed His flock. He showed me that the very situations that had seemed like death to me would in fact be vehicles of life to many. He promised me that my fervency would be restored, only it would be driven by His love, not by my attempts to prove myself worthy.

And it has been so.

CHAPTER

# UNTIL HE RETURNS $11$

THE PLACE OF 24-HOUR
INTERCESSORY WORSHIP

I remember a time in the early days of the International House of Prayer in Kansas City, when someone was leading a worship set one day, and their musical
style was bugging me. I'm an old Vineyard guy, and I love
the casual intimacy of laid-back love songs to Jesus. My own
personal style of worship is more contemplative than aggressive.

The person who was leading had a different style, more
strident and assertive in declaring the glory of the Lord and
His purposes in the earth, and I was feeling cranky and superior. I remember standing at the back of the room, a critical
spirit oozing out of every pore, and feeling very righteous
about it. At one point in the worship set, I actually asked the
Lord if I could talk with this leader and fix what I didn't like
with his style.

Now, I am not unaccustomed to hearing the instructive
voice of the Lord, but I seldom have had an answer land on
my heart as quickly and clearly as this one did. It was as
though the Lord spoke directly into my spirit, *"Gary, every
human worship style is a condescension of my goodness to human
weakness. I love people so much that I will allow them to come to me
with every conceivable expression of worship. And know this:*

*Compared with what is going on here in the heavenly worship center, nothing that happens on earth is all that exciting."*

With this rebuke ringing in my spiritual ears, I realized that my worship style was not *right* because I liked it, but rather in the mercy of God, He has made a way for me to come to Him that I can embrace with joy. And I understood in that moment that He has done this for every person, group, tongue, tribe and nation. If I truly want to know Him, I will embrace those whose love for Jesus is expressed in ways different from mine, so that my own understanding of His character, grace and love may grow and mature.

In fact, God releases "new" forms from time to time that by departing from routine can shake the slumbering spirit to wakefulness and give individuals the opportunity to touch the heart of God. The present move of God is no different. The emerging prayer movement is taking place in a variety of structures in various places. What is essential, I believe, at the beginning stages in which we find ourselves, is that all believers acknowledge the various methodologies and diverse forms that give expression to the adoration exploding in the hearts of people of every tongue, tribe and nation.

As we find the grace to acknowledge the legitimacy of many forms, we will at the same time find liberty to embrace the form that best gives expression to the fire burning in our own breast and in that of the community in which we find ourselves.

The forms I enjoy, which are a blessing to those who make up the community at the International House of Prayer in Kansas City, may not be for everyone but they will be helpful to some, and it is for that reason that I am concluding this book with this focus.

What has been somewhat surprising to us at the House of Prayer is that there is a definite liturgical feel to what we do here from day to day. We evangelicals, especially as we have adopted an increasingly charismatic style of worship and ministry,[1] have lost the appreciation for the value of a predictable and repeated form of worship that, if approached with faith, can serve as a launching pad, an "on-ramp" to the spontaneous life of the Spirit of God. The forms of liturgy were never intended to replace life, but to be inhabited by life in such a way that encounters with the powerful presence of God could be routine occurrences.

To me, many of the contemporary attempts at spontaneity sometimes seem more a reflection of a cultural attention-deficit disorder than a reflection of the life of God. For others, however, they may be the very vehicles that open the door to the life of God. The Lord uses anything He chooses to touch the hearts of those who seek Him, and if we will come with faith into the place of seeking, He promises to meet us there with an outpouring of His presence.

I believe God intends for this current prayer movement to expand and multiply until the earth is filled with believers seeking the face and hand of God in this final hour of natural history.[2] Jesus' question to the disciples in the context of exhorting them to "always pray and never give up"[3] was whether at the end of the age, when the Son of Man would return to the earth, He would find faith being exercised.

In the context of the parable in Luke 18, the implied definition of "faith" is unceasing and persistent prayer rooted in the heart conviction that our God delights in us as His elect, and therefore will speedily grant justice as we call out to Him. Because it is His intent to have universal, unceasing prayer among all believers everywhere, I am convinced that we will need models, rooted in adequate value systems, that will liberate God's people to call upon Him with joy until He comes again.

Therefore, this chapter outlines the values and the model of the International House of Prayer in Kansas City as one "on-ramp" into the presence of the Lord in intercessory worship.

## THE VALUE OF NIGHT-AND-DAY PRAYER

An intriguing dimension of what God's Spirit is stirring in the hearts of His people is the longing to see prayer happen 24 hours a day, seven days a week. In the spring of 1983, as Mike Bickle, now the director of the International House of Prayer in Kansas City and at that time the pastor of South Kansas City Fellowship, was meditating upon *Psalm 27:4.* He asked the Lord to grant him the joy of ministering in the beauty of the Lord all the days of his life.

The Spirit of God spoke to Mike in an unusual way that a day would come when he would lead a ministry of unceasing prayer "in the spirit of the Tabernacle of David." During the intervening 16 years, this vision was held before the Lord in an extravagant way by the people of Mike's congregation, until the House of Prayer became a reality in 1999. Several biblical factors have given rise to this night-and-day ministry.

First, there is the simple and awesome fact that Jesus Christ is worthy of extravagant praise and adoration. In the fourth chapter of the book of *Revelation,* John the apostle is drawn into an overwhelming experience of the eternal worship taking place around the throne of God. He becomes a first-hand witness to the intensity of adulation and exaltation that goes on continually in God's presence. In that place, the fundamental motivation for worship is the overarching worthiness of the Lord. Consider this text:

**The four living creatures, each having six wings, were full of eyes around and within. And they do not rest day or night, saying: "Holy, holy, holy, Lord God Almighty, who was and is and is to come!"**

**Whenever the living creatures give glory and honor and thanks to Him who sits on the throne, who lives forever and ever, the twenty-four elders fall down before Him who sits on the throne and worship Him who lives forever and ever, and cast their crowns before**

**the throne, saying: "You are worthy, O Lord, to receive glory and honor and power; for You created all things, and by Your will they exist and were created."**

**Revelation 4:8-11**

The seraphim, those magnificent creatures whose very name means "burning ones,"[4] and the 24 elders, who represent human government through all of history, spend their full time—night and day they do not rest—declaring the holiness and worthiness of the Lord Jesus. This is significant for us because the seraphim represent the highest order of non-human creation, while the elders represent the highest level of human authority.

Right now in heaven, these magnificent creatures see the beauty and majesty of the Lord, and consider their time well spent as they worship Him night and day. In fact, they are compelled to do so not through coercion, but because the transcendent beauty of Lord captures them and drives them to their knees, and they know without a doubt the wisdom and value of ceaseless adoration.

Once again, as I write this chapter, the Holy Spirit is encouraging my heart in the House of Prayer as the musicians are singing a song entitled "Burning." Here are the lyrics to the first verse:

*I have found the love of my desire*
*I'm caught up in the passion of an ever-flaming fire*
*I'm blinded by His pure and holy gaze*
*Captured by His beauty, and I just can't look away.*[5]

This is why we minister to the Lord night and day— because He is worthy of our praise and His beauty compels us. But He is also worthy because of His work of redemption:

**And they sang a new song, saying: "You are worthy to take the scroll, and to open its seals; for You were slain, and have redeemed us to God by Your blood out of every tribe and tongue and people and nation, And**

**have made us kings and priests to our God; and we
shall reign on the earth."**
**Revelation 5:9-10**

The wondrous reality of our Lord Jesus is that as the eternal Son of the Father, He carries all authority in heaven and on earth,[6] and the way He chose to exercise that authority as God incarnate was to lay down His life in the work of redemption for every tongue, tribe and nation of the earth.

He is a human being with *all* authority, and He chose to use that authority to redeem me! Since repaying Him is outside the realm of possibility, the only thing left to do is to worship Him night and day with my whole life. Since this is what we will be doing for eternity, the Holy Spirit is giving us opportunity to begin now and join with the saints and angels in the heavenly worship center, giving glory to the One Who is worthy.

Since volumes have been and still could be written concerning the worthiness of Jesus, these two hymns from the book of *Revelation* must suffice for this work. But to those who begin to explore the wonder of the Lord Jesus, there are vast realms of glory still to explore as the Spirit of God opens to us the infinite beauty and worthiness of our Savior.

The second reason for night-and-day ministry before the Lord is that it has characterized the life of the saints throughout the history of the Church. Whenever the Lord has seen fit to reveal to His people the beauty of what goes on in heaven, there have been attempts to re-create that beauty on the earth. From the Tabernacle of David to the night-and-day ministry of the priests in the temple, from the 300-year ministry of the Bangor Monastery in Ireland to the 125-year prayer meeting of the Moravians, human beings have ministered to the Lord around the clock, approximating what they have seen in heavenly visions.

Third, there is the sobering fact that before the throne of God there also stands an accuser, who night and day brings condemning testimony before the Father concerning human beings.[7] Since the Judge is our Father and the Advocate is our Lover,[8] these accusations have no effect on the mind of God. But they do have an effect on the minds and hearts of people, for the enemy also accuses God to us, and us to ourselves and to one another, and he pursues his task night and day. The antidote to his accusations is to stand before the Lord night and day and agree with Him concerning His character and His assessment of the human race. As our minds and hearts are conformed to what He sees, we find the strength to agree with Him, and the voice of the accuser is silenced. This is the blessing of night-and-day intercessory worship.

## THE VALUE OF CITY-WIDE PRAYER

The human throng standing before the throne of God is made up of people from every tongue, tribe and nation on the earth. The heart of God is burning with love for every person of every race, every people group and every linguistic expression, that they would come to know His heart for them and become part of His Bride. The beauty of the Lord is so varied in its expression, so multi-faceted, that there is no way one race, one doctrinal system, one worship style or one language can ever hope to express His praises adequately. The writer of the old hymn understood it well:

> *Oh, for a thousand tongues to sing*
> *My great Redeemer's praise!*
> *The glories of my God and King,*
> *the triumphs of His grace.*

While this dimension of every tongue, tribe and nation certainly speaks of the worldwide ministry of reconciliation that is happening, it also addresses us at a city level. Many cities of the earth represent not only the world's ethnic and cultural diversity, but also many varieties of expression in worship, ministry, doctrine, style—all things that partially represent the nature of God, but of themselves are inadequate to accurately represent Who He is.

A commitment to the city-wide expression of the House of Prayer is essential in order to begin to more fully represent the character and nature of God. Part of what needs to happen in the Body of Christ is a turning away from the perspective that *because I happen to prefer a particular style, it must be the right one.*

The Lord is interested in revealing His own beauty to us, and one of the main ways He is doing this is to show us His beauty reflected in the lives of others in His family. When we embrace those who love Him, we are in fact embracing Him, and He is pleased with that.[9]

Part of the genius of the Harp and Bowl model of intercessory worship is that it is adaptable to virtually every kind of worship style, and every kind of intercessory style. From the antiphonal choirs of classical era cathedrals to the home groups of the contemporary church, this model of intercessory worship is adaptable to the settings God's people love. Part of the joy of learning to know His heart is realized in the task of embracing the city-wide church as an important element of this ministry.

I believe with all my heart that the significant fronts on which the Lord wants to address this issue are the centuries-old schisms among those of the Catholic, Orthodox and Protestant expressions of faith. While I understand that there are real issues that must be addressed from all sides, I believe unity in the body of Christ will never come until we are ready to embrace one another in the place of worship, and then from that place, begin to address our differences with humility and grace.

*Psalm 133* speaks powerfully about the place worship holds in bringing about the unity of the faith:

> **Behold, how good and how pleasant it is**
> **for brethren to dwell together in unity!**
> **It is like the precious oil upon the head,**
> **running down on the beard, the beard of Aaron,**

**running down on the edge of his garments.**
**It is like the dew of Hermon,**
**descending upon the mountains of Zion;**
**for there the LORD commanded**
**the blessing-life forevermore.**
**Psalm 133:1-3**

One of the key revelations of this passage that God is quickening at this time in history is the truth that unity, a good and pleasant thing that leads to the commanded blessing of God in a city, is a function of the *priesthood*. The anointing of unity comes on Aaron's head, not on the head of Moses, who represents kingly authority, leadership in a task-driven ministry. This speaks to the reality that God's unifying presence comes in the place of worship, not in the context of task. It is in the priestly ministry of worship and adoration that God will visit unity upon His people, not in the task-oriented ventures we so readily embrace.

For decades, the apostolic and catalytic leaders of the Church have attempted to build unity around programs and it has seldom (if ever!) produced the desired result. Whether focused on a Billy Graham crusade, a youth outreach or a ministry to the poor, the body of Christ has never affected lasting unity centered on a task, because the task is invariably tied to the vision of some particular leader.

Worship, however, is focused on the Person of the Lord Jesus Christ and as such draws us all as one in adoration before the feet of the Lamb.

I believe this was one of the surprising elements of the Promise Keepers movement that turned out to be a powerful key to its success. I attended several of these events with men from various churches, and in the wake of those times together, it was never the teaching that gripped the hearts of the men over the long term. The dynamic thing that thrilled our hearts was always the experience of worshipping the Lord of glory in a stadium with tens of thousands of other men of other tongues, tribes and nations.

Men would come to those events carrying banners with church names on them, wearing all sorts of ball caps, advertising their churches, their teams or their clothing manufacturers—symbols of what divides, not what unites. But when the worship began, the hats would come off, the banners would be laid aside, hands would be raised (whether that was a "normal" expression of worship for the individuals or not—it didn't matter), and the total focus of the gathering was to minister to the Lord. The sense of unity and power was palpable, and it is the chief thing I remember from those events.

How much more will God command blessing on a city where men and women, young and old come into His presence to worship and adore Him! When we come together not to advance an agenda, but to worship and agree with the Lord's purposes as revealed in the Word of God, surely He will be pleased to release justice and mercy in that city.

## THE VALUE OF THE PRAYERS OF SCRIPTURE

When one takes the time to consider the logic of using the prayers of the Scriptures in the context of an ongoing prayer meeting, it seems as though there would be immediate agreement with that strategy. Yet while there are many who pray from the Scriptures, the use of the specific prayers of the Scriptures is limited. In this section, I want to lay out some reasons the use of the explicit prayers of the Scriptures is wise, and explain how these prayers are instrumental in sustaining a 24-hour ministry of intercessory worship.

A common perspective among many who pray expresses itself in this language: *"I simply want to pray what's on my heart."* This is certainly acceptable, for we know that the Father loves to hear what's on our hearts and is tender and responsive to these matters. Often, however, what is on our hearts is the resolution of horizontal issues, the needs of our families, our communities and cities, moral issues that need to be addressed and other important matters.

Make no mistake: I understand that these things are important. But if our hearts and minds are focused primarily on issues that need to be resolved, we eventually will find ourselves right back in the widow's posture of prayer, overwhelmed and anxious, measuring our success in prayer and our personal identity in God by the rate at which these issues are resolved.

The other dimension of having our prayers rooted primarily in "what's on our hearts" is that these prayers tend to depend on a certain intensity of emotion that is looking for release. Again, this is a perfectly legitimate way to pray. The Lord loves it when we release the emotions of our hearts in His presence, and He is delighted to touch our emotions with the comfort of His love and grace.

The down side, however, is that it is difficult to sustain prayer for extended periods of time when the primary driving force is the release of pent-up emotion. Often, when we have released the pressure, the motivation to pray is released as well, and either we don't pray with intensity or we conjure false emotion that may not reflect the actual condition of our hearts before God at all. This results in prayer times that are boring and emotionless or that carry an aura of falseness that is not pleasing to us or to the Lord.

It is helpful to be reminded that what the Lord has in mind for the end of the age is unceasing, night-and-day, 24-hour, seven-day-a-week intercessory worship. It never stops. What is emerging is not a series of several intense intercessory meetings during any given week, but a never-ending participation in the ceaseless worship and intercession going on in heaven at this very moment.

At the International House of Prayer in Kansas City, we have divided every day of the week into 12 two-hour prayer meetings. Over the course of the week, that comes to 84 prayer meetings every week, 168 hours every seven days. This schedule is not sustained by emotion, nor can it be sustained by prayer that is focused on the resolution of issues. Unceasing prayer must be rooted in something positive, something that exhilarates and feeds the soul, and that something is the beauty and glory of the Person of God.

The prayers of the Scriptures are primarily rooted in and focused on the release of the glory of the Lord upon the earth. As we focus on His beauty and on His passion for the peoples of the earth and the situations that surround them, our hearts are lifted up because of His majesty, and we find the exhilaration that sustains us over the long term. In the House of Prayer, our model is to focus on two primary realities: the glory of the Lord as declared in the Word of God, and His agenda for the restoration of all things through the release of His Holy Spirit among the peoples of the earth.

On a typical day, we spend about 70 percent of our time declaring the beauty and glory of the Lord, ministering to Him through songs of worship and the spontaneous singing of the *Psalms,* or by praying and singing through the worship hymns of the book of *Revelation.* The other 30 percent of each day is spent agreeing with His purposes as revealed through the Word of God. In this methodology, we find the exhilaration of His revealed beauty that fuels night-and-day prayer. But we also find that the issues of our hearts—the daily needs and concerns—are addressed as we agree with His larger purposes, for the Word of God is marvelously and thoroughly practical.

I'm reminded of one question that came to me as I was teaching an orientation seminar in the House of Prayer. Asked by a mom who was concerned about the teen-agers in her city, including her own children and their friends, her passion and concern were evident. The eyes of her heart had been focused on the pressures facing these kids, and she felt overwhelmed and pressed by the enormity of the issues. She had prayed much and was not encouraged. She was desperately looking for relief.

As I began to respond to her, the Holy Spirit brought to mind one of the prayers penned by the Apostle Paul to the Thessalonian believers:

**Finally, brethren, pray for us, that the word of the Lord may run swiftly and be glorified, just as it is with you, and that we may be delivered from unreasonable and wicked men; for not all have faith.**

**But the Lord is faithful, who will establish you and guard you from the evil one. And we have confidence in the Lord concerning you, both that you do and will do the things we command you.**

**Now may the Lord direct your hearts into the love of God and into the patience of Christ.**
**2 Thessalonians 3:1-5**

I shared this with her as a prayer inspired by the Holy Spirit not just for that time and place, but for every time and place. We began to pray, focusing on the swift and glorious ministry of God's Word, the faithfulness of God to establish and guard His people from wickedness, and His agenda to direct people's hearts to God's love and Christ's patience. As we worked our way through this prayer, we made the focus of it the teen-agers in her city, especially her own children.

I tell you, this mother experienced tremendous release in her heart because her prayer was no longer focused on the troublesome issues her kids were facing, but on the glory and power of the Lord to have His way with her children. It's a marvelous way to pray.

We also can study the prayers of the Scriptures and mine the wealth stored in the Word of God concerning His character and power. Oh, Beloved, I tell you we have a resource in the Word of God that is staggering! It is a sea of majesty into which we may plunge without fear of exhausting its resources. Even as Hezekiah commanded his musicians and singers to sing the *Psalms* of David and Asaph[10] and the songs were sung with gladness, so we want to study and go deep in the knowledge of the Lord as revealed in His own Word. The more clearly we see Him, the more confidently we will pray. The more we understand His beauty, the more our hearts will find the joy that motivates us to night-and-day prayer. Therefore, we want to disciple musicians, singers and intercessors in the knowledge of the Word of God.

Unfortunately, the knowledge of God's Word typically is not a high priority among musicians and singers. Our songs are often focused on the experiences of our hearts, not on the glory of the Lord. This is because we have not led our songwriters into the deep understanding of the Word that gives them fuel for their writing. But this is changing.

Our methodology for study is to take any given prayer in the Scriptures and break it down into short segments. Then, using such aids as cross-referencing tools, concordances and topical Bibles, we search the Scriptures concerning the various topics. Over time, the reservoir of understanding grows in powerful ways. For example, I have included below a sample study of just one phrase from *Ephesians 1:17-19* that I use for praying in the House of Prayer:

### Prayer for the Revelation of Jesus' Beauty and the Bride's Destiny for the Transforming of Our Hearts

*(I pray that) the Father of glory may give to you the SPIRIT OF WISDOM AND REVELATION IN THE KNOWLEDGE OF HIM, the eyes of your understanding being enlightened; that you may know what is the HOPE OF HIS CALLING, what are the riches of the GLORY OF HIS INHERITANCE IN THE SAINTS, and what is the exceeding GREATNESS OF HIS POWER TOWARD US . . . (Eph. 1:17-19).*

- **Father of glory**—appealing to the greatness of God as our source of power
  - ➤ God has all glory and power, is exalted as head over all

    *Yours, O LORD, is the greatness, the power and glory, the victory and the majesty; for all that is in heaven and on earth is Yours; yours is* the kingdom, O LORD, and You are exalted as Head over all. (1 Chronicles 29:11)

➤ **He is the King of glory, the Lord of hosts**

Lift up your heads, O you gates! And be lifted up, you everlasting doors! And the **King of glory** shall come in. Who is this **King of glory?** The LORD strong and mighty, the LORD mighty in battle. Lift up your heads, O you gates! Lift up, you everlasting doors! And the **King of glory** shall come in. Who is this **King of glory?** The LORD of hosts, he is the **King of glory.** Selah (Psalm 24:7-10)

➤ **His voice thunders over all creation to bring it forth**

The voice of the LORD is over the waters; the **God of glory** thunders; the LORD is over many waters. (Psalm 29:3)

➤ **He is the glory of His people Israel**

Has a nation changed its gods, which are not gods? But My people have changed **their glory** for what does not profit. (Jeremiah 2:11)

➤ **Other scriptures—Matthew 6:13; Luke 2:14; Acts 7:2; 1 Corinthians 2:8; James 2:1; Revelation 7:12**

The point is that the phrases of Scripture, like icons on a website, are doorways into magnificent depths of truth about the character and beauty of our Lord and God. As we focus on those realities, our minds and hearts are brought to a place of faith and confidence. When I focus on the term "the Father of glory," my mind recalls this study[11] and my heart is filled with the assurance and joy of being cared for by a Father such as this.

I am then able to pray from the place of knowledge about and confidence in His nature as the Lord of all glory. The Word of God strengthens my soul as I articulate His greatness, and my heart is filled with faith. Then, like a bride fully alert and convinced of the strength of her beloved, I can simply mention any issues in my life that need to be dealt with and the passion of His heart takes over. He addresses my issues by His intense and focused activity on behalf of His Bride.

As a result of praying these biblical prayers, we find it increasingly easy to come to agreement with the Spirit of God concerning His nature and His agenda. We begin to desire what He desires, confident in His ability to bring it all to pass. Also, as we pray the prayers of the Scriptures, we find it easy to come to unity and agreement with other believers. We are not praying for our own agenda or the success of our own programs. We are not praying for our political convictions to be established as the norm. Rather, we are focused on the establishment of His rule and reign, and that is an agenda with which all believers are in agreement.

The prayers of the Scriptures—the best way to pray!

## THE HARP AND BOWL MODEL

A central value at the House of Prayer is the use of the Harp and Bowl model of intercessory worship. This term is taken from *Revelation 5:*

> **Now when He had taken the scroll, the four living creatures and the twenty-four elders fell down before the Lamb,** *each having a harp, and golden bowls full of incense, which are the prayers of the saints.*
> **Revelation 5:8**

The four living creatures—the seraphim—and the 24 elders are before the throne of God night and day, and they carry with them worship (the harps) and intercession (the bowls of incense, the prayers of the saints). The picture is of unceasing worship carrying the prayers of the saints on the wings of ministry to the Lord Jesus. This is what happens in heaven night and day, and our desire is to emulate that reality here on the earth.

When Jesus taught His disciples to pray that the Kingdom of God would come *"on earth as it is in heaven,"*[12] I believe this was an integral part of what He was asking of the Father. The release of a heavenly model of worship and intercession, with music and prayers woven together in a tapestry of ministry to the Lord, is key to the release of revival upon the earth. The Lord in His grace has revealed to us in the Word how He enjoys receiving ministry from us, and we neglect this revelation to our own loss.

During recent years, there has been somewhat of a separation between intercessors and worshippers, as though the two groups were competing. Thankfully, that wedge is being removed and there is an increasing awareness that both ministries belong together in the same room, at the same time, with worship and intercession wafting up toward the Lord's presence like the smoke of the incense in the Tabernacle of David.

What we are beginning to understand is that worship is the essential warfare of the saints, for it releases the presence and power of God. From *Psalm 22:3* we know that the praises of the people of God make up the throne on which He establishes His rule and authority, and so as we minister to Him we are confident that His power is released in the earth.

Another passage that reflects the awesome effectiveness of worship to release God's power is found in this beautifully poetic text:

**Sing to the LORD a new song,
and His praise from the ends of the earth,
you who go down to the sea, and all that is in it,
you coastlands and you inhabitants of them!**

**Let the wilderness and
its cities lift up their voice,
the villages that Kedar inhabits.
Let the inhabitants of Sela sing,
let them shout from the top of the mountains.**

**Let them give glory to the LORD,
and declare His praise in the coastlands.**

**The LORD shall go forth like a mighty man;
He shall stir up His zeal like a man of war.
He shall cry out, yes, shout aloud;
He shall prevail against His enemies.
Isaiah 42:10-13**

In this passage, the whole of creation is enjoined to praise the Lord of glory. Both the citizens of the earth and the created order around them join in exalting the Lord and declaring His praises. The Lord Himself responds to such a majestic and unified outcry of worship, and He does so in the personality of the Man of War. He stirs up His zeal, His jealous love, on behalf of His Bride, and goes out to prevail against *His* enemies.

This is precisely the model of warfare that Queen Esther used in her strategy to deal with the evil Haman. She ministered to the king (the Banquet of Wine really is an affectionate worship service, a re-presentation of the betrothal ceremony), and as in that context she mentioned her need, the king arose like a man of war, the queen's enemy became the king's enemy and the issues were settled. When worship and intercession are mingled together, there is power and effectiveness in ministry.

This marriage of intercession and worship also sets up a wonderful dynamic of teamwork in the House of Prayer. In the Harp and Bowl model, we encourage the intercessors and the singers to minister to the Lord in dialogical fashion—one praying and the other echoing the prayer in a song of agreement, leading to frequent crescendos of joyful intercessory song. The instruments join in with periodic *selah* sections (times of spontaneous instrumental music), and as we work our way through the phrases of the prayers, there is a creative and exciting dimension to it all.

We believe the Lord intends to strengthen team ministry, and the Harp and Bowl model of intercessory worship is one way that can happen. In addition to being an effective way to pray, it is eminently enjoyable and provides the maximum opportunity for fresh experiences in the beauty and joy of the Lord. It is the desire of our hearts that the beauty and presence of the Lord would increase in the land, and we are convinced that this is one means His Holy Spirit will use to accomplish that purpose.

This is the central reality of Bridal Intercession: human beings, hearts ravished by beauty and love, standing in the gap for those who do not know Him. They declare the heart and mind of Christ over those people, holding them before the throne of God that His grace might be poured out upon them. This is the place of authority that arises from intimacy with Jesus. It is the gracious place of Bridal Intercession in which we have been invited to stand.

# AND THEY LIVED
# HAPPILY EVER AFTER
## THE ETERNAL REVELATION
## OF THE BEAUTY OF JESUS

The blessed hope that we as believers in Jesus Christ will one day be with Him in heaven forever has been a part of my belief system and my expectation for as long as I can remember. It is only in the past few years, though, that the reality of our eternal existence with Christ has gripped me with fresh power.

In my life, the primary result of spending extravagant amounts of time in the place of prayer, considering the beauty of the Lord, calling out to Him to establish His Kingdom on the earth, has been the awakening of a yearning in my soul to be with Him face to face. The aching reality of a love that is real but not yet fully realized is the single most powerful motivating factor in my life. If the anticipation of seeing Jesus was not a reality, I would be among all men the most miserable.

Like you, I was created for His enjoyment. I was made to be in His presence worshipping Him, exalting Him, being thrilled by Him and ruling with Him. You, too, were made for that very reason. All of the longings of our hearts will be fully realized when we see Him. We will know as we are known, we will understand all things, and yet we will gaze upon His beauty with an ever-increasing wonder at the infinite nature of His glory and grace.

Across the prayer room from where I am sitting, there is a large picture of the crucified Christ, hanging on the wall above a little table that is set with the elements of the Lord's Supper. I gaze upon that picture often as I sit in this place, and the longing in my soul increases—the longing to know Him more, to be fully conformed to His image, to have a body with the capacity to receive more and more of His presence and glory. My heart belongs to Him, and my life is spent waiting in eager anticipation for His return.

This face-to-face reality is the Beatific Vision, the anticipation that has motivated the devotion of the saints through history. It is the power that provoked Paul the apostle,[1] and it is the reality behind the love that Peter knew for the Lord, and from which he strengthened the suffering Church of the first century.[2] The revelation of the beauty of the Lord Jesus was so overwhelming that His beloved disciple was stunned into immobility,[3] and the theme of the culmination of human history is that we will be with Him in unmitigated glory and blessing.[4]

The future fulfillment of this longing has been part of the consciousness of human beings throughout history. I chose to title this little epilogue, "And They Lived Happily Ever After," precisely because that fairy-tale ending is in fact the truth; it is really what will happen. We have been assured that this life is not the end, that there is an ever-after and that it will be a place of bliss and exhilaration in the presence of the One we adore. Standing in His presence with all who make up His Bride, we will fall before Him night and day, staggered by His beauty in ever-increasing ways as He forevermore reveals new dimensions of His infinite glory. It is the ultimate reality, the smallest touch of which is sufficient to send us into ecstasy. Every tear will be dried,[5] there will be no sickness or death, no disappointment. Every dream and promise will be realized beyond our wildest imaginations.[6] We will reign with Him in His power and glory, and all the longings of our heart for significance and influence will be realized fully in the heart of God.[7]

It is toward this end that we give ourselves night and day to the glorious work of intercessory worship. The longing of our heart is that the Spirit of God would be released to accomplish His purposes in the earth, that the nations would come to the knowledge of the Lord, so that the Lamb might be satisfied and receive the just reward of His passion. Our hearts ache to see that day, and to that end we say, "Amen! Even so, come Lord Jesus!"

# NOTES

## Chapter 1

[1]This information is taken from research done by George Barna and his associates, and can be researched on his website at www.barna.org.

[2]See the website at www.ifa-usapray.org.

[3]See *Romans 8:34* and *Hebrews 7:25.*

[4]*Protocol.* Don Sullivan, 1990.

[5]For biblical examples of these acts, see *2 Kings 2:21* and *Joshua 6:4.*

[6]*Needless Casualties of War,* by John Paul Jackson. Streams Publications, Fort Worth, TX, 1999.

[7]*Transformations.* The Sentinel Group, 1999.

[8]*The Prayer of Jabez*, by Bruce Wilkinson. Multnomah Publishers, Inc., 2000.

[9] "Sons" is certainly intended here to be gender inclusive. The wonderful dynamic of the biblical imagery of God's family is that women are the sons of God and men are the Bride of Christ!

[10]See *Ezekiel 16:1-14* and *Ruth 2:17-4:17.*

[11]See *Matthew 3:17* and *Mark 9:7.*

[12]Consider *2 Samuel 6:12-23,* where in v.21 King David uses this word to describe his celebrative activity before the Lord as the Ark of the Covenant was brought up to Jerusalem.

[13]See *Romans 8:15-17; 28-30.*

[14]*Prayer,* by Hans Urs Von Balthasar. Ignatius Press, 1986, p. 40.

[15]See *Isaiah 9:7;* also *Romans 8:17; 2 Timothy 2:12; Revelation 1:6; 5:10; 20:4.*

[16]See *Deuteronomy 10:8* for a wonderfully concise description of the intercessory (priestly) role.

[17]See *Romans 5:12-21.*

[18]*Psalm 24:3-6* speaks to this.

[19]See *Colossians 2:9.*

[20]See *Romans 5:17.*

[21]See *Ephesians 1:4; Titus 1:2; 1 Peter 1:19-20;* and *Revelation 17:8* to better understand this concept.

[22]See *John 1:12-13.*

[23]See *Hebrews 1:3.*

[24]See *Colossians 1:1-3.*

[25]See *Revelation 21:1-3.*

[26]See *Ephesians 5:27.*

[27]See note [3] above.

[28]See *Romans 8:31-35.*

[29]See *2 Corinthians 3:18.*

[30]See *Hebrews 10:19-22.*

[31]See *Lamentations 3:23.*

[32]See *Hebrews 4:16.*

[33]For example, see Paul's apostolic prayer in *Ephesians 1:17-19,* in which Paul prays the purposes of God over the Ephesian believers.

[34]See *1 Corinthians 2:9-12.*

[35]See *Isaiah 42:1-4.*

## Chapter 2

[1]This was certainly true within other movements besides the Vineyard. During that season, many groups were experiencing the same dynamic of the presence of God in their midst that we were.

[2]I'm not speaking here of the offense of the Gospel. There is sufficient offense in simply speaking and doing the truth, without adding the offensiveness of cultural dynamics that are not central to the Gospel message.

[3]See *Ephesians 5:30-32.*

[4]See *Revelation 13:8.*

[5]The text of *Genesis 22:8* is profoundly and accurately translated by the American Standard Version, when it says that *"God will provide Himself the Lamb for a burnt offering. . . ."* God Himself was the Lamb, provided in the Person of Christ.

[6]See *Mark 10:42-45; Philippians 2:5-11.*

[7]See *1 Peter 1:8.*

[8]See *Isaiah 53:2.*

[9]For a more in-depth consideration, I would recommend *The Bride of Christ,* an audio tape series by Mike Bickle of the International House of Prayer in Kansas City. This series can be ordered at the *Friends of the Bridegroom* website, www.FOTB.com, by selecting the bookstore link.

[10]See *Deuteronomy 24:21-22.*

[11]See *Ruth 3:8ff.*

[12]See *Ruth 2:8-9.*

[13]See *Ephesians 3:14-17* and *Ezekiel 16:1-14* for an additional example of this dual role of father/bridegroom.

[14]*Ruth 3:10.*

[15]See also *Ezekiel 16* for a fuller explanation of the condition of God's people. The explicit nature of the language is used to make clear to us how God sees the relationship, and the impact it has on His own emotions.

[16]See *Ezekiel 16:31-34.*

[17]This word in Hebrew is *"ba-al,"* and is a clear reference to the slavery the Israelites experienced in relationship to the false gods.

[18]See *John 8:1-12.*

[19]See *Isaiah 61:3,10.*

[20]See *Isaiah 62:7.*

## Chapter 3

[1]These eight "Faces of Jesus" are taken with some editorial liberty from *The Song of Songs,* an audio-tape series with workbook by Mike Bickle, available through the Friends of the Bridegroom bookstore, www.FOTB.com

[2]Many commentators agree on this interpretation of the divine kiss. For example, see Matthew Henry's commentary on *The Song of Solomon 1:2.*

[3]Literally *the House of Wine*, which speaks of the most intimate realities, the initiation and maintenance of the marriage relationship, a renewable intimacy based on the recurring stimulus of romantic inclinations.

[4]See *Revelation 21:2*.

[5]See *Philippians 3:7-11*.

[6]See *Acts 7:55-56*.

[7]See *Hebrews 11:35-40*.

[8]See *The Song of Solomon Volume I,* an instructional workbook by Mike Bickle, Session 8, p. 16.

[9]See *Romans 8:14-17*.

[10]See *Colossians 3:1-4*.

[11]See *Song of Solomon 3:4-5*.

[12]See *Isaiah 62:8* as a representative verse of the power of God working salvation for His people.

[13]See *Zechariah 8:2* as a representative verse of God's zeal working for the redemption of Zion.

[14]See *Revelation 13:8*.

[15]See *Mark 3:14*, NIV.

[16]See Jamieson, Fausset, and Brown Commentary on *The Song of Solomon 5:2;* See also Bickle, *The Song of Solomon, Session 13*.

[17] See such passages as *Isaiah 63:1-6* and *Ezekiel 22:29-31*.

[18] I will address this topic more extensively and personally in the chapter entitled, "The Restoration of Fervency."

[19] Again, in my opinion the best resource for this kind of interpretation is Mike Bickle's audio-tape and workbook series entitled *"The Song of Solomon,"* available at www.FOTB.com, by clicking on the Bookstore link.

[20] See *2 Timothy 1:12*.

[21] See *Habakkuk 2:14*.

## Chapter 4

[1]*Justice* is a wonderful word, taken from the Hebrew word *mishpat*, that speaks about the total restoration of all things to the perfection of God's original design. It is a word that should and does strike fear in the hearts of the unrighteous, but it should not be mistaken for a merciless thing born out of wrath. Rather, *justice* is seen as the primary work of the anointed Servant in Isaiah 42:1-4, and as such should be joyously anticipated by those who seek the Kingdom of God.

[2]It is for this reason that the miracle of Jesus raising the son of the widow at Nain in *Luke 7* is such a tender and compassionate portrayal of the heart of God.

[3]See the story of Naomi and Ruth in the Old Testament book of *Ruth.*

[4]Such was probably the case with Anna, whom we meet in *Luke 2:36-38.*

[5]See *Jeremiah 31:32* and *Ezekiel 16* as examples of this accusation.

[6]See *Jeremiah 30:12ff.*

[7]See *Isaiah 62:1-5.*

[8]See *Hosea 2:16.*

[9]We will consider one of the major prophetic portraits in the next chapter, in the story of Esther as a metaphor for Bridal Intercession.

[10]See *Ephesians 1:3-4*. Note that the verb is past tense, and the spiritual blessings have been released "just as" we were chosen in Christ from the beginning.

[11]See *John 5:19-20.*

[12]See HUVB, *The Glory of The Lord,* Ignatius Press, 1982, Vol. 1, p. 160, italics mine

[13]I am not here primarily concerned with the external model of the prayer as much as with the emotional root systems. Energetic prayers with loud voices and obvious passion are fine. What I am contending for is that they be rooted in intimacy, not in fear and distance.

[14]See *Psalm 46:10.*

## Chapter 5

[1]The exegesis of these specifics is beyond the scope of this chapter, but is a study that is deeply worthwhile in understanding the preparatory processes of the Bride of Christ. For more information, see "The Reigning Bride," part of *The Bride of Christ* audio tape series by Mike Bickle, Friends of the Bridegroom, 1999.

[2]The Agagites were an accursed people to the Jews, and had been a thorn in their side for many centuries. King Saul had been commanded to kill King Agag but had disobeyed, and the fruit of his disobedience plagued the nation for hundreds of years.

[3]See the stories of Job, Peter, and even the Lord Jesus, all of whom were harassed and harmed by the enemy *with God's clear permission.*

[4]On a recent trip to Israel, I received some instruction from a Messianic Jewish pastor on the meaning of the Banquet of Wine. What I am sharing in this section is derived from that instruction. Further information on this topic can be found in a little booklet by Richard Booker entitled, *Here Comes the Bride: Jewish Wedding Customs and the Messiah,* published by Sounds of the Trumpet, Houston, Texas.

[5]See *John 14:1ff,* where Jesus so specifically followed through on this prophetic picture as He spoke to the disciples after the Last Supper about going to prepare their place of eternal dwelling.

## Chapter 6

[1]See *Mark 6:5-6.*

[2]The reader is reminded that faith is defined as "the habitual agreement with God's opinion of how things really are." This is not merely a factual perception, but is a truth established in the heart in the place of intimacy.

[3]See *Matthew 6:23.*

[4]See *John 18:11.*

[5]See *Acts 4:23-28.*

[6]This term was coined by some folks in the Youth with a Mission movement as a way of emphasizing the relational dimension of developing a prayer and financial support team for ministry activity.

[7]See *Isaiah 53:10.*

[8]The Greek word used here is *"doxas,"* which literally means "the glorious ones."

[9]See *John 14:30.*

[10]See *Job 42:8.*

[11]See *Strong's Exhaustive Concordance,* Greek definition #3794.

[12]See *Isaiah 42:10-12.*

## Chapter 7

[1]This story is told in more detail in the following chapter.

[2]*The New Unger's Bible Dictionary.* Moody Press, Chicago, Illinois, 1988.

[3]Mary's inheritance, which was the pound of spikenard referenced in John 12, comes into play later in the story.

[4]See the NIV text of this passage.

[5]This interpretation of the Genesis account is given in *Hebrews 11:19.*

[6]There are certainly times in which the binding and loosing of spiritual entities is appropriate, but I am speaking here of using these terms in an automatic way, as though they were some sort of mantra. There is no command of prayer that is effective unless it is what the Father is doing in the moment, and the understanding of His strategies comes only in the context of intimacy.

## Chapter 8

[1]See *1 Corinthians 2:9.*

[2]See *Philippians 3:12.*

[3]See *Philippians 3:14.*

[4]I am indebted to Jack Frost of Shiloh Place Ministries in Myrtle Beach, SC, for the term.

[5]I highly recommend the audio tape series, *The Life of David,* by Mike Bickle, available through the FOTB bookstore, www.FOTB.com.

[6]See *Song of Solomon 1:5.*

[7]See *Psalm 132:17-18.*

[8]In point of fact, Mike's testimony is that he was not nearly patient enough, and that out of his pressing to accomplish what God was saying came significant difficulty. At this point in the journey, however, it is clear that Mike and the team in Kansas City exercised wisdom as they waited for the Lord to establish what He had promised.

[9]See *Psalm 25:4,* noticing that this request is framed in the context of waiting upon the Lord all the day (v. 5).

[10]See *2 Samuel 8:13.*

[11]See *2 Samuel 8:6,14.*

[12]See *Psalm 2.*

[13]This is one meaning of *Isaiah 61:6-7,* where we are told that we will boast in the glory of the Gentiles. Through the partnership ministry of the redeemed Bride, the Gentiles come to comprehend their own beauty and glory, and that becomes our gift to the Lord, the crowns of glory laid at His feet.

## Chapter 9

[1]See *Matthew 11:6.*
[2]See *Isaiah 53:10.*
[3]See *Psalm 62:11.*
[4]This statement is based on the Christian doctrine that all people are born into sin, having inherited the sin nature from Adam and Eve. Thus they are deserving of death under the demands of the law. See *Romans 5:12.*
[5]See *2 Corinthians 5:21.*
[6]See *Hosea 2:15.*

## Chapter 10

[1]See *Romans 8:21.*
[2]See *The Online Bible Greek Lexicon,* definition of *Strong's Exhaustive Concordance,* #3954. There is another powerful passage, *Hebrews 10:19,* that uses this same term and concept to strengthen our faith.
[3]See *Hebrews 1:3.*
[4]See *Hebrews 11:6.*
[5]This designation refers specifically to James and John, as referenced in *Mark 3:17.* See also *Luke 9:53-54* for an indication of their thunderous personalities.
[6]See *2 Kings 1.*
[7]See *Mark 9:33ff; Mark 10:35ff; Luke 22:24ff.*

## Chapter 11

[1]My intent in using this phrase is to be purely descriptive, not to spark a theological debate about who has the Holy Spirit and who doesn't. Our conviction is that all believers have the Holy Spirit (see *Romans 8:9ff*), and that the term "charismatic" has come to include a certain style of worship.

[2]There has been a false romantic notion around the body of Christ that somehow it is better to seek the face of God than to seek His hand, as if His character and His power were different things. Our desire is that God would shine forth in all His glory, and release the full extent of His character and power upon the earth.

[3]See *Luke 18:1ff*, and reference Chapter 4 of this book.

[4]See *Strong's Exhaustive Concordance*, OT:8314.

[5]"Burning," by Monty Poe, 2000. All rights reserved.

[6]See *Matthew 28:18*.

[7]See *Revelation 12:10*.

[8]See *Romans 8:33-34*.

[9]See *Matthew 10:40*.

[10]See *2 Chronicles 29:30*.

[11]We encourage the liberal use of study notes as we sing the prayers, so that if a particular phrase or concept captures our heart, we can use it in the prayer room without fear of forgetting it. If someone else in the prayer room uses a phrase we like, it immediately goes in the notebook. I use it the next time I pray from that passage.

[12]See *Matthew 6:10*.

## Epilogue

[1]See *Philippians 1:23*.

[2]See *1 Peter 1:3-9*.

[3]See *Revelation 1:9-20*.

[4]See *Revelation 22:1-5*.

[5]See *Revelation 21:4*.

[6]See *1 Corinthians 2:9*.

[7]See *Revelation 22:5*.

# ALSO BY GARY WIENS

*Songs of a Burning Heart*

A collection of contemplative poems with artwork by David Costello. This book also includes a CD, with the poems read by the author and interpretive music by renowned violinist Ruth Fazal.

*Songs of a Burning Heart (CD only)*

*Before Your Feet: A Contemplation on the Seven Last Words of Christ on the Cross*

A compact disc with nine poems read by the author, "Before Your Feet" is a consideration of the crucifixion of Jesus, written from the perspective of John the apostle.

**Ordering Information**
**Burning Heart Ministries, Inc.**
13309 Corrington Ave.
Grandview, MO 64030

www.burningheartministries.com
816-965-9336